HARMONY AND NORMALIZATION

HARMONY AND NORMALIZATION
US-Cuban Musical Diplomacy

TIMOTHY P. STORHOFF

University Press of Mississippi · Jackson

The University Press of Mississippi is the scholarly publishing agency of the Mississippi Institutions of Higher Learning: Alcorn State University, Delta State University, Jackson State University, Mississippi State University, Mississippi University for Women, Mississippi Valley State University, University of Mississippi, and University of Southern Mississippi.

www.upress.state.ms.us

The University Press of Mississippi is a member of the Association of University Presses.

Copyright © 2020 by University Press of Mississippi
All rights reserved

First printing 2020
∞

Library of Congress Cataloging-in-Publication Data

Names: Storhoff, Timothy P., author.
Title: Harmony and normalization: US-Cuban musical diplomacy / Timothy P. Storhoff.
Description: Jackson: University Press of Mississippi, 2020. | Includes bibliographical references and index.
Identifiers: LCCN 2020013731 (print) | LCCN 2020013732 (ebook) | ISBN 9781496830876 (hardback) | ISBN 9781496830883 (trade paperback) | ISBN 9781496830890 (epub) | ISBN 9781496830906 (epub) | ISBN 9781496830913 (pdf) | ISBN 9781496830920 (pdf)
Subjects: LCSH: Music and diplomacy—United States. | Music and diplomacy—Cuba. | Music—Political aspects—United States. | Music—Political aspects—Cuba. | United States—Foreign relations—Cuba. | Cuba—Foreign relations—United States.
Classification: LCC ML3916 .S87 2020 (print) | LCC ML3916 (ebook) | DDC 780.97291/0973—dc23
LC record available at https://lccn.loc.gov/2020013731
LC ebook record available at https://lccn.loc.gov/2020013732

British Library Cataloging-in-Publication Data available

CONTENTS

Acknowledgments IX

Introduction XI

1. US-Cuban Musical Relations before and after the Revolution 3

2. A New Beginning: US-Cuban Relations in the Obama Era 30

3. The Politics of Cuban Music in the United States 55

4. Jazz as Intercultural Dialogue at the Havana Jazz Plaza Festival . . . 81

5. New Musicians and Travelers in Cuba. 112

6. 2016 and the Sounds of Normalization 137

Epilogue: Dissonance and Diplomacy under Donald Trump 165

Notes. 176

References. 197

Index. 203

For Kate

ACKNOWLEDGMENTS

The initial ideas for this book began when I was an undergraduate music student with a burgeoning interest in Afro-Cuban music, and I realized how difficult it would be to pursue those interests. There are many people who made this book possible by encouraging my interests, providing guidance, sharing their insights, providing criticism, and allowing me to have a glimpse into their world. I am particularly grateful to the faculty at Florida State University who helped guide this research, including Frank Gunderson, Michael Bakan, Denise Von Glahn, José Gomáriz, Joseph Hellweg, and everyone in the Musicology Department. Additional thanks go to Ben Coelho, Cynthia Schmidt, Jim Dreier, Paul Cunliffe, and the musicologists at the University of Iowa. As the following chapters explain, traveling to Cuba is logistically challenging, expensive, and unpredictable. I depended on the help of numerous individuals to make it happen. I would like to thank the various administrators and staff at FSU who supported my field research, Cuba Tours and Travel, and everyone at the Friendship Association.

Thank you to the University Press of Mississippi, especially Craig Gill, who saw the value in this book, Emily Bandy for her assistance throughout the process, and Lisa McMurtray, who helped get it to publication. I am indebted to the anonymous readers of this manuscript for their constructive feedback and suggestions.

I am grateful to the kind individuals who made my time in Cuba so memorable, particularly Carlos, Anier, Amparo, and Leo. I also need to thank all of the musicians, artists, and travelers who took their time to speak with me, whether it was while they were trying to enjoy their time in Havana or over the phone months later in the United States. Thank you to Lisa Hittle, Will Magid, Isaac Peña, Nachito and Aurora Herrera, Joanne Connolly, Neeta Helms, Tania León, Richard Blanco, Chi Saito, Jeff Smith, Norah Long,

Melissa Deal, Conner Gorry, Eric Amada, Leonid Fleishaker, Yosi McIntire, Soledad Pagliuca, and all of the individuals at the Kauffman Center, the Krannert Center, the Kravis Center, and the Afro Latin Jazz Alliance.

Most importantly, thank you to my friends and family. This project would not have come to completion without the support and encouragement of my amazing wife.

INTRODUCTION

On Friday, December 21, 2012, during the colloquium of the 28th Havana Jazz Plaza Festival, Cuban jazz musician Bobby Carcassés spoke about improvisation. It's "something we all already do every day," he said. "It's something insects do, the mosquitoes and cockroaches." His point was that jazz improvisation is not something that should intimidate young musicians nor should it be approached cautiously. He invited a few musicians from the small audience in the auditorium to join him in an improvisatory jam session to prove his point. Scarcity has forced Cubans to make nonmusical improvisation a survival technique and part of their daily lives. Common goods and products taken for granted on the other side of the Straits of Florida are in limited supply. When purchasing groceries, it is unknown what the store will have in stock and what will be missing. When the 1950s cars that drive up and down Havana's streets have trouble, the necessary parts for repairs can be impossible to find, so a driver takes what he can get and modifies it until it works.

When Obama administration (2009–2017) policies made legal US-Cuban travel easier, musicians increasingly visited Cuba from the United States but were often forced to improvise to make such trips possible. After his first inauguration, President Obama directed his administration to gradually create opportunities for travel between the United States and Cuba, which had been restricted by President George W. Bush (2001–2009). These policy changes gave the people of both countries the ability to interact through music and culture, but travel and musical exchanges continued to be challenging. The Cuban government attempted to meet the needs of increasing international visitors, but Cuba's economy, inefficient bureaucracies, and burdensome US regulations often forced travelers to alter their plans.

My interests in traveling to Cuba had been piqued after performing in the Afro-Cuban Drum and Dance Ensemble at the University of Iowa and hearing about the group's travel to the island before President Bush restricted academic travel in 2004. I realized that I was unlikely to visit Cuba legally until a new administration occupied the White House. After Barack Obama's election, I closely followed his approach to Cuba and formulated my own plans to visit the country for the Havana Jazz Festival in December 2010. Those plans fell through when I was unable to obtain the license permitting travel for academic purposes.[1] In 2011 the White House announced additional policy changes that made academic travel to Cuba possible without submitting a license application. I visited Havana that July to study Afro-Cuban percussion and made plans to return for the jazz festival in December 2012.

I intended to join an organized tour for musicians with the company Cuba Tours and Travel. Their website said the Havana Jazz Festival trip was designed to help American musicians, music teachers, music producers, and anyone in the noncommercial music world visit Cuba.[2] The travel opportunity was offered to full-time American professionals in the field of music because they could use professional research as a justification for legal travel. The trip was initially scheduled for December 12 through 19 and cost $2,390. These fees included all visa and travel license paperwork, chartered air service from Miami to Havana, seven nights at a hotel, festival registration, and guided tours of the city. Cuba Tours and Travel promised additional perks such as a special party for American musicians and a special "music guide" to assist and provide recommendations to participants on where to go. I filled out an online reservation form, but when I inquired about how to mail my deposit in mid-October, I received a response saying, "That trip has been cancelled because the Havana Jazz Festival's dates were inexplicably moved up a week by its organizers. Consequently, our trip could not be reorganized because of lack of flexibility on the hotel rooms."[3]

The festival dates listed online had been inconsistent even on official Cuban Ministry of Culture pages, and my attempts to contact anyone associated with the festival in Cuba were dead ends. Once I knew the festival dates had been moved to December 20–23, I had two months to make new plans. The group trip was canceled, but the staff at Cuba Tours and Travel still helped me secure a visa and plane ticket. I flew from Miami to Havana on December 16 on a large plane mostly filled with Cuban Americans visiting family. The flight itself was short and smooth, and I was surprised to find a bilingual magazine in the seat-back pocket specifically aimed at US-to-Cuba travelers, filled with general advice about visiting the island and an article about the jazz festival.

A few weeks before departure, I made a reservation at a *casa particular*, a private Cuban home where the owner is licensed by the government to rent out rooms to foreign visitors. This was the same *casa* I used on my previous trip to Havana, but when I arrived, the owner told me that he did not have a room for me. Thankfully, he brought me inside, and his wife made me some fresh juice as he called around to other *casas particulares* in the neighborhood. He then insisted on carrying my suitcase three blocks to the apartment he found where I would be staying for the duration of the festival. I was exhausted but gratefully accepted the offer to join my new host, Amparo, and her neighbors when they offered me some beer and *tostones* (fried plantain slices) immediately upon my arrival. The circumstances surrounding my arrival in Cuba were significantly different from what I had initially planned, but I was settled in Havana and prepared to take in the jazz festival. Over the next few days and throughout my research, I met musicians from the United States who all had stories about the improvisation required in making their way to Cuba.

Two years after I heard Bobby Carcassés describe the significance of improvisation and more than fifty years after the United States and Cuba had severed formal political and economic ties, US President Barack Obama and Cuban President Raúl Castro announced that their governments would restore diplomatic relations. This book examines musical exchanges during this period as a lens through which to view not only US-Cuban musical relations in particular, but also the larger political, economic, and cultural implications of musical dialogue between these two nations. My research methods were largely shaped and determined by the US-Cuba travel restrictions discussed throughout this text. From when I first proposed studying US-Cuban musical relations as a graduate student, I faced many hindrances in conducting fieldwork in Cuba. Various financial and travel restrictions made extended research stays on the island impossible. I altered my plans and improvised when necessary in order to gather all of the information that was needed despite these challenges. In addition to three trips to Cuba, I attended performances by Cuban musicians in the United States. I conducted interviews with performers, travel providers, managers, and audience members, and phone interviews with individuals who were at concerts I could not experience in person. As the number of musicians traveling between Cuba and the United States increased, it was impossible to be everywhere. I analyzed video and audio recordings of performances and gathered news articles and online resources containing first-person accounts. Library, archival, and internet research elicited a significant amount of the data discussed in the following chapters and allowed me to cover the breadth of musical interactions related to this topic. In the end, the barriers and obstacles I faced while investigating US-Cuban musical diplomacy only reinforced the importance of this study, and the hindrances themselves became an integral and relevant aspect of the work, as they exemplify the difficulties faced by musicians who wish to act as cultural diplomats.

PAN-AMERICANISM AND US MUSICAL DIPLOMACY

In the twentieth century, while folk, art, and popular musics promoted US interests throughout Latin America and the Caribbean, the United States effectively ignored Cuba both before and after the 1959 revolution. A study of state-sponsored musical diplomacy in the Americas illustrates how Cuba has typically been treated as a point of exclusion. A greater Pan-American consciousness developed as more political leaders, artists, and scholars in the Western Hemisphere rejected a Eurocentric focus in their work and instead emphasized shared postcolonial histories and challenges. Musical diplomacy, defined as an effort to use music as a designated representative of one nation or culture while interacting with representatives from another to strengthen relationships, enhance sociocultural cooperation, or promote national interests, became a common tool to promote Pan-Americanism.[4] The analysis of historical US musical diplomacy efforts, including their origins in the 1930s, provides a useful point of comparison for the contemporary US-Cuban musical exchanges that are the focus of this book.

In the book *Culture and International Relations*, Estelle Jorgensen (1990) cites seven international processes in which music plays a part: image preservation, loyalty maintenance, personification, socialization, information exchange, cooperation, and competition. All of these processes have been found in US musical diplomacy efforts at one time or another. Musical diplomacy, like all forms of cultural diplomacy, is built upon the assumption that good international relations can be built in the context of mutual understanding and respect. Cultural diplomacy efforts also rest on the idea that the arts and education are one of the most important avenues to connecting with and understanding another culture. Today, US cultural diplomacy is often practiced with little to no direct government oversight. Traditional ideas of cultural diplomacy maintain that one of the actors be a direct representative of the state, but contemporary efforts are directed by private-sector contractors, not-for-profit organizations, and multinational corporations.[5] Sometimes they are government-funded as official public-private partnerships, but often they are not (Goff 2013, 419–29).

Before the late 1930s, the US government did not have any direct financial involvement in musical and cultural exchanges with other countries (Campbell 2010, 3–12). Private foundations and organizations facilitated connections between performers, composers, and music students within the Americas, usually under the auspices of educational institutions and promoting American musicians to compete with their European counterparts. Official US efforts to promote Pan-American ideals were institutionalized under President Franklin D. Roosevelt's administration (1933–45) through the adoption of a "Good Neighbor" policy with Latin America. Pan-Americanism, or the belief that American nations are bound by common aspirations, often has its origins traced to the beginning of the nineteenth century, when Simón de Bolívar penned his 1815 Jamaica Letter, or when the Monroe Doctrine was adopted in 1823. These two conflicting views on the beginning of Pan-Americanism reflect two separate readings of the concept: Bolívar's anti-imperialist vision and the history of US hegemony in the Western hemisphere. US officials became newly committed to Pan-Americanism in the late nineteenth century, when north–south relations were stressed by events including the US-Mexican War. One initiative under President Benjamin Harrison was the formation of the Commercial Bureau of American Republics in 1890, which was later known as the Pan American Union and was designed to open up potential Latin American markets to US commercial interests (Hess 2013, 195).

These imperialist attitudes were criticized by José Martí, a Cuban poet, writer, and intellectual who became a key figure in the island's fight for independence from Spain. He spent much of his life in the United States, first in New York and then in the Cuban communities of Tampa and Key West, where he raised money and support for the Cuban independence movement. Martí was killed by Spanish troops in 1895 at the age of forty-two, but before his death he wrote about the North American threat to Cuba's sovereignty. In his last letter, Martí wrote of the United States, "I have lived in the monster and I know its entrails" (Martí 1895, 347). Although the US military helped Cuba escape Spanish control, Martí's fears about US attitudes toward Latin America and Cuba were realized after his death.

Political relations with Latin America largely deteriorated after the Spanish-American War, when the United States annexed Puerto Rico with the Treaty of Paris (1898), established political control over Cuba through the Platt Amendment (1903), destabilized the Colombian government in order to construct the Panama Canal (1903), and intervened militarily in countries including Nicaragua (1912), Mexico (1914), the Dominican Republic (1916–24), and Haiti (1915–34). These actions coincided with increased US business interests throughout Latin America that took advantage of cheap local labor and natural resources. Businessmen, government officials, and academics justified US political, economic, and military interference at the time by using social Darwinist concepts in describing the "sick nations" to the south. Another concept that encouraged US interest in Latin America was the idea of "newness" and "freshness." After World War I had devastated Europe, the idea of the Western Hemisphere as a place filled with unspoiled territories with people free from European dogmatism became a foundational myth for the United States that was easily extended to all of the Americas. This continuation of nineteenth-century Manifest Destiny contributed to the appeal of Pan-Americanism.

In his inaugural address on March 4, 1933, President Franklin D. Roosevelt outlined the essentials of his Good Neighbor policy, which institutionalized Pan-Americanism as a part of his administration. Discussion about the Americas' shared history of overcoming colonialism, mutual commitments to democratic ideals, and the ties of geographic proximity replaced the previous terminology that had exoticized and infantilized the people of Latin America. This attitude both reflected and willfully ignored the position espoused by José Martí in his 1891 essay "Nuestra América" ("Our America"), in which the poet points out the shared history of America's disparate nations and cautions against adopting North American approaches to democracy and governance (Martí 1891). Roosevelt declared that the United States would reverse its military interventionist conduct in the hemisphere; instead, the White House began to condone economic and social policies adopted by Latin American governments even if they disrupted US capitalist investments, and New Deal support for writers and artists extended to sponsoring cultural efforts intended to win the hearts and minds of populations throughout the hemisphere (Pike 1995, 164–76). Cultural and musical diplomacy was in its infancy at that time in the United States, but it soon became coupled with Pan-Americanism to make Latin America a testing ground for expressing soft power through culture while simultaneously combating leftist populism and the increasing presence of Axis propaganda throughout South America.

In 1938, the same year that the Platt Amendment was repealed, the State Department established the Division of Cultural Relations (DCR) and its own music committee, which acted as a facilitator and clearinghouse for performance groups that wished to undertake international tours and matched them with donors and organizations willing to finance them, while easing the bureaucratic requirements related to overseas travel. The DCR concentrated initially on Latin America, a region of the world where they perceived that more doors were open to them and where their efforts could have greater impact (Ninkovitch 1981, 30). Before the DCR could spend any federal dollars to directly sponsor any tours, Roosevelt supplanted it with the Office of Inter-American Affairs (OIAA) in 1940 (Campbell 2010, 54–58). The OIAA's Music Committee membership included musicologist Carleton Sprague Smith and composer Aaron Copland, among others. Together, they created the basic blueprint for what cultural diplomacy through music would look and sound like during ensuing decades. The Music Committee carefully considered how to have the greatest impact by promoting music that would have a degree of popular appeal while also encouraging hemispheric bonding, so they decided they needed music accessible to the masses and that sounded Latin American (Hess 2013b, 113–15). As a result, the Committee agreed they should not fund concerts with only classical and European music, but they also did not go so far as to sponsor performances of only folk or commercial music.[6] The OIAA Music Committee's activities ended with their last meeting in the fall of 1941, but the cultural diplomacy model they established for selecting, organizing, and promoting musical events continues to inform international musical exchanges today.

Musical diplomacy resumed in the postwar years. Initially, music was primarily used for de-Nazification efforts in Europe, but as the Cold War intensified in the 1950s the geographic arena for using music to combat Soviet ideology extended around the world. A number of US government institutions arranged musical performances for the purpose of cultural diplomacy, including the executive branch's US Information Agency (USIA), the Congressional Fulbright Program to fund international arts projects, various divisions within the Department of State, and the attempts to use music for propaganda as psychological operations (psyops) by the CIA.[7] However, these initiatives did not reflect any desire for hemispheric goodwill and made previous efforts at being a Good Neighbor appear to some as nothing more than the result of crisis-driven self-interest instead of genuine compassion (Hess 2013, 217).

The US government emphasized jazz in Cold War cultural diplomacy tours because it was a distinctly American style of music that had already gained popularity around the world and that countered Soviet propaganda about the United States as a racist country. Therefore, state sponsors of musical performances were particularly drawn to integrated groups that promoted an image of racial harmony, even though that was not an accurate depiction of the postwar United States. Many popular jazz groups received funding from the USIA or State Department to tour overseas, and these tours were accompanied by the promotion of jazz as US propaganda over the international radio station the Voice of America.[8] Dizzy Gillespie performed in state-sponsored tours of the Soviet Union and the Middle East before being asked to tour South America and the Caribbean in 1956. He had popularized Latin jazz in the United States, so he seemed especially fitting for such a tour. Duke Ellington also visited Latin America on a state-sponsored tour of Mexico, Puerto Rico, and South America in 1971. Although it was near the end of his life, Ellington still toured extensively and was held up as an ideal musical diplomat because of his music, poise, and demeanor (Von Eschen 2009, 215).

State-sponsored cultural diplomacy tours at this time generally had a number of elements in common. Tour organizers emphasized musical ability, style, and repertoire and had little concern about the political leanings of participating musicians. Musical diplomats rarely had explicitly political duties while abroad, but organizers expected them to maintain good diplomatic demeanor and manners that would positively represent the United States. The government wanted musicians who would be able to interact with foreign media without getting flustered, and who would not negate the attempts at cultural diplomacy with ill-mannered behavior. Organizing institutions also realized early on that the planning and coordination of performances could be just as important as the performances themselves. Successful concerts required efficient interaction between US musicians and managers with foreign government officials as they collaborated to achieve a mutual goal.

The George W. Bush and Obama administrations emphasized the importance of cultural diplomacy and musical exchanges in the twenty-first century, but Cuba was not a country where the Department of State's Bureau of Educational and Cultural Affairs supported exchanges until the end of Barack Obama's final term in office. Despite the lack of diplomatic relations, Patricia Goff uses the United States and Cuba as an example in the entry on cultural diplomacy in *The Oxford Handbook of Modern Diplomacy* (2013). She writes:

> There may be no official relations between two governments, but artists can communicate with each other and forge meaningful ties. The United States and Cuba have been involved in artist exchanges—many high profile—including the New York Philharmonic, the New York City Ballet, and the Jazz at Lincoln Center musicians, despite chilly official diplomatic relations between the two governments. These exchanges arguably create fertile ground for traditional diplo-

macy; maintain links when official relations are imperiled; and remind citizens of the two countries that they have things in common despite official policy to the contrary. (Goff 2013, 421)

US musicians wishing to legally travel to and perform in Cuba require a license from the Department of the Treasury. The Obama administration made it easier to qualify for travel licenses with the hope that increased travel would create connections and build understanding between US and Cuban citizens. The following chapters describe in detail how different musicians qualified for licenses and engaged in musical diplomacy to create cultural bridges.

Before the collapse of the Soviet Union, few Cuban musicians were able to travel abroad and perform in international tours, but the Cuban government did engage in limited musical diplomacy before that time. Nueva trova is a genre of Cuban protest music that rose to prominence in the 1970s and drew upon the political nueva canción songs that were popular in South America. As the Cuban government began to promote *trovadores*, musicians like Pablo Milanes and Silvio Rodriguez became international symbols of socialist culture, and Cuban cultural institutions allowed them to perform in festivals throughout Latin America, Spain, and the Soviet Bloc (Moore 2006, 153–58). Some Cuban jazz musicians were also permitted to perform internationally beginning in the late 1970s. Musical diplomacy efforts increased in the 1980s and took on new significance in the 1990s as a way to attract tourists. Today, the Cuban Ministry of Culture operates the majority of the music festivals in Havana, and they are engaging in musical diplomacy when they choose to invite an international musical group to participate. Living in a socialist state, prominent Cuban musicians are typically employed by or in some manner affiliated with the Cuban government and Cuban government institutions. When traveling to the United States as musical diplomats, they sometimes meet opposition from groups who are against renewed US-Cuban relations because these musicians are seen as representatives of the Castro government.

Many of the musical interactions and performances that took place from 2009 to 2016 were informal musical diplomacy efforts with only tacit government approval or involvement. When these exchanges were first given a legal window to take place, musicians leapt at the opportunity to traverse the Straits of Florida, make cross-cultural connections, and start to rebuild the once thriving US-Cuban musical relationship. These efforts demonstrated the desire for cultural interaction in both countries and quieted the fears of a political backlash to engagement, which laid the groundwork for the formal modes of cultural diplomacy (and political diplomacy) that would follow. In this way, music is not only reflective of socioeconomic and political realities but can also be predictive of future realities; through music, Thomas Turino explains, "new possibilities leading to new lived realities are brought into existence in perceivable forms" (2008, 17). The performances themselves have reflected the promise and tensions of US-Cuban relations. These dynamics manifest themselves in music through the styles and genres musicians choose to present while abroad. In selecting music that represents a more harmonious international relationship or subverts listeners' musical expectations, performers can be critical of the status quo without making overt political statements and can reach new audiences and individuals by avoiding simple political classifications.

US-CUBAN MUSIC AND POLITICS

The following chapters describe how US policy changes spurred musical exchanges and cultural diplomacy efforts, which in turn created contact zones that were multifaceted and multivocal. In contrast with cultural diplomacy narratives that emphasize unidirectional action in which one nation brings its cultural practices and expressions to an outside population in an effort to export ideas and encourage cooperation, the examples described in this text emphasize the complexity of these multidirectional interactions. The cultural exchanges and musical diplomacy initiatives that took place during the Obama years were not available to all people equally; even as the policies governing US-Cuban travel changed, the institutions and bureaucrats administering them did not always do so consistently. As a result, the connections created by these US-Cuban musical interactions are awkward, uneven, and discontinuous; they consist of both areas of dense interconnections and others of exclusion and immobility. The uneven nature of the musical interactions, combined with the often disparate goals and intentions of the individuals and institutions involved, gave rise to friction. As anthropologist Anna Tsing describes it, friction is a metaphorical image that illustrates how "heterogeneous and unequal encounters can lead to new arrangements of culture and power" (2005, 5). It is common in anthropological discourse focusing on transnational connections such as these to describe them with the word "flow," but as Stuart Rockefeller (2011) points out, the term "flow" elicits harmonious overtones that ignore the discontinuity of these connections and removes the agency of individual actors. The policy changes during the Obama years did not create a flow of music between the United States and Cuba, but they did facilitate musical interactions that both caused and highlighted cultural and political friction.

Over the last three decades, musicologists have acknowledged and studied the political meanings that can be found in any performance or composition (Ballantine 1984; Bohlmann 1993, 1996; Goehr 1994; Leppert and McClary 1987). Susan McClary argues that "Music is always a political activity" (1991, 26), but in describing US-Cuban musical interactions during the Obama years, I have strived for an ethnographic understanding of what is and is not political. Many US musicians who have been given the opportunity to perform in Cuba have been asked about the politics of their performance, and almost always claim their performance is nonpolitical. Cultural anthropologist Matei Candea (2011) suggests that instead of immediately dismissing these claims and assuming everything is political, we should take into account what is considered political and nonpolitical by our informants with the same ethnographic sensitivity anthropologists traditionally accord to their informants during fieldwork.

In saying that they are not performing for political reasons, the musicians are not lying. Definitions of what is and is not political varies from person to person, but many of the musicians I spoke with consider a performance to be political when it is intended to support or oppose a specific policy, party, candidate, or political ideology. The musicians involved in these exchanges typically had no such intentions, but they also believed that their performances had the potential to make a political impact by fostering international goodwill. Furthermore, because of the status of the US-Cuban relationship, musicians cannot avoid having their music politicized. Suspicions of nonpolitical claims can be justified because all musicians traveling between the United States and Cuba must be granted some level of political permission to do so. Castro's 1961 "Words to Intellectuals" speech, in which he declared, "Within the Revolution everything, against the Revolution nothing," further complicates any claims of nonpolitical intentions (Moore 2006, 277). By understanding how musicians attempt to distinguish the political and nonpolitical in their performances, additional elements and themes emerge that would be overlooked with a premature critical reflex. This political gray area helps illuminate the greater political implications of US-Cuban musical exchanges during this time period.

Musical interactions between Cuba and the United States have significantly impacted musical developments in both countries, particularly in the first half of the twentieth century. Following Fidel Castro's rise to power after the 1959 revolution, the relationship between Cuba and the United States became openly antagonistic. When Castro allied Cuba with the USSR, the United States responded with an economic embargo and travel ban. These actions seemed momentarily to bring the long history of musical interaction between Cuba and the United States to a halt. Musicians in the exile community and the ongoing availability of recordings from the island ensured that a range of Cuban musical genres continued to be accessible and at times even enjoyed immense popularity in the United States. Popular US musicians could also be heard in Cuba through international broadcasts and recordings brought into the island from overseas. But direct human interactions were stifled and the circular migration of musicians between the United States and Cuba came to an end.

In order to understand the role of music in Cuban culture throughout the twentieth century and today, it must be put into the larger context of how music has functioned in socialist states more generally. One unifying element of socialist musical policies and initiatives is a push for musical nationalism and a more unified music-culture (Askew 2002; Baranovitch 2003; Edmondson 2007; Manuel 1987; Moore 2006). The two examples most relevant in comparison to Cuba are the Soviet Union, for its close economic and political relationship to revolutionary Cuba before perestroika, and modern-day China, which provides a valuable contemporary parallel. Both China and Cuba are socialist states that have developed their own approaches to dealing with the outside world, and various scholars (Hernandez-Reguant 2009; Kinkley 2007) have adopted the speculative label of "late socialism" for these countries in reference to processes of economic liberalization and their strained but necessary ties to the globalized outside world. Cuba's use of music to collect royalties internationally and attract tourist dollars from overseas is a key part of how the island nation is attempting to sustain a socialist economic system while adapting to the modern world.

This book is not an attempt to provide an overview of Cuban musical genres. There is significant existing musicological scholarship on Cuban music, both by scholars from Cuba (Acosta 2003; Carpentier 2001) and the United States that address a range of musical styles including Afro-Cuban religious music (Hagedorn 2001; Rodriguez 1998), rumba and son (Moore 1997; Sublette 2003), hip-hop (Baker 2011; Fernandes 2006), timba (Perna 2005), and other popular musics after the revolution (Manuel 1987; Moore 2006).[9] While I do describe the musical qualities of some Cuban genres and artistic movements, I am primarily concerned with how they figure into the US-Cuban relationship. Chapter 1 provides a historical context for the rest of the book and demonstrates that the United States and Cuba had a vibrant musical relationship before the Cuban Revolution. A description of the rich prerevolutionary musical relationship that existed in art music, popular song, and jazz shows how that relationship has been muted since 1960. When the United States instituted a trade embargo and travel ban on Cuba, musicians continued to seek opportunities for musical interaction and pushed the boundaries of what travel policies permitted. The chapter outlines how the US-Cuban relationship has changed under various US presidents, and how musical exchanges have been both stifled and briefly sanctioned under different administrations.

Chapter 2 picks up where the first chapter leaves off, with the election of Barack Obama. After his inauguration, President Obama enacted numerous policy changes that gradually moved toward improved relations with Cuba. The Cuban government and economy also underwent transformations instituted by President Raúl Castro during this period. Together these changes created opportunities for increased musical exchanges. One of the first high-profile musical exchanges of the Obama administration took place in September 2009 when Miami-based Colombian American rock star Juanes headlined his "Peace Without Borders" concert in Havana with the blessing of the State Department and the Cuban Ministry of Culture. Other musical exchanges that were made possible because of policy changes included Cuban American composer Tania León, who heard her music played in Cuba for the first time, students and academics who performed as part of educational programs, and other ensembles who went through the arduous process of obtaining a Specific License to participate in a cultural exchange. While US and Cuban officials began meeting in secret in June 2013 to discuss normalization, musical performance functioned as the primary public forum for cross-cultural interaction throughout the Obama Administration.

Chapter 3 describes the history of Cuban politics in the United States, their recent transformations, and how they have impacted musical production and interaction. The politics and musical prominence of Miami has resulted in reactions to Cuban musicians in South Florida ranging from controversy to acceptance. Divisive Florida performances are contrasted with appearances by Cuban artists elsewhere in the country. The 2011 ¡Sí Cuba! Festival in New York City, which brought over 125 Cuban artists to the city over several months and received significant acclaim, and the first US tour of the National Symphony Orchestra of Cuba illustrate the desire for increased musical interaction and normalized political relations. Yet while these musicians claimed apolitical intentions, it was impossible for Cuban musicians visiting the United States to avoid questions about politics and political interpretations of their performances.

Chapter 4 consists of an in-depth analysis of jazz in US-Cuban musical exchange along with an ethnographic description of Havana's International Jazz Plaza Festival. Cuba's relationship to jazz became complicated after the revolution. Performers on the island had to carefully negotiate their desire to play jazz with the Castro government's descriptions of jazz as imperialist music. The 2012 Havana Jazz Plaza Festival and the US musicians who played at the event are analyzed in depth to show how participants navigated US-Cuban relations to perform in a festival that uses jazz as a form of intercultural dialogue. The example of Arturo O'Farrill, a New York musician of Cuban heritage who was regularly featured in the jazz festival, illustrates the significance of jazz in musical diplomacy and how the definition of jazz is redefined through the festival lens.

Chapter 5 focuses on why musicians want to visit Cuba, how social networks help them get there, and how the influx of new visitors impacted US-Cuban musical relations. An analysis of the social network that has brought various Minnesota musicians to the Cubadisco Festival in 2013 and 2015 shows how Obama-era policies spawned and strengthened transnational musical networks. Both US and Cuban musicians drew upon some amount of previously accumulated social capital or other human resources available to them in order to navigate the complicated bureaucracies that govern travel across the Straits of Florida. Through participation in musical exchanges they gained access to an emerging transnational social network and the various contacts and resources it contains. The knowledge and resources provided by the social network has continued to expedite and encourage additional musical exchanges. US lawmakers ostensibly instituted the Cuban embargo to isolate the Castro regime, but it has had the effect of isolating US musicians from their Cuban counterparts. The Obama administration's travel policies reduced that isolation by allowing performers to tap into transnational social networks. Beyond being a resource for individual musicians, these networks can be understood as a reflection of US and Cuban aspirations for diplomatic and transnational ties. The brief musical interactions between actors during these musical exchanges have given rise to a network whose shape extends over international boundaries, is constantly transforming yet durable, and has ongoing political implications.

The final chapter focuses on official and unofficial cultural diplomacy efforts that have been organized to celebrate the United States and Cuba restoring diplomatic relations. Spring 2016 included a visit to Cuba by Barack Obama and free concerts by Major Lazer and the Rolling Stones in Havana. The following month, the President's Committee on the Arts and Humanities led a delegation to Havana with representatives from the National Endowment for the Arts, the National Endowment for the Humanities, and the Smithsonian Institution along with artists and musicians including Dave Matthews, Usher, Joshua Bell, and Smokey Robinson. At the end of the trip, the leaders of the participating institutions announced new programs and initiatives to fund and support further artistic engagement between the two countries. Unofficial musical diplomacy initiatives continued as well, and I describe my trip to Cuba with Musicians Across the Straits, a program that brought performers from St. Augustine, Florida, to Havana for a residency at the Fábrica de Arte Cubano. Normalization also presented new challenges, and the increased presence of international visitors and musicians exposed and contributed to growing inequalities in the Cuban economy.

The cultural exchanges and musical diplomacy initiatives I describe in this book are only a sample of the many musical interactions that have occurred between Cuba and the United States. There were many I do not mention because there have been far too many to create a comprehensive list. The examples also lean more heavily on the experiences of performers from the United States than those of Cuban musicians, as it was primarily changes in US policies that created opportunities for US-Cuban musical interactions to resume. My research experiences have led me to encourage others to participate in a US-Cuban exchange if possible; the opportunity to enjoy Cuba's music and interact with its people is something I want more individuals to experience. While I present arguments both for and against the policy changes during the Obama years, I do not hide my belief that musical and cultural engagement is a good thing.

Cuban music holds a special significance for performers, music consumers, and music scholars in the United States because of Cuba's geographic proximity and its pervasive influence on broader cultural conceptions of "Latin music." Because cultural exchanges are the basis for this ethnography, I hope that this research can potentially benefit individual musicians in the United States who want to perform in Cuba and Cuban musicians interested in sharing their talents with US audiences. Despite the hopes of the Obama years, the Trump administration (2017–) has been intent on cutting US-Cuban ties. The near future may see a return to US-Cuban cultural and diplomatic engagement or it could produce a further deterioration of relations. Either way, the political and economic relationships between these two nations, which are only ninety miles apart, and the policy decisions that govern that relationship (many of which have been made by near-mythic figures in modern history), affect the lives and careers of musicians on both sides of the Straits of Florida.

HARMONY AND NORMALIZATION

1

US-CUBAN MUSICAL RELATIONS BEFORE AND AFTER THE REVOLUTION

On August 13, 2013, Chucho Valdés, the best-known jazz pianist, composer, and arranger in Cuba today, appeared live in concert with singer Natalie Cole at the Hollywood Bowl in California. Valdés toured the United States multiple times after 2009 and has been the highest-profile Cuban musician to do so with regularity. His concert at the Hollywood Bowl, however, was special because it marked a reunion of sorts. Earlier in the year, Cole released her first Spanish-language album *Natalie Cole En Español*, which followed in the tradition of her father Nat King Cole's Spanish albums recorded in the late 1950s as a collaboration between US and Cuban musicians. One of Nat King Cole's primary collaborators was Chucho's father, Bebo Valdés. Although concert promoters billed both Cole and Valdés as headliners for the 2013 concert, each played separate sets and came together for only one song, a rendition of "Quizás, Quizás, Quizás" ("Perhaps, Perhaps, Perhaps").

When Nat King Cole recorded "Quizás, Quizás, Quizás" for his 1958 album *Cole Español* it was common for musicians from Cuba and the United States to visit one another's countries to record and perform. Despite political strains between Cuba and the United States in the early twentieth century, musical connections were thriving until 1959. Interaction between musicians became increasingly difficult after the Cuban Revolution, which was followed by the US trade embargo and travel ban on Cuba. This chapter provides a brief history of the US-Cuban musical relationship and the once rich prerevolutionary ties in art music, popular song, and jazz that deteriorated under shifting US policies toward Cuba from 1960 through 2008. An analysis of how US presidents from John F. Kennedy to George W. Bush approached Cuba illustrates that while musicians were unable to traverse the Straits of Florida with any consistency for over fifty years, the desire for musical interaction between these two countries continued to grow since its prerevolutionary peak. The period between 1958, when Bebo Valdés and Nat King Cole collaborated, and 2013, when their children performed together, had seen other musicians from Cuba and the United States make music with one another, but politics restrained the US-Cuban musical relationship and kept it from thriving.

PREREVOLUTIONARY US-CUBAN MUSICAL INTERACTIONS

The transnational relationship between the United States and Cuba was important to the development of music in both countries.[1] Beyond their close geographic proximity, political and economic ties dating to the colonial period led to a variety of musical interactions. After Cuba won its independence from Spain at the end of the nineteenth century, it was occupied and politically controlled by the United States. The 1901 Platt Amendment gave the United States the ability to intervene in Cuban affairs, and US politicians maintained sway over Cuban leaders throughout the first half of the twentieth century. The Cuban people reacted to North American hegemony in various ways; one of these was the cultivation and promotion of distinctly Cuban, specifically Afro-Cuban, musical forms. As the *afrocubanismo* movement of the 1920s and 1930s pushed African-influenced musical forms and mass-mediated images of dark-skinned Cubans into the national mainstream, Cuban conceptions of race and nation were transformed (Moore 1997). This period saw the popularization and commodification of Afro-Cuban dance genres such as rumba and son. As Afro-Cuban musical elements began appearing in middle-class music such as light opera and salon piano music, composers from both the United States and Cuba joined organizations to learn from one another and promote their music throughout the hemisphere.

The Pan American Association of Composers (PAAC) was founded by Edgard Varèse in 1928 with the goal of promoting and connecting composers from throughout the Western hemisphere (Root 1972). When Henry Cowell assumed leadership of the organization in 1929, he began establishing connections with Cuban musicians and recruited composers Alejandro García Caturla and Amadeo Roldán. In 1933, the organization's most active year in the Western Hemisphere, PAAC gave five concerts in New York and seven in Havana. Caturla and Roldán both conducted orchestras in Cuba that they used to promote PAAC, making them the most active Latin American members of the organization (Stallings 2009, 91). PAAC disbanded in 1934, however, because of a lack of organization and an inability to remain solvent under the pressures of the Great Depression. Individual performers and composers, however, continued to visit Cuba. One of the most prominent individuals to represent the United States abroad, which included some trips to Cuba, was former OIAA Music Committee member Aaron Copland. He visited Cuba twice in 1941, after which he composed *Danzon Cubano* for two pianos (Hess 2013, 203).

Other musical connections grew out of travel, economics, and the prohibition of alcohol in the United States after the passage of the Eighteenth Amendment. Irving Berlin, one of Tin Pan Alley's most prolific composers, played on the US-Cuban connection in some of his songs that were marketed to white North American audiences. In 1911 he collaborated on "There's a Girl in Havana" with lyricist E. Ray Goetz. A year later, Berlin married Goetz's twenty-year-old sister Dorothy, and they vacationed in Havana for their honeymoon. While there, Dorothy caught typhoid, and died five months later in New York (Sublette 2004a, 329). Although this trip ended tragically, it was also one of the few memories that Berlin had of his brief marriage to Dorothy. These experiences would help inspire his 1920 song "(I'll See You in) Cuba." This song was a direct response to the recent passage of the Eighteenth Amendment and alcohol prohibition in the United States, as it advertises the island where "wine is flowing." It also reflects the status of Cuba as "America's playground" at that time, which many Cubans would come to resent over the ensuing decades. Like most Tin Pan Alley songs, "(I'll See You in) Cuba" features simple rhythms and melodies and no direct Cuban musical influences. Although most US consumers were not yet familiar with actual Cuban music, the tropical topic was appealing and the song was a success.

Perhaps the most influential song in terms of introducing US listeners to Cuban music and showing the potential for marketing Latin music to North American audiences was "El Manisero," or "The Peanut Vendor." Cuban pianist Moisés Simons wrote the song in 1928; he based it on a *pregón* or vendor's call. It gained popularity among Cuban audiences after Rita Montaner recorded it for Columbia Records for distribution on the island. The real money at this time, however, was still in music publishing, not recording. After Herbert Marks, the son of music publisher E. B. Marks, purchased a copy of the song while in Havana for his honeymoon in 1929, he acquired the publishing rights from Simons. The song was released in the United States the following year (Pérez 1999, 203). "The Peanut Vendor" found huge success after being performed by Don Azpiazu and his Havana Casino Orchestra in 1930 at the Palace Theater in New York City. A costumed

Antonio Machín, who had been billed as the Cuban Rudy Vallee, sang the piece as he pushed a vendor's cart and threw peanuts into the audience. The popularity of the performance prompted a recording by the group for RCA Victor, which became an international hit in 1931. Marion Sunshine, who toured with Azpiazu's group as a singer, wrote English lyrics for the song with the help of L. Wolf Gilbert, and "The Peanut Vendor" gained further popularity among non-Spanish speakers. The song was marketed as a rumba, although it was actually a Cuban son. It sold over a million copies of sheet music in the 1930s, and the E. B. Marks Company who published it made Latin songs a major part of their catalog. In his autobiography, E. B. Marks wrote: "The blow of the depression was softened, for our firm at least, by our introduction of a new popular musical genre—the rumba.... Although the catchiness of the Cuban rhythms was at once apparent, I had to get danceable arrangements and singable translations to put them over in the United States" (Marks 1934, 219). The song's success encouraged multiple publishing companies to open offices in Havana for the purpose of signing Cuban composers, and a songwriting industry reminiscent of New York City's Tin Pan Alley quickly gained a foothold in Cuba's capital. Most of the songs that came out of Cuba's Tin Pan Alley, however, did not find significant popularity on the island even if they became hits abroad.

The presence of US tourists in Cuba during Prohibition also created a demand for dance bands both from Cuba and the United States. North American jazz bandleaders such as Jimmy Holmes, Max Dolin, Ted Naddy, and Earl Carpenter all led groups in Havana in the 1920s, and they began hiring Cuban musicians to perform with them; they found they could get away with paying them less than their US counterparts. At the end of the 1920s and through the 1930s, the number of American bands in Cuba would drop off and be replaced by Cuban groups. Moisés Simons had been leading a jazz band in Havana's Plaza Hotel from the mid-1920s until the release of "El Manisero" changed his career. Even Roldán occasionally played violin with some jazz bands and Caturla was a huge jazz enthusiast, leading a jazz band while at the University of Havana (Acosta 2003, 18–30). Geographic proximity, instantaneous radio broadcasts, and the ease of travel between Havana and New York City allowed popular tunes to appear in Cuba shortly after they premiered in the United States, and Cuban musicians used those songs as a point of reference to entertain visiting North American tourists (Acosta 2003, 57).

The genre of Latin or Afro-Cuban jazz developed simultaneously and gradually in both New York and Havana, although in Cuba it was an almost imperceptible process because no one was intentionally seeking a new fusion. Alternatively, in New York, Latin jazz exploded in the 1940s because the musicians were consciously bringing these musical styles together, and the music they created was widely disseminated and popularized through records and broadcasting.[2] The musicians who fused these styles included Cuban and Puerto Rican immigrants as well as black and white US citizens already living in New York City. In the late 1930s and early 1940s, a number of Cubans moved to New York City and impacted the city's popular culture. While the influx of Cubans to the city was much smaller than the growing Puerto Rican population, they established an identifiable Cuban community, which made the city more attractive to jazz musicians, including Machito, Mario Bauzá, and Chano Pozo, who hoped to have successful recording careers (Abreu 2015, 58–61; Sublette 2004a, 459–64). Through the first half of the twentieth century, there was a large influx of Puerto Ricans migrating into New York City. Puerto Ricans had already appropriated Cuban dance music into their own traditions, so Puerto Rican jazz musicians like Juan Tizol, who wrote "Caravan" for Duke Ellington's band, brought those influences with them (Manuel 1994, 249–61).

Established New York jazz musicians began working with these Cuban and Puerto Rican performers, and they brought Cuban elements to the forefront of their music. Together they popularized the genre that eventually became known as Latin jazz. Bebop pioneer Dizzy Gillespie was central to this process. Gillespie had the opportunity to form a big band in the mid-1940s, and when he was looking for a conga player in 1947, Mario Bauzá recommended Chano Pozo. With Pozo in the group they performed Latin tinged pieces like "Cubana Be, Cubana Bop" and "Manteca," which became Gillespie's biggest selling record. Pozo, who could not speak English, composed "Manteca" by singing out the individual lines for the instrumentalists and the arranger, and Dizzy wrote the bridge, creating a fusion of aesthetics in the piece. After "Manteca," bongos and congas became standard in jazz bands, and the addition of Latin jazz pieces to repertoires was widespread (Sublette 2004a, 536–42).

While Latin jazz was developing in the United States, Arsenio Rodríguez and Pérez Prado were experimenting in Cuba with son to include jazz orchestration. Prado divided his band into two registers that provided ongoing counterpoint while emphasizing melody and rhythm over harmony (Acosta 2003, 88–89). The mambo emerged from Prado's arrangements, which incorporated rumba and son rhythms around a constant clave, and it enjoyed broad popularity in the United States shortly after emerging in Cuba. In fact, mambo's marketability in North America, led by musicians like Machito, Tito Rodríguez, and Tito Puente, far outweighed its appeal in Cuba in the early 1950s. New York City's Palladium Ballroom became the center of the mambo craze, and it was the place to be seen for aspiring socialites (Garcia 2006, 64–65). Couples danced the mambo competitively at the Palladium, and it was thoroughly covered by the nation's media. There was a mambo section in *West Side Story*, and Desi Arnaz appeared with his Cuban band on *I Love Lucy*. Cuban music and dance expanded well beyond New York City in the early 1950s and could be found all over the country. The connection between Cuban musical elements and Latin music had been cemented in the minds of the American public.

Records by Cuban artists and music production in Cuba were flourishing, but the profits from record sales were largely going to North American companies such as RCA Victor and Columbia. By the 1950s, US corporations controlled the majority of radio, television, and record distribution in Cuba, and they used Cuban media to disseminate North American songs instead of Cuban genres (Moore 2006). The domination of the US culture industry exacerbated anti-US sentiments on the island, which had been particularly strong since 1952, when Fulgencio Batista organized a successful coup to reassume control of the country. Batista was backed by the United States during his rule, but his right-wing dictatorship polarized Cuban society. Musical diplomacy was being used to counter growing leftist ideologies elsewhere in Latin America, but any perceived threat to US interests in Cuba was seen as a military issue for the Batista regime to deal with and not a cultural or social issue. The revolutionary movement that would eventually topple Batista began on July 26, 1953, when charismatic revolutionary Fidel Castro staged a failed attack on the Moncada military barracks in Santiago de Cuba. Almost two-thirds of his revolutionary force was captured or killed, and Castro himself was arrested within a week of the attack. He was given a fifteen-year prison sentence but was released in 1956 under a general amnesty granted by the Batista government. Castro traveled to Mexico, where he met Ernesto "Che" Guevara, an Argentine doctor and ardent socialist; together they reorganized the 26th of July Movement. In December of that year, Castro led a force of just over eighty dissidents back to Cuba on the yacht named the *Granma*. While only twelve individuals survived the landing and initial clash with the Batista military, they were able to flee to the Sierra Maestra Mountains. For the next three years they instigated a bloody guerrilla war while spreading socialist ideology across the Cuban countryside. On December 31, 1958, Batista fled the country for the Dominican Republic, and Fidel Castro took control of the capital shortly thereafter. Following his victory, Castro gave a speech in Santiago de Cuba outlining the foundation for the new government that, at that time, he said would guarantee civil liberties, including freedom of speech and the press, and be based upon the popular will of the Cuban people.[3] However, it soon became clear that Castro would be in direct control of this new government and those who opposed the new totalitarian regime were jailed or killed.

Within months of the revolution, the fledgling Cuban government established new centers of music, film, theatre, and literary production. They instituted a free educational system with a curriculum including the arts, worked to preserve Cuba's folklore, and allocated a significant amount of money to training professional musicians and organizing and sponsoring musicological research. Enterprises were created for contracting and programming the nation's musicians, who were guaranteed steady employment and pay. These organizations initially fell under the auspices of the Consejo Nacional de Cultura or the National Culture Advisory, which was later replaced by the Ministry of Culture. Cuba's government organizations enacted various initiatives like the Amateurs' Movement as an effort to democratize music and the other arts. Castro and the socialist thinkers he surrounded himself with came to believe that there was a divide between artists and workers, and they tried to correct it by encouraging as many people as possible to participate in the arts (Moore 2006). The institutionalization of music, however, led to various complaints from musicians about bureaucratic delays and restrictions on the ensembles with which they could perform or the number of live concerts permitted. Unlike many other socialist states at the time, the Cuban government actively promoted popular music because Cuba had its own vital popular music styles, while in the Soviet bloc, popular music consisted mostly of styles imported from the capitalist West. Cuban authorities banned North American and British rock and pop for the first decade of the revolution; by the late 1970s international popular music was accepted and even broadcast on Cuban radio in order to keep young fans from tuning into US-based stations that could be picked up on the island (Manuel 1987).

The US government under the Eisenhower administration (1953–1961) was initially ambivalent regarding the changes taking place in Cuba—until Castro's leadership started to seize property and nationalize American companies. These actions followed a speech in 1960 in which Castro openly rejected US Pan-Americanism and announced Cuba's alliance with the Soviet Union.[4] As a result, direct, reciprocal US-Cuban musical interaction stopped. Eisenhower declared an economic embargo against Cuba in October 1960.

The revolutionary government began instituting greater socialist and anti-imperialist reforms, and many of the country's most prominent musicians fled the island nation to continue their careers abroad. International travel for Cubans became difficult if not outright impossible, and "foreign" music was shut out of the Cuban media (Moore 2006, 13). During Fidel Castro's tenure as head of the Cuban government, he faced off against ten different US presidents. While specific policies toward Cuba would vary between administrations, allowing for occasional musical interactions, the overall antagonistic relationship between the United States and Cuba remained in place.

US–CUBAN RELATIONS FROM KENNEDY TO FORD

US-Cuban relations underwent some of their tensest moments during President John F. Kennedy's administration (1961–63). As a result of Cold War–fueled antagonism from both sides, the United States strengthened its embargo against Cuba and instituted a travel ban. In April 1961, executing a plan conceived during the Eisenhower administration, Kennedy oversaw the failed mission by CIA-trained exiles attempting to invade Cuba at the Bay of Pigs. The hopes were that the Cuban people would rise up against Castro and aid the invasion, but the exiles grossly underestimated Castro's popularity at the time and instead of initiating a revolt, the invasion actually bolstered his support. The attempted invasion resulted in a radicalization of the revolutionary government as Castro quickly began rounding up and imprisoning suspected counterrevolutionaries. In November of that year, as Soviet weapons and military advisors began arriving on the island, Castro declared that he had always been a socialist and affirmed Cuba's relationship with the Soviet Bloc.

On September 26, 1962, Congress passed a joint resolution giving the president the right to intervene militarily in Cuba if US interests were threatened. The Trade Expansion Act of 1962 followed on October 11, which extended the Cuban embargo and prohibited the US government from pursuing diplomatic relations with Cuba until it was "no longer dominated or controlled by the foreign government or foreign organization controlling the world Communist movement" (Crandall 2008, 169). Days later, US reconnaissance planes discovered Soviet missile construction sites in Cuba, setting off the Cuban Missile Crisis. The tense thirteen-day confrontation ended with an agreement between Kennedy and Soviet Premier Nikita Khrushchev that the United States would not invade Cuba again, and the Soviet missiles were removed from the island. However, covert missions to destabilize the Cuban government and attempts to assassinate Castro as part of Operation Mongoose continued to be authorized by the administration. Kennedy further curtailed opportunities for US citizens to visit Cuba in February 1963 when his administration directed the Department of Treasury's Office of Foreign Assets Control (OFAC) to institute and enforce stronger anti-Cuba policies. On July 9 of that year, the OFAC issued a comprehensive set of prohibitions in the Cuban Assets Control Regulations that did not outlaw the act of visiting Cuba directly but restricted any financial transactions incident to visiting Cuba, which effectively resulted in a travel ban.[5] The OFAC's Cuban Assets Control Regulations continue to be the primary legal mechanism for restricting US travel to Cuba.

Attorney General Robert Kennedy sent a memo to the Secretary of State that argued for lifting the travel ban only a few weeks after his brother was assassinated and Vice President Lyndon Johnson assumed the presidency. He claimed that "the present travel restrictions are inconsistent with traditional American liberties," and that "it would be extremely difficult to enforce the present prohibitions on travel to Cuba without resorting to mass indictments."[6] However, the policy preventing travel by US citizens to Cuba remained in place, and there was little change in the isolationist policy toward Cuba during the Johnson (1963–69), Nixon (1969–74), and Ford administrations (1974–77).

While it was illegal for US citizens to spend any money traveling to Cuba, more Cuban exiles, including musicians, arrived in the United States each year. Starting in November 1965, the Freedom Flights program airlifted Cubans seeking asylum, enabling 250,000 Cubans to come to the United States by 1971. President Johnson signed the Cuban Adjustment Act into law on November 2, 1966, which gave legal status to Cubans who arrived on US soil and allowed them to remain in the country. US politicians intended to isolate Cuba with these policies, but Castro was expanding Cuba's influence around the world with calls for Pan-American unity and a worldwide fight against imperialism. In January 1966 Cuba convened the inaugural meeting of the Organization of Solidarity of African, Asian and Latin American Peoples, bringing 483 delegates from 82 countries to Havana. The goal of the organization was "to increase the anti-imperialist battle on three continents" while rebuking US involvement in Vietnam. Over the next decade, Cuba expanded its international influence by sending arms, aid, and troops to regions of Africa and Latin America (Gronbeck-Tedesco 2008, 659). President

Ford would later cite Cuba's attempts to interfere in the US relationship with Puerto Rico and Cuba's intervention in Angola as the primary factors precluding any improvement in US-Cuban relations during his administration.[7]

Despite the active travel ban, folk singer Pete Seeger flouted the law and traveled to Cuba in 1971 through Spain. As a popular musician with socialist sympathies, he received VIP treatment on his trip, which included a suite in the Havana Hilton and a chauffeured car. What he wanted, however, was time interacting with the Cuban people; he looked forward to offering his labor cutting sugar cane but was only able to spend about two hours in the fields (Dunaway 2008, 371). Seeger had some earlier connections with Cuba and Cuban music, as his version of the Cuban song "Guantanamera" became an international hit in 1966 when it was recorded by vocal group the Sandpipers. US laws, however, prevented royalties from being sent to Joseíto Fernández, the Cuban musician credited with setting José Martí's verses to music. Seeger had the opportunity to meet Fernández during his 1971 visit. Yet the payment of royalties to the Fernández family is still prevented by the embargo.[8]

The 1970s saw the consolidation of the Cuban government's socialist bureaucracy as the island turned to the Soviet Union for increased support. The failure to reach the goal of 1970's Ten Ton Sugar Harvest initiative left the Cuban economy in a weakened state, and the government responded by ending many of the economic experiments and voluntary programs from the 1960s in favor of a Soviet model (Arús 2019, 189–95). International travelers to Cuba during this period were low in general, and the number of US musicians visiting Cuba continued to be minimal until President Carter attempted to improve US-Cuban relations in 1977.

THE HAVANA JAM AND THE CARTER YEARS

US president Jimmy Carter, who promised a new foreign policy less obsessed with preventing possible Soviet communist expansion, began moving toward improved relations with Cuba soon after his inauguration in 1977. The travel ban was lifted and, in lieu of embassies, "interests sections" were created to permit limited diplomatic contacts (Loiacano 2010). The Carter administration's (1977–81) actions allowed musicians to travel between the two countries, but the US government was largely uninvolved in the musical diplomacy efforts that took place. The first US performers to freely travel to Cuba during this period consisted of a group of jazz musicians led by Dizzy Gillespie. Musicians on the cruise included Gillespie's quartet, Earl Hines,

Stan Getz, Lionel Hampton, Roberta Flack, Ry Cooder, and Joe Williams. They were originally scheduled for stops in Jamaica and the Bahamas, but the tour promoter substituted Havana as a port of call after Carter eased travel restrictions. The performers were nervous about this prospect after Juanita Castro, Fidel's sister, had organized a dockside protest of exiles in New Orleans as the musicians' ship, the *Daphne*, was leaving. Hampton, Flack, and Williams even pulled out of the tour because they believed a performance in Cuba could hurt their careers, so multi-instrumentalist David Amram's group was brought in to replace them (Maggin 2005, 347). The Carras Lines cruise, when initially announced, sold fewer than one hundred bookings, but the cruise became a sellout with 320 booked passengers after the Cuban stop was added.

Although the revolutionary government enacted multiple policies to support Cuban musicians and musical production on the island, Fidel Castro saw little worth in jazz and was skeptical of music by US performers. The cruise ship was permitted to dock, but official dignitaries did not greet it and the visit was not promoted in the Cuban media. Moreover, the Cuban government expressed that no Cuban exiles would be welcome and that none should be on the ship. The musicians aboard played in multiple jam sessions, put on a concert, and met the Cuban Vice-Minister of Culture. Despite the stop in Havana lasting little more than twenty-four hours, the US musicians also spent time with the Cuban group Irakere, led by Chucho Valdés and featuring, among others, Arturo Sandoval on trumpet and Paquito D'Rivera on saxophone. Sandoval met the US jazz cruise when it arrived in port and drove Dizzy Gillespie around the island, showing him Havana and introducing him to musicians, before explaining that he was a trumpet player himself. They had the chance to jam together in the Hotel Habana Libre's Caribe Room, and at one point Gillespie reportedly waved a white handkerchief in surrender to Sandoval's playing.[9]

Reporter Arnold Jay Smith, who covered the tour for *Down Beat* magazine, described the highlight of the stop in Havana as the end of the concert at the Teatro Mella. The extended concert peaked with a performance by David Amram, who was accompanied by Cuban musicians from Irakere and Los Papines de Cuba, a four-person percussion group. The whole concert had been dedicated to Chano Pozo, but the theme was not announced to the crowd until Amram, who spoke fluent Spanish, took the stage. Smith wrote:

> The finale was not to be believed, and it may never be topped anywhere in the world save right back here in Cuba. Everyone was

on stage—there were nine percussionists playing 25 drums, with Los Papines giving a dazzling display of their own. The tune was "Manteca," but they literally marched off to "Straight, No Chaser." It was all they could do, march off. It's a cinch they weren't going to get off any other way. The audience was on its feet screaming the Cuban equivalent of "more!" It sounded like a demand rather than a request. [Gillespie] thanked everyone from Bird to Mao and off we marched to the ship and our disembarkation point, Nassau, Bahamas.[10]

Most Cuban jazz fans, however, were not able to attend the concert because tickets were not made available to the public and were distributed on an invitation-only basis. As a result, the audience primarily consisted of sons and daughters of Cuban officials, while others were turned away at the box office, and the Cuban press did not promote it. Composer Leo Brouwer, who was involved in the decision to keep it private, defended it on the basis of how quickly the evening was put together. Despite the private nature of the event, the jazz cruise visit to Havana created relationships between musicians and opened the door for Irakere to enter the international jazz festival circuit. Upon returning to the United States, Gillespie and the other musicians spoke so highly of Irakere that they were invited to perform in the Newport Jazz Festival and the Montreux Jazz Festival in 1978. An agreement between Columbia Records and Cuba's EGREM (Empresa de Grabaciones y Ediciones Musicales) label then paved the way for Irakere to release a self-titled LP that was sold in the United States with selections from these festival performances (Acosta 2003, 216–17).

Other musical interactions following the jazz cruise included a late 1978 US tour of major Cuban performers headed by the legendary Orquesta Aragón, but their performance at Lincoln Center was canceled when the Cuban American terrorist group Omega 7 set off a bomb in the performance hall. Trova musicians Pablo Milanés and Silvio Rodríguez then played a tour throughout the US East Coast in February 1979 (Sublette 2004b). One of the most significant events took place the following month, when a group of high-profile US musicians traveled to Cuba for the Havana Jam festival. Following the positive response to the 1977 jazz cruise, Columbia Records with the help of officials in the US State Department and the Cuban Ministry of Culture organized Havana Jam '79. The three-day festival included performances by US musicians such as Weather Report, Kris Kristofferson, Rita Coolidge, Stephen Stills, the CBS Jazz All-Stars, the Trio of Doom (a group created just for this occasion consisting of John McLaughlin, Jaco

Pastorius, and Tony Williams), the Fania All-Stars, and Billy Joel. Cuban groups Irakere, Orquesta Aragón, and the Cuban Percussion Ensemble also performed. Like the previous performance with US musicians, tickets were not made publicly available and the event was not widely promoted in Cuban media beforehand, so the audience was primarily made up of individuals with connections to the government. The performances were covered in the communist state newspaper, the *Granma*, with article headlines declaring "Desde hoy, encuentro musical con artistas cubanos y norteamericanos en el Carlos Marx" (From today, Musical Encounters with Cuban and North American Artists at the Karl Marx).[11]

Despite the audience not being wholly representative of the Cuban public, a number of the US musicians made special efforts to connect with the Spanish-speaking audience in attendance at the 4,800-seat Karl Marx Theater. Stephen Stills wrote a new song in Spanish, entitled "Cuba al Fin" ("Cuba at Last") for the audience (Zimmer 2000, 209). For his part, Kris Kristofferson added references to the Cuban Revolution in Spanish while performing his song "Living Legend" with the accompaniment of a Cuban *tres* guitar. After singing the line "Was it bitter then with our backs against the wall?" he asked, "¿En Oriente?" (In the east?), and he responded to the line "Say, if she came again today, would you still answer to the call?" with "¿En la Sierra Maestra?" (In the Sierra Maestra?). Both references were to Castro's guerrilla war against Batista's forces in Cuba's eastern mountain range. The Fania All-Stars, who had recently popularized salsa in the United States by playing a combination of Cuban son and other Latin genres, closed the first night of concerts but were not as enthusiastically received as Fania president Jerry Masucci had hoped. Fania's biggest star, Cuban-born singer Celia Cruz, did not travel to Cuba, and her absence could explain the response to the Fania musicians.[12] Instead, the audience was most excited about US pop musicians like Rita Coolidge and Billy Joel, whose current hits could be picked up from Miami radio stations (Perna 2005).

People magazine speculated about the potential impacts of the Havana Jam, stating it "might do the same thing for Cuban relations with the US that Ping-Pong diplomacy did for the Chinese."[13] Although Columbia Records had some cooperation with the State Department in this endeavor, their primary goal was not to actively influence US-Cuban relations. Instead, their intentions were much more practical and commercial: the production of a concert film and record. Billy Joel, however, refused to allow his performances to be used on either project. He told *People*, "I'm not down here on some capitalist venture. I'm here to play music for these people." Despite the wide variety of intentions among those involved, it had some important musical and commercial results. The *Havana Jam* album was so successful that Columbia released a sequel album with additional performances from the festival, and many of the participating musicians fondly recalled their experiences in Cuba through interviews and written accounts. Irakere, now Cuba's best-known jazz group, followed the performers back to North America to go on tour in the United States as an opening act for fellow Havana Jam performer Stephen Stills. In Cuba, the Havana Jam performances received little mention outside of two articles in the *Granma*, and musical recordings were not made available. Pedraza Ginori, a Cuban stage director for the concerts, later wrote, "It could be classified as the most hidden musical festival of all time in our national history."[14]

The liner notes for the album release of *Havana Jam* by *Variety* music editor Frank Meyer boldly and hyperbolically declared:

> If music hath charms to soothe the savage beast, "Havana Jam '79" also proved it hath charms to blow away cobwebs from years of non-communication and to help start a small breeze of change blowing across the waters between Cuba and the United States which can someday lead to a roaring wind which will return our peoples to complete understanding of each other and our music.[15]

However, that breeze of change failed to grow. More than twenty-five years later when Sony reissued the *Havana Jam* album, the travel ban had been reinstated, and former Irakere member Paquito D'Rivera, who played in the concert but had since defected to the United States, criticized the political statements of his fellow performers. In a 2005 open letter to Stephen Stills and Kris Kristofferson, D'Rivera wrote:

> So I wonder if after all these years of repression, divided families and innocent people killed by firing squad or dying in the sea, still you guys really want to keep those lamentable songs to the oldest dictator on this planet on that Sony reissue? I would really think about it![16]

D'Rivera left Cuba permanently in 1981. Irakere flew to Spain for a European tour, and instead of boarding the band's connecting flight to Sweden, D'Rivera fled the airport; he eventually made his way from Madrid to New York. Since that time, D'Rivera has been an outspoken critic of the Cuban government's totalitarian practices and has denounced other artists who travel to Cuba and meet with government officials (D'Rivera 2005, 281–313).

THE 1980S: REAGAN, DIZZY, AND THE COLD WAR

Any lasting political results failed to materialize from the musical exchanges during the thaw in US-Cuban relations under Carter. In April 1980, following a sharp downturn in the Cuban economy and thousands of Cubans requesting asylum, Fidel Castro announced that any person wishing to leave Cuba had free access to depart from the port city of Mariel. As a result, hundreds of boats left Miami to pick up refugees. With the cooperation of President Carter, the flotilla eventually brought 125,000 Cubans to the United States over a period of five months. When it was later revealed that the boatlift contained numerous "undesirables" released from Cuban prisons and mental institutions, it had negative political implications for Carter and created challenges for Reagan's Cuba policy. The initial wave of immigration in 1959 and the early 1960s was largely made up of white professionals and their families who established the Cuban presence in Miami. In contrast, the influx of Cubans in 1980 brought many working-class individuals of African descent and created new tensions in the Cuban American community that continue into the present. There was a fear that the new arrivals, who had grown up under communism, would not assimilate into the Cuban exile community. Over time, this generational gap led in part to the divisions between anti-Castro hardliners and the *"dialogueros"* more open to negotiating with Cuba. The Mariel Cubans were also stigmatized by the US media and politicians, as they arrived during an economic recession when there was little sympathy in the United States for the plight of immigrants (Garcia 1996, 69–74).

Following President Reagan's inauguration, his administration (1981–89) had to address both the Mariel boatlift and the flow of Soviet weapons through Havana to Marxist guerrillas in Nicaragua. Following failed talks to repatriate the Mariel undesirables and end Cuban military shipments to Central America, the relaxed Cuba policies established by Carter were reversed. By April 1982 the travel ban was reinstated and charter flights between Miami and Havana were halted (De la Cova 1997, 381–83). Attempts to challenge these restrictions failed in the Supreme Court. Diplomatic communications were suspended, and Cuba was placed on the US list of "state sponsors of terrorism." Reagan's national security advisor Richard Allen then assisted anti-Castro Cuban Americans in the formation of the Cuban American National Foundation, which gained easy access to politicians and has exercised great influence over Washington's Cuba policy ever since (Sublette 2004b, 9). Reagan's Presidential Proclamation 5377 in 1985 prohibited entry for any aliens deemed detrimental to US interests, specifically those "considered to be officers or employees of the government of Cuba or the Communist Party of Cuba," which made it more difficult for Cuban musicians to perform in the United States. Because the Cuban government controlled all industry in the country, the restriction against government employees could be applied to nearly all Cubans, and US-Cuban musical interaction was hindered yet again.

Yet in the same year that Reagan issued Proclamation 5377, Dizzy Gillespie was granted permission to perform at the Havana Jazz Festival. His trip is documented in the 1988 film *A Night in Havana*.[17] Cutting between Gillespie's festival concert, his travels in Havana, and interviews, the film captures musical performances as well as Gillespie's opinions about Cuba and the close connections he feels to the country's people and music. While there is some political content, it is largely glossed over and not a focus of the film. During this trip, Fidel Castro met personally with Gillespie and treated him like an honored guest. The film shows them discussing the history of jazz and connections to Cuban music, and at the end of their conversation the dictator encouraged the musician to come back to visit Cuba's beautiful beaches. Early in the film, Gillespie recalls being anxious and concerned going to Cuba the first time on the 1977 jazz cruise, but on this trip eight years later he was very comfortable and excited to spend more time in the country. There are short clips of Gillespie playing with Arturo Sandoval for Cuban students and interacting with the Conjunto Folklórico Nacional, the country's national Afro-Cuban folkloric ensemble. As he walked around Havana with a cigar in his mouth, Gillespie described the similarities and differences in race relations between Cuba and the United States and reflected on his own role in popularizing Afro-Cuban music through jazz forty years earlier. In that spirit, he visited Chano Pozo's sister in her home to discuss Pozo's journey from Cuba and his musical impact.

While in Havana, Gillespie appeared on a television talk show to promote his appearance at the jazz festival, which marked a clear difference from the earlier performances by US musicians in the Carter years, when they were not publicized and only individuals with political connections could attend. This gave Gillespie the opportunity to speak directly to Cuban citizens during his mainstage performance, when he announced, "Ladies and gentlemen, we are here tonight to demonstrate what one brother can give to the other in the spirit of unity. If our respective governments cannot join hands in the spirit of brotherly love, we will demonstrate to them how tonight." That performance included appearances by Arturo Sandoval and pianist Gonzalo Rubalcaba. A number of other US jazz stars followed Gillespie's lead to perform at the jazz festival in the late 1980s and 1990s. Gillespie himself returned to Cuba for the jazz festival the following year and again in 1990, while retaining his political connections and receiving the National Medal of the Arts from President George H. W. Bush in 1989.

When in Cuba for the 1990 Havana Jazz Festival, Gillespie was informed that Arturo Sandoval wished to defect with his wife and young son. Dizzy pledged Sandoval his support and assisted by creating a long European tour for the United Nation Orchestra, which allowed Sandoval to obtain permission for his family to be based in London for a couple of months. With the assistance of a member of President Bush's National Security Council, Sandoval and his family were able to declare asylum in US embassies and then be flown to the United States (Maggin 2005, 373–76). Gillespie's trips to Cuba reinforced his other international travel experiences and encouraged him to share intercultural music with listeners around the world. The resulting United Nation Orchestra included Cubans Paquito D'Rivera, Arturo Sandoval, and Ignacio Berroa, along with performers from Panama, Brazil, the Dominican Republic, Puerto Rico, and the United States. Dizzy Gillespie died in January 1993 of pancreatic cancer, but his musical legacy of bringing US and Cuban music together survives him on both sides of the Straits of Florida.

While Gillespie and a small number of other US jazz greats were able to visit Cuba under the Reagan and Bush (1989–93) administrations, traveling between the countries was nearly impossible for most everyone else. In 1988, however, members of a Cuban dance troupe from the Tropicana nightclub were granted two-week visas for performances in New York and Los Angeles. Their visa requests were initially denied, but the State Department reversed its course following positive US-Cuban talks regarding the withdrawal of Cuban troops from Angola and the shortening of the visa request from sixteen to two weeks.[18] That same year, an amendment to the otherwise unrelated Omnibus Trade and Competitiveness Act exempted "information and informational materials, including but not limited to, publications" from the Cuban embargo. Intended to protect the First Amendment rights of US citizens, it also legalized the import and sale of records from Cuba in the United States. While this policy only allowed the licensing of already-made recordings and did not permit US companies to create and sell new records of Cuban artists, the law facilitated the release of hundreds of albums by Cuban musicians and created new audiences for Cuban music (Sublette 2004b, 11). Yet the ability of those artists to perform in the United States remained difficult. Although the Cold War only had a few short years left, Cuban travel restrictions would outlast the global conflict by decades.

CLINTON, THE SPECIAL PERIOD, AND THE *BUENA VISTA SOCIAL CLUB*

When the Soviet Union collapsed in December 1991 and the Cold War came to a close, Cuba lost an estimated $5 billion in annual Soviet aid. The end of the Cold War also erased the original justifications for the Cuban embargo and travel ban, which were established to isolate Cuba until it was no longer aligned with the USSR and the world Communist movement. Many US politicians hoped and assumed that a collapse of the Cuban economic and political system was inevitable, and they strengthened the embargo in an attempt to ensure an end to the Castro regime. During his presidential campaign, Bill Clinton endorsed the Cuban Democracy Act of 1992, commonly known as the Torricelli Bill, which was passed by Congress and signed into law by then President George H. W. Bush. The legislation prohibited foreign-based subsidiaries of US companies from trading with Cuba, banned foreign ships that had carried goods to Cuba from entering US ports, and strictly limited remittances and the sale of medical supplies to Cuba. The United States' policies on Cuba had changed from countering the Soviet Union and stopping Communist expansion to concerns for human rights and democratic reform. These policies faced little resistance and were supported by both Democrats and Republicans in attempts to win votes from the powerful Cuban American voting bloc in Miami.

While Bill Clinton was campaigning for president in October 1992, Los Muñequitos de Matanzas were on their first US tour. Los Muñequitos originally formed in 1952 in the town of Matanzas and are one of the best-known folkloric ensembles in Cuba. The drum and dance group primarily performs traditional rumba and staged re-creations of Afro-Cuban religious music and dance. Organized with the help of writer and record producer Ned Sublette, the 1992 tour was carefully planned for two years to comply with the strict US regulations. The itinerary required approval by Washington officials, and each participating musician needed an exemption from Reagan's Presidential Proclamation 5377 (Sublette 2004c, 76). Despite the organizational challenges, the nine-week tour was a great success. Groups like Los Muñequitos de Matanzas took on new importance during this "Special Period" as the Cuban government began to increasingly depend on tourism dollars to sustain the island's economy, and the Cuban tourism industry found some success marketing Afro-Cuban folklore to international visitors.[19] The musical practices of Santería (also known as Lucumí and Regla de Ocha), a syncretic Cuban religion with African origins, had filtered into Cuban popular music over the years, but the ritual elements had long been open only to practitioners of the religion; in the 1990s it became common for folkloric ensembles to perform choreographed and staged versions of Santería ritual dances for tourists and to give workshops in which visitors learned the rhythms and dances (Hagedorn 2001). In the 1970s and 1980s, tourism was minimal, as officials believed it could be a threat to national security and that foreign visitors would spread unhealthy capitalist ideas or anti-revolutionary ideologies. After the collapse of the Soviet Union, however, tourism became an important source of hard currency for the country. The Cuban government expanded the José Martí International Airport, opened new restaurants and bars catering to tourists, and started to advertise Cuban tourism packages overseas. As a result, musicians had new performance venues and more opportunities to make a better living. Overall, however, much of Cuba's population did not benefit from the increased tourism. Cities were divided between tourist zones where foreign currency was accepted and the poorer areas that ran on Cuban pesos.

Additional reforms included limited privatization and foreign investment, which helped the Cuban political and economic system endure. The state's control of foreign trade was relaxed, opening Cuba up to foreign investment and offering investors up to 49 percent ownership in joint ventures. Economic reforms extended to art and culture as well; the Cuban government shifted its position in signifying authorship and applying copyright during the Special Period. In order to bring money to the island, Cuba's culture industries entered the global economy and started to function largely as "copyright industries" designed to create copyrighted material, distribute it internationally, and collect royalties (Hernandez-Reguant 2004). As a result, professional musicians started to profit from working in contact zones where transnational corporate capitalism and state socialism meet.[20] Along with strict rations on food, gas, and oil, Cuban authorities instituted periodic power blackouts to decrease energy consumption. While Castro opened some of these reforms for ratification by public referendum, public dissent was forcefully suppressed and exit visas were denied to individuals wishing to leave the country. Tensions reached a peak on July 13, 1994, when the Cuban Coast Guard attacked seventy-two dissidents on a tugboat they had commandeered to escape to Florida. The boat was sunk and forty-one people on board were killed. Major political demonstrations followed over the next month, and Castro responded by opening the borders to those who wished to leave. As a result, over thirty thousand Cubans fled for the United States. Concerned about the social and economic repercussions of a massive influx of Cuban refugees, President Clinton altered the formerly welcoming immigration policy towards Cubans. The resulting "wet foot, dry foot" policy allowed Cubans who made it to shore to remain in the country, but the US Coast Guard would apprehend, detain, and return Cuban refugees caught in the water (Crandall 2008, 172).

The Clinton administration (1993–2001) adopted a two-track policy overall toward Cuba that tried to keep the island economically isolated while also encouraging cultural and musical exchange.[21] In 1996 Congress passed the Cuban Liberty and Solidarity Act, more commonly known as the Helms-Burton Act, which further codified existing sanctions against Cuba and placed power over altering or ending the embargo in the hands of Congress instead of the president. The law stipulates that trade restrictions will not be lifted until Cuba has a democratically elected government not affiliated with either of the Castro brothers. It also requires that the new government will have to undertake measures to return property that was seized and nationalized in the 1960s to its original owners. Clinton initially threatened to veto the bill because it was controversial and limited the president's ability to conduct foreign policy (Crandall 2008, 174). Then, on February 24, 1996, the Cuban government shot down two planes operated by Brothers to the Rescue, a group of Cuban exiles who assisted distressed rafters fleeing the island but also violated Cuban airspace to drop anti-Castro leaflets. Clinton signed the Helms-Burton Act on March 12, 1996, as families of the Brothers to the Rescue pilots stood behind him. The act undermined Clinton's authority and that of future presidential administrations to make Cuba-related policy changes. The action also helped Clinton win reelection by securing Florida's Electoral College votes. After taking a hard line against Cuba by signing Helms-Burton into law but no longer concerned about winning another election, the Clinton administration used what authority it had in its second term to increase cultural connections between the US and Cuban people (LeoGrande and Kornbluh 2014, 304–15).

Music played a significant role in the Clinton administration's use of soft power in attempting to improve relations with Cuban citizens. In 1996 the Clinton administration approved visas for Los Van Van, Cuba's most popular dance band at the time, to perform in the United States. Their six-city tour was a commercial success, as many fans were already familiar with this progressive Cuban band's timba music, which combined traditional Cuban dance music with elements of rock and other foreign influences. They returned to the country again in 1999, but the band faced large protests outside their first Miami concert. Los Van Van was just one of many groups to visit the United States in the late nineties during a massive influx of Cuban musicians after the Clinton administration eased visa restrictions for Cuban artists and musicians in 1997.[22] The president exempted Cuban artists from Proclamation 5377, making it much simpler for Cuban musicians to perform in the United States and for promoters to arrange their visits and concerts. Additionally, the Clinton administration allowed US citizens to visit Cuba for religious, humanitarian, and academic purposes, and many musicians were able to justify trips as educational experiences. Legal travel to Cuba by US citizens was made easier by traveling with an organization that possessed a "people-to-people" license from the OFAC. These licenses specifically forbade tourism as an acceptable activity, so trips to beaches and resorts were not permitted, and travelers were instead required to have itineraries with educational activities (Sublette 2004b, 12). Specific musical activities were also permitted. In 1999, a group of US musicians and songwriters were granted a license to participate in the Music Bridges project. US songwriters including Bonnie Raitt, the Indigo Girls, Montell Jordan, Jimmy Buffett, Mick Fleetwood, and others traveled to Cuba for a week to write songs with the Cuban counterparts Chucho Valdés, Silvio Rodríguez, Amaury Perez, Miriam Ramos, and others. The week ended with a large invitation-only concert at the Karl Marx Theatre, where the collaborators performed their new compositions.[23] By permitting these exchanges, the Clinton administration was actively working to build a political constituency for improved US-Cuban relations in both countries.

Exposure to and awareness of Cuban music became much more prominent following the release of the *Buena Vista Social Club* album and documentary film in 1997 and 1998, respectively. Recorded in 1996 at Havana's EGREM studio, the album featured primarily elderly Cuban musicians performing traditional son and Cuban dance music from the prerevolutionary era. American guitarist Ry Cooder, who had visited Cuba with the aforementioned 1977 jazz cruise, produced the album and accompanied some of the tracks on slide guitar. It was recorded for the British World Circuit label and released in the United States on Nonesuch Records in September 1997. The album became a runaway hit in the United States and Europe and spawned a feature-length documentary film the following year. Together, these productions largely redefined how those outside of Cuba perceived Cuba and Cuban music, even though the full album was never released for sale on the island. As a result, "Chan Chan," the album's opening track, overcame "Guantanamera" as the song most commonly played by Cuban bands in tourist hotels. While the Clinton administration had been facilitating US-Cuban musical exchanges and was not overly concerned with punishing individuals who illegally traveled to Cuba through a third country, the impact of *Buena Vista Social Club* was too much to ignore. Many US citizens began calling the Department of Treasury seeking the same permission Ry Cooder had received. However, Cooder traveled without a license, so to make an example of him he was fined $25,000 in 1999 for flouting the travel ban. Had he financed the production of the record himself, he likely would have faced an even greater punishment (Sublette 2004c, 79).

The hardline Cuban exile community was already unhappy with Clinton's reforms when the US Coast Guard picked up eleven-year-old Elián González floating in the Straits of Florida. The young boy was found alone after the boat his mother and several other Cuban refugees were on sank off the Florida coast. After an extended custody battle between the boy's father, who was still in Cuba, and some of his relatives who had settled in Miami, the Supreme Court ruled that he should be returned to his father. Clinton's enforcement of that decision with armed troops led to a harsh backlash from South Florida Cubans. When Florida became the deciding state in the 2000 US presidential election between Al Gore and George W. Bush, Gore won a paltry 18 percent of the Cuban American vote compared to the 39 percent Clinton had won in 1996, and many pundits speculated that the Clinton administration's handling of the González case and opening of people-to-people travel likely caused the swing in South Florida votes.[24] Following the controversial 2000 election, President George W. Bush modified Cuban policy to be one of confrontation and curtailed many of the policies that had allowed musical interactions in the preceding years.

BEYOND THE AXIS OF EVIL: US-CUBAN MUSICAL INTERACTION AND GEORGE W. BUSH

At the beginning of the George W. Bush administration, Cuban musicians were still performing in the United States with regularity and the OFAC was issuing licenses for educational and people-to-people exchanges. However, the OFAC and Treasury Department under Bush quickly became much more stringent on licensing Cuba travel while also prosecuting individuals who violated the travel ban. In the last year of the Clinton administration, the OFAC filed 188 Cuba cases; the next year, the George W. Bush administration more than tripled that number by penalizing 788 parties for illegal travel to Cuba (Bardach 2009, 239–40). After terrorists attacked the United States on September 11, 2001, international policies changed drastically. It became much more difficult for Cuban performers to enter the United States because each individual needed to pass a stringent security check in addition to receiving a visa. The new requirements and related delays forced many musicians to miss their scheduled performances, essentially having the same impact as an outright visa denial. In 2001 the State Sponsor of Terrorism list included Cuba, Iran, Iraq, Libya, Syria, Sudan, and North Korea.[25] Cuba had been on the list since the Reagan administration, and the island's inclusion after September 11 meant an increase in aggressive rhetoric and talk of regime change from the United States. In May 2002 Undersecretary of State John Bolton gave a speech titled "Beyond the Axis of Evil: Additional Threats from Weapons of Mass Destruction" to the conservative Heritage Foundation. He announced that Cuba was harboring terrorists from other countries, was actively collaborating with Iran and other state sponsors of terror, and had an active biological weapons program. The evidence presented for this weapons program was merely that Cuba had a "well-developed and sophisticated biomedical industry" that was "one of the most advanced in Latin America and leads in the production of pharmaceuticals and vaccines that are sold worldwide."[26] In essence, Bolton was claiming that any country capable of producing its own pharmaceuticals was a threat. While Secretary of State Colin Powell later backed away from these allegations, the message received by the Castro regime was that the Bush administration considered Cuba a threat.

The Bush administration's growing anti-Castro propaganda efforts and stated intentions to seek regime change in other countries pushed Fidel Castro to repeatedly voice his concern that the United States was preparing to invade Cuba. As a result, in a 2003 meeting of the Communist Party, new military contingency plans on how to respond to a possible attack were drafted (Bardach 2009, 63–64). Castro simultaneously cracked down on political dissidents by arresting opposition leaders, activists, and journalists, and on April 11, 2003, he ordered the execution of three individuals who had commandeered a ferry in an attempt to flee to the United States. The Cuban leader also reversed many of the reforms from the Special Period. The US dollar was removed from the Cuban economy to be replaced by the new "convertible peso" that would be used in tourist zones, and almost half of the nation's private entrepreneurs who emerged in the nineties were forced back into public employment when their licenses were revoked (Crandall 2008, 183).

Much of the George W. Bush administration's Cuba policy was shaped by Representative Lincoln Díaz-Balart, a Miami Republican and Fidel Castro's nephew by marriage. Díaz-Balart had worked with fellow representative and exile hardliner Ileana Ros-Lehtinen to win Bush the 2000 election, and as a result they helped draft the administration's anti-Castro programs and ensured that they were well funded (Bardach 2009, 61). Amendments ending the Cuban embargo and travel ban were added to the House Treasury-Transportation Bill in 2003 and it was on track to pass in both the House and Senate; the provisions were eventually removed because Bush threatened to veto the whole bill if it contained any references to Cuba (Crandall 2008, 184). The next year during the run-up to the 2004 election, the Bush administration enacted some of the most stringent measures against Cuba since the Cold War, criminalizing travel to Cuba for most Americans and severely limiting the ability of Cuban Americans to visit their families. The administration stopped issuing licenses for purposeful travel by slightly changing the regulations and instructing the Treasury Department to deny all applications. At the same time, the OFAC made a point to target violators of the travel ban. A 2007 government report found that since 2000, 61 percent of the OFAC's investigations meant to enforce sanctions against countries harboring terrorists had been aimed at Cuba, and a 2004 congressional hearing revealed that tax dollars earmarked for the war on terrorism were being spent to track unauthorized travelers to Cuba. In that same hearing, the OFAC acknowledged that while they had only four employees following the funds of Osama bin Laden and Saddam Hussein, they had twenty full-time investigators devoted to probing individuals violating the Cuban embargo (Bardach 2009, 239–40).

Restrictions on travel to Cuba were also passed at the state level in Florida, where the President's brother, Jeb Bush, was governor at the time. In 2006 the Florida Legislature passed a law banning the use of any state resources for academic travel to Cuba. Florida Senate Bill 2434, described as an "act relating to travel to terrorist states" and known as the Florida Travel Act, was instituted after Florida International University professor Carlos Alvarez and his wife were arrested and admitted to spying for Cuba for almost thirty years.[27] The resulting law prohibits the use of public or private funds by Florida colleges and universities from being used to "implement, organize, direct, coordinate, or administer activities related to, or involving, travel to a terrorist state" and tying the definition of a terrorist state to the US Department of State's list of state sponsors of terrorism. After the bill was passed, the Florida American Civil Liberties Union filed suit against the state and in 2008 a South Florida US District Court ruled the law unconstitutional. A US Circuit Court of Appeals overturned that decision and the Supreme Court declined to hear the case, affirming the law's constitutionality. As a result, no money that was handled by a state university in Florida, even a private grant, could be used to fund travel to Cuba.

In a statement issued by the US Interests Section in Havana on February 6, 2004, it was announced that Cuban artists would once again be subject to Reagan's Proclamation 5377. According to the statement, "'We decided to return to the policy in effect before March 1999, because the Castro regime has taken advantage of the exemption to enrich the government, not to enhance people-to-people exchanges."[28] In 2004 alone, major Cuban musicians including Chucho Valdés, Carlos Varela, Los Van Van, Los Muñequitos de Matanzas, and Buena Vista Social Club singers Ibrahim Ferrer and Omara Portuondo canceled performances in the United States following visa denials. During the 2004 Grammy Awards, all five nominees in the Traditional Tropical Latin category were Cuban, but none of them could enter the United States for the ceremony. While these restrictive policies were a victory for South Florida Representatives Mario and Lincoln Díaz-Balart and Ileana Ros-Lehtinen, US musicians criticized the Bush administration. In a March 2004 op-ed in the *New York Times*, singer-songwriter Jackson Browne expressed his dismay that Carlos Varela's visa was denied. Browne and Varela had previously toured together in Europe, but they were forced to cancel their US performances. Browne wrote:

> I believe in justice and human rights in the United States and abroad. I am saddened by the treatment by the Cuban government of the political dissidents in their country. I long for the day when there is freedom for both Cubans and Americans to travel in both directions across the Straits of Florida without undue interference by their governments. I want this freedom not just for artists but for all people, American and Cuban, who live each day in the hope for a just and prosperous future. Giving Carlos Varela a visa to sing in America would be a good way to begin.[29]

Cuban American jazz musician and leader of the Lincoln Center Afro Latin Jazz orchestra Arturo O'Farrill echoed that sentiment stating, "My father was betrayed by the Castro regime, and I am not a Castro supporter. But to play with a Cuban musician does not mean you are supporting the regime. Playing music should transcend politics. And right now I feel betrayed by the Bush administration and the stance it is taking toward Cuba."[30]

There was one significant exception to this policy, however, and in May 2005, American rock band Audioslave received a license to perform a concert in Havana. The only explanation for why this band was granted a license is that, according to their lawyer who helped arrange the trip, it was a coincidence of agendas as both governments wished to reach Cuban youth.[31] The band members made it clear that they were not there to make a political statement. It was particularly ironic for Audioslave to claim an apolitical stance because of the band's close association with the non-profit organization Axis of Justice, which uses music to promote social justice, and the instrumentalists' previous membership in the very political band Rage Against the Machine. Over sixty thousand Cubans attended the concert at the José Martí Anti-Imperialist Plaza (which sits right in front of the US Interests Section in Havana), and Audioslave was able to claim the title of the first US rock band to play an open-air concert in Cuba.[32]

In the final days of the George W. Bush administration, the United States and world economy were in shambles, and despite the administration's best efforts, Bush became the tenth American president to be outlasted by the Castro regime. The Cuban political and economic system remained in the hands of the Communist Party even though Fidel Castro was functionally no longer in power. In July 2006 Fidel Castro provisionally relinquished the office of President of the State Council to his brother Raúl because of poor health. Despite the celebratory parties in Miami's Little Havana and the Bush administration's previous statements that the Cuban succession process was unstable, the transition was smooth and the Cuban system continued. With the Coast Guard on standby to prevent a potential refugee crisis, the White House urged Cubans on both sides of the Straits of Florida to remain where they were. Press Secretary Tony Snow issued a statement to both Cubans and Cuban Americans that reflected what the administration had been telling most musicians since 2001: "Stay where you are. This is not a time for people to try to be getting in the water and going either way" (Erikson 2009, 12).

CONCLUSION: THE PROMISE OF CHANGE

Hopes were high for US proponents of Cuban policy reform during the 2008 presidential election, as Democratic nominee Barack Obama stated that the United States should begin normalizing relations and easing the embargo.[33] Musicians and fans of Cuban music alike began tentatively planning for the resumption of US-Cuban musical exchanges in the event of Obama's election. While the United States and Cuba had close musical ties in the prerevolutionary period, it was not the result of coordinated musical diplomacy. Music and musicians flowed across the Straits of Florida with regularity, and the musical relations reflected the uneven economic and political relationship between the two countries. When a market for Cuban songs was discovered in North America, music publishers and record companies set up shop in Havana to find musical resources that could be profitably exploited. At the same time, US commercial interests started shaping Cuban radio to push North American popular music and products while the most successful Cuban musicians left their home country behind for more lucrative careers in New York City.

Following the Cuban Revolution, the musical connections between the United States and Cuba appeared to be severed. The embargo and travel ban established by Kennedy would continue with few exceptions for more than fifty years. When US policy toward Cuba changed in sometimes subtle and sometimes dramatic ways under different presidential administrations, musicians were often some of the first people to test new policies and start creating new transnational connections. The 1977 jazz musicians' cruise was the first major interaction between US and Cuban musicians on the island since 1960, and it led directly to further interactions with Cuban groups visiting the United States and the Havana Jam Festival in 1979. During periods when restrictions were relaxed and Cuban groups were able to tour the United States, some musicians claimed political asylum and defected while others often sought to extend their stays without completely defecting. Most, however, returned home after making international connections and taking new musical ideas back to Cuba with them. Their performances for US audiences, along with albums like *Buena Vista Social Club*, fed a growing curiosity about Cuba among US citizens who were unable to visit the country legally. It often seemed that as soon as it was possible to satisfy that curiosity, political forces would again bring the US-Cuban relationship to a standstill.

⊕

As opportunities for increased musical interaction became available under Presidents Barack Obama and Raúl Castro, it was unclear if they were a sign of a larger transformation or yet another chapter in the continuing cycle of starts and stops. Despite, or perhaps because of, these uncertainties musicians quickly and actively sought to travel over the Straits of Florida and renew the once thriving musical relationship between the two countries. The ongoing history of US-Cuban musical interaction exhibits how musicians passionately believed in these exchanges before the revolution and continued to pursue them afterward, whether or not they were a part of more extensive sociopolitical changes.

2

A NEW BEGINNING

US-Cuban Relations in the Obama Era

Cuba policy was not a defining issue in the 2008 US presidential race between the Democratic candidate Barack Obama and his Republican opponent John McCain. Neither candidate advocated dramatic changes to the embargo or Washington's relationship with Havana, but there were stark differences in how the candidates responded to questions about the US-Cuban relationship. In separate speeches on Latin American policy for Cuban American audiences in South Florida, each made their positions clear. McCain advocated for continuing the strict policies of George W. Bush and used Cold War–era rhetoric to gain the support of prominent anti-Castro politicians. Obama alternatively pledged to engage in dialogue with the Castro government and called for dramatically expanding the ability of Cuban Americans to travel to Cuba (Erikson 2009, 305–8). Following Obama's election and inauguration, gradual policy changes created new opportunities for US-Cuban musical exchanges. At the same time that the Obama administration enacted policies to permit a greater number of US citizens to travel to Cuba, the Cuban government under Raúl Castro began updating many long-held positions to support a changing economy and adapt to the increasingly connected world of the twenty-first century.

Even as legal options for "purposeful" travel to Cuba became available, US citizens continued to face bureaucratic challenges. Musicians wishing to visit Cuba required authorization, and their options varied depending on their occupation, political connections, and relationship to the island. Throughout most of the Obama administration, US citizens were primarily forced to travel under the auspices of a license from the Department of Treasury's Office of Foreign Assets Control (OFAC). An analysis of how US-based performers justified and legally obtained OFAC licenses shows that regulations treated would-be travelers inconsistently and unequally even after reforms expanded legal travel options. Despite these challenges, US musicians and music fans increasingly wished to visit Cuba during the Obama era. The performers who made that journey and their reasons for doing so were as varied as the musical genres they performed. As musicians and nonmusicians from the United States were increasingly drawn to Cuba beginning in 2009, it became more apparent that restrictions on travel did not reflect the will of the US public and failed to benefit the people of either country.

CULTURAL POLICIES AND ECONOMIC TRANSFORMATION IN CUBA

In July 2006 at the age of seventy-nine, Fidel Castro handed control of the Cuban government over to his younger brother Raúl in what was meant to be a temporary measure to allow the elder Castro time to recover from intestinal surgery. While some Cuba watchers speculated about Fidel's death and waited for a collapse of the country's socialist system and revolutionary government, the Cuban system endured. Fidel made occasional public appearances and regularly wrote his "Reflections" column in the *Granma* about the state of the revolution and other issues. Then on February 19, 2008, *Granma* published a message from Fidel in which he addressed his recovery and his brother's time as interim president. In the conclusion, he declared that he would neither accept nor aspire to the position of president, and with that he brought his forty-nine-year tenure as Cuba's leader to a close. Days later, Raúl Castro was confirmed as president of Cuba by the National Assembly, which marked a historic but anticlimactic transition. While news of Fidel's illness had sparked celebrations in South Florida, the official end of his presidency was greeted quietly. It did not signal the grand changes in Cuban society the exile community had desired. Yet Raúl Castro's first five-year term as president was marked by a series of cautious but deliberate changes to Cuba's economic and political system.

Raúl Castro publicly stated that the revolutionary government had made errors, such as fostering an "excessively paternalistic, idealistic and egalitarian approach instituted by the Revolution in the interest of social justice," and he acknowledged that the centralized model of the Cuban economy had become more of a problem than a virtue. The new Cuban president declared that the island would move away from a model inspired by the former Soviet

Union to something uniquely Cuban with "a socialist feature of management, albeit without ignoring the current market trends" and learning from other nations, even capitalist ones (August 2013, 143). An admission of fault alone was something the Cuban people were not accustomed to hearing from the government, and the announcement of potentially dramatic economic changes brought an air of uncertainty to Cuba. Raúl Castro and other top officials have argued, however, that their reforms were not rejections of Cuban socialism but were intended to safeguard it.

The economic changes generally involved the relaxation of government control and more opportunities in the private sector, with early reforms focused on small business and farmland. Cuban residents can buy and sell homes and used cars, where previously they were only allowed to trade for items of equal value. As a result, some home-run businesses have flourished, including small restaurants known as *paladares* and *casas particulares*, the private homes licensed to rent out rooms to foreign travelers. In October 2013 it was announced that the state-run tourism industry had been authorized to contract with private businesses to provide lodgings, meals, excursions, and other activities. At that time 400,000 Cubans worked in the budding private sector of small business and self-employment, up from 150,000 in 2010. Farms were also transitioned into the private sector. Large state farms broke up into smaller units including co-ops and private farms that could sell their surplus produce to hotels and restaurants.[1] In late 2013 the Cuban government announced a plan to unify Cuba's dual currency system, which had been in place since the Special Period.[2] Under this system, most state-owned cafeterias and shops set prices in Cuban pesos (CUPs), which is also how Cuban citizens working in the public sector are paid. At the time of the announcement the exchange rate was approximately twenty-five CUPs to a dollar, so the average monthly wage of a state-employed worker of 466 CUPs was worth just $19. The tourist economy, on the other hand, operated with "convertible" pesos (or CUCs) equal to the dollar. Income inequality rose dramatically as a result of this dual system, with more Cubans obtaining CUCs, either as remittances from relatives abroad or because they worked in tourism or the growing private sector. As a result, a waiter in a popular tourist restaurant who was tipped in CUCs could make more than a highly trained doctor working in a state-run hospital. The timeline for the currency unification, however, remained unclear and inconsistent in the years following the announcement.

Political changes accompanied these economic reforms. Raúl Castro's government made efforts to rout out corruption in government and state-run operations. While there were no efforts from within the government to significantly change how leaders are elected, Castro called for a limit of two five-year terms in top political positions, including his own. He also called for younger leadership in government, as ten of the fifteen Politburo members (the top committee in the Communist Party of Cuba) were in their seventies or eighties when the younger Castro assumed power.[3] Most significantly for US-Cuban musical diplomacy, Raúl Castro's government increased Cubans' ability to travel abroad. Previously, if a Cuban wished to leave the country, they had to apply to the government for an expensive and rarely issued exit permit. The cost and requirements of these permits made such travel nearly impossible for most Cubans. Following the travel reforms, individuals no longer needed to purchase the $150 permits or have letters of invitation from their foreign hosts. They did, however, still need a passport and a visa for the country they planned to visit; the visa process remains time-consuming and prohibitively expensive for most Cubans. The amount of time Cubans can spend outside of the country without losing rights and property has also been extended from eleven to twenty-four months.[4] Previously, only musicians favored by the government had been able to tour outside the country, but this change has made it easier for all musicians to perform in other countries, including the United States.

Despite political and economic changes, the Castro government refused to acknowledge human rights issues on the island. Castro freed fifty-two long-term political prisoners in his first five years, but in 2012 alone there were a record 6,200 short-term detentions for political dissent.[5] The livelihood of Cuban musicians continues to depend on their willingness to comply with the government and not publicly criticize elements of the revolution. Jazz musician Roberto Carcassés (son of jazz musician Bobby Carcassés) discovered firsthand that this was still the case when he expressed his discontent at a major concert in Havana on September 12, 2013. The concert was held outside the US Interests Section to demand the release of the Cuban Five on the fifteenth anniversary of their arrest. The Cuban Five are a group of Cuban intelligence officers arrested in Miami in 1998 after infiltrating anti-Castro Cuban American groups. Cuban officials claim that they were only monitoring violent exile groups to prevent terror attacks on the island, and their imprisonment became one of Havana's chief grievances against the United States. The concert calling for their release featured more than a dozen popular Cuban musicians and was televised live throughout the country. Carcassés performed with his group Interactivo in the concert's finale. Their song featured a call and response between Carcassés and his backup singers, but mid-song the singer called for marijuana legalization, freedom of information, direct elections, and an end to the embargo.[6] The next day, Carcassés was informed that he was banned from performing in all venues governed by the Ministry of Culture for making comments that went against the revolution. As a result, all scheduled Interactivo performances were canceled. The punishment caused a stir, receiving attention throughout Cuba and in the Cuban American community. It reached a resolution after Silvio Rodríguez issued a statement disagreeing with both how Carcassés made his comments and with the excessive sanctions that followed. Six days after the scandal erupted, the Ministry of Culture announced that Interactivo and its director could again perform in state-operated halls and theaters.[7] Carcassés had spoken out against elements of the government and was able to return to his professional routine, but many others remain imprisoned or have been forced to leave the country for dissent. This case is a musical example of how the Cuban government struggles with balancing previous practices of regulating all aspects of public life and a potential future that is more open to individual autonomy.

OBAMA'S NEW BEGINNING WITH CUBA

Less than nine months after Raúl Castro became president of Cuba, Barack Obama was elected in the United States. One of the new administration's first opportunities to address its relationship with Cuba was at the April 2009 Summit of the Americas, held in Trinidad and Tobago. Cuba was the only country in the Americas not invited to participate, as it had previously been expelled from the Organization of American States. A 1962 resolution stated that "adherence by any member of the Organization of American States to Marxism-Leninism is incompatible with the inter-American system and the alignment of such a government with the communist bloc breaks the unity and solidarity of the hemisphere" and therefore "the present Government of Cuba, which has officially identified itself as a Marxist-Leninist government, is incompatible with the principles and objectives of the inter-American system."[8] Despite Cuba's absence, the US-Cuban relationship became the defining issue for the summit after Obama announced he would attend.

Four days before the summit, the White House announced a series of policy changes under the label "Reaching Out to the Cuban People." The updated guidelines lifted restrictions on Cuban Americans visiting relatives and sending remittances to family members on the island.[9] When Obama addressed the gathered Latin American leaders on the opening night of the summit, he said, "I'm here to launch a new chapter of engagement that will be sustained throughout my administration," echoing many of the sentiments that were previously a part of Franklin Roosevelt's Good Neighbor policy. He later addressed Cuba policy more directly:

> There's been several remarks directed at the issue of the relationship between the United States and Cuba, so let me address this. The United States seeks a new beginning with Cuba. I know there's a longer journey that must be traveled to overcome decades of mistrust, but there are critical steps we can take toward a new day. I've already changed a Cuba policy that I believe has failed to advance liberty or opportunity for the Cuban people. We will now allow Cuban Americans to visit the island whenever they choose and provide resources to their families—the same way that so many people in my country send money back to their families in your countries to pay for everyday needs.[10]

Although Cuban Americans were quickly able to take advantage of the changing policies, starting a "new beginning" was a gradual process. Most US citizens who wished to visit Cuba were still unable to do so. Possibilities for greater developments in the two countries' relationship contracted when US communications specialist Alan Gross was arrested in Cuba in December 2009. Gross had been bringing communications equipment to Cuba's Jewish community that helped them bypass the Cuban government's blocks on internet access. His employer, Development Alternatives, Inc., had been hired as a US government contractor for a controversial USAID (United States Agency for International Development) democracy-promotion program. While the US government argued Gross was not working as an intelligence agent, Raúl Castro defended Gross's fifteen-year prison sentence.[11] Opponents of rapprochement with Cuba cited Gross's imprisonment as evidence that the Cuban state could not be trusted and that no further actions toward Cuba should be taken until his release.

Despite the measured and seemingly slow changes in US policies regarding travel to Cuba, the administration's pro-engagement attitude facilitated valuable cultural exchanges. The Office of Foreign Assets Control was instructed to once again start issuing licenses for Cuba travel to qualifying applicants, and the administration made it easier for Cubans to visit the United States. The administration's early overtures led music promoters to apply for permission to bring increasingly more Cuban musicians stateside. By October 2009 the State Department had issued 5,500 more visas for Cubans to visit the United States than were issued in 2008.[12] The Obama administration was no longer applying Reagan's Presidential Proclamation 5377 to all Cuban musicians across the board, but as the policy was still technically in place it continued to create some problems. When Cuban singer-songwriter Silvio Rodríguez applied to visit the United States for Pete Seeger's ninetieth birthday concert in May 2009, his visa application was delayed, causing him to miss the event.[13] In a public letter to Seeger, Rodríguez wrote, "I tried to come back to be with you today, but, as you well know, I was not allowed to get there by those who do not want the US and Cuba to get together, to sing to each other, to talk to each other, to understand each other."[14]

THE STATE DEPARTMENT'S BLESSING: JUANES AND PEACE WITHOUT BORDERS

On September 20, 2009, Miami-based Colombian American rock star Juanes headlined a major US-Cuban musical collaboration in the form of his Peace Without Borders concert in Havana, which required cooperation by the US State Department and the Cuban Ministry of Culture. The concert took place in the Plaza de la Revolución, where large, three-dimensional murals of revolutionaries Che Guevara and Camilo Cienfuegos adorn the sides of government buildings lining the plaza. The massive open cement courtyard surrounds the José Marti Memorial tower, and the plaza regularly hosted political rallies where Fidel Castro gave long, anti-imperialist speeches. On this day, however, it became home to an event that brought together Cuban musicians and a range of stars from Latin America and the United States.

Juanes was born Juan Esteban Aristizábal Vásquez in Medellín, Colombia. He initially earned acclaim singing and playing guitar in the heavy metal band Ekhymosis, but his songwriting has transformed over time to combine rock with popular Latin styles and Colombian traditional music. In the late 1990s he relocated to the United States and settled in South Florida, but he continues to tour extensively around the world. *Time* magazine named Juanes one of the world's 100 most influential people in 2005, and Quincy Jones praised his abilities to cross cultural, linguistic, geographic, and political boundaries with his music. Much of the Colombian rocker's impact comes from his work as a political activist around the globe; his Fundación Mi Sangre (My Blood Foundation) was founded to fight against the use of anti-personnel mines in Colombia and has been involved in numerous humanitarian causes.[15] The 2009 Havana event was Juanes's second Peace Without Borders concert. The first was held in 2008 on the border between Colombia and Venezuela. At that time, a diplomatic standoff and a growing military presence along the border led to increased tension in the region. The concert drew over two hundred thousand fans from both countries and was seen by millions of viewers throughout Latin America on television. The Cuba concert, like the original, had a goal of uniting citizens across borders and advocating peaceful conflict resolution.

Raúl Castro's government permitted Juanes to organize Peace Without Borders and provided logistical and technical support for the event. In planning the concert, Juanes and the event planners met with Obama administration officials and spoke directly with Secretary of State Hillary Clinton. According to Juanes, Secretary Clinton and Department of State officials were very supportive of the idea.[16] The Department of State facilitated the concert by ensuring that the performers and their support staff had the required licenses and authorizations for travel. The musicians performed without compensation and financed the costs of shipping the massive concert's stage and sound equipment from Miami.

When it was announced that Juanes intended to perform in Cuba, there was a storm of controversy in Miami's Cuban exile community, as some believed that such a performance would lend credibility to a dictatorial government while ignoring the plight of political dissidents. Anti-Castro groups publicly destroyed Juanes records, and the performer even faced death threats requiring police protection outside his home in Key Biscayne. The responses from musicians in the exile community were generally more nuanced. Cuban-born musician Willy Chirino, who came to the United States in 1960, released a statement that supported Juanes's efforts to provide a needed distraction to the Cuban people, but he also called out what he considered to be a dual moral standard of musicians willing to perform in Cuba who likely would not have performed for other authoritarian regimes.[17] Juanes responded to the controversy in an interview with the *Miami Herald*, saying:

> This is not about politics. Nobody called us, nobody invited us to Havana. I am not a communist. I am not aligned with the government. I'm not going to Cuba to play for the Cuban regime. Our only message is one of peace, of humanitarianism, of tolerance, a message of interacting with the people . . . We are musicians, not politicians.[18]

Amaury Pérez, a Cuban singer and part of the *nueva trova* movement, was also scheduled to perform at the concert. In responding to the backlash Juanes was facing in Florida, Pérez argued that the exile community in Miami had politicized the show, not Juanes or Cuba.[19] Despite the contention, the concert went on as planned. Fourteen artists from six countries performed. It was estimated that just over one million people attended the concert, making it the largest gathering for an international visitor in Cuba since the visit of Pope John Paul II in 1998. One Miami station nicknamed it the "Concert of Discord," but it was the first Havana concert to be televised live in Miami, allowing Cuban nationals and exiles to watch the event simultaneously.[20]

After seeing the broadcast, many in Miami who had previously opposed the concert changed their opinion and viewed the exchange favorably. Beforehand, only 27 percent of Cuban Americans supported the event while 47 percent opposed it. In a poll taken afterwards, however, 53 percent of respondents had a favorable opinion of it as opposed to 29 percent who saw it negatively.[21] Although Juanes and the other musicians claimed apolitical intentions and agreed to not make overtly political statements, political meaning was read into many of their words and lyrics. A female rapper performing with Cuban artist X Alfonso chanted "Down with the control. Down with those who manipulate you," and Spanish pop singer Miguel Bosé said, "We're all here together for the dream of concord, for the dream of dialogue!"[22] During Juanes's performance he called for peace and unity multiple times. He told the youth of Latin America the future was in their hands, and he dedicated a song to anyone who was unjustly imprisoned. The most powerful moment came near the end of the show when all of the performers were gathered on stage, and Juanes shouted "¡Cuba *libre!*" (Free Cuba!) and "¡Una *sola familia Cubana!*" (One Cuban family!). These words avoided any direct political criticism, but they were still enough to convince some in Miami that the concert was a positive, worthwhile event.

Just two days later, Massachusetts Representative Jim McGovern praised the concert on the floor of the House of Representatives. He said:

> I applaud Juanes and all the participating artists for their courage, their vision and commitment to working together to communicate directly to the Cuban people through the language of music. More than just a rock concert, this massive cultural event in Havana was a moving and emotional testament, even to many of its critics, about the power of the human spirit to reach across barriers during times of tension and opportunities. The ripples and waves created by this

concert are just beginning to be felt in Cuba, the United States and throughout the hemisphere. I very much look forward to supporting other Paz Sin Fronteras initiatives in the future.[23]

However, his Republican colleague, Representative Ileana Ros-Lehtinen, a Cuban American from Miami, said the concert was a triumph for the Castro regime because there was no direct mention of Cuba's human rights violations or demand to free political prisoners. Discussion about Cuba policy in the US Congress has typically been dominated by the Cuban American politicians who support aggressive policies targeting the Cuban regime. During the Obama administration, however, an increasing number of politicians from both parties and different states started to express pro-engagement stances.

Besides Juanes, two other groups had high-profile trips to Cuba under the auspices of the Obama administration's Department of State: funk and disco band Kool and the Gang in December 2009 and the Jazz at Lincoln Center Orchestra in October 2010. Kool and the Gang performed in Havana just three months after the Peace Without Borders concert, but their performance avoided even brief statements that could be interpreted politically. In an interview, Robert "Kool" Bell made it clear that they were visiting the island as musicians and not politicians, adding, "We are all about the music. We travel the world and our message is love, understanding and unity."[24] Although the band claimed their performance had no political intentions, it still depended upon government authorization, which they received from the US State Department and the Cuban Institute of Music. The day after their performance, the band received the 2009 Honorary Cubadisco Award from the Cuban Minister of Culture in a meeting at the Cuban Music Institute. Robert Bell was also given a Cuban *tres* (a guitar with three sets of double strings used in Afro-Cuban music), and the band pledged to return and perform in Cuba again sometime in the future.[25]

Wynton Marsalis and the Jazz at Lincoln Center Orchestra already had a connection with the State Department through the Rhythm Road: American Music Abroad cultural diplomacy program, which they had facilitated since 2005. Yet this was the first time the famous jazz orchestra performed in Cuba. While in Havana, Marsalis and his fellow musicians participated in numerous concerts and workshops as part of a five-day residency with the Cuban Institute of Music. They performed with Chucho Valdés and then invited Valdés to perform with them in New York the following month. These celebrity musicians had their licenses secured with the help of the

Obama administration, but less famous performers and those without political connections depended on policy changes and faced more challenges in traveling to Cuba.

VISITING FAMILY: TANIA LEÓN AT THE LEO BROUWER FESTIVAL

Cuban Americans have legally been able to travel to Cuba in some capacity since the 1980s, but the guidelines for visiting relatives have been inconsistent. Even under the George W. Bush administration, Cuban Americans were able to travel on a general license when visiting a "close relative," but there were restrictions on the duration and frequency of trips to Cuba for that purpose. Travelers who qualified for a general license did not need to submit an application to the OFAC before traveling to Cuba; if someone met the qualifications, they were automatically licensed without an application. By easing the general license qualifications for Cuban Americans in 2009, Obama facilitated the travel of all Cuban Americans, including musicians such as composer Tania León. This allowed Cuban American musicians to avoid much of the red tape endured by other musicians who wanted to visit the island; but the Cuban government has long had an unfavorable view of artists who left the island, so performance opportunities in Cuba were rare.

As a composer and conductor residing in the United States since the late 1960s, León has witnessed multiple presidential administrations and the variations on US-Cuban travel policies that have accompanied them. Changes in the political relationship between the United States and Cuba have had a direct impact on León's life by limiting her connections to family and her home country. Tania Justina León was born in Havana, Cuba, on May 14, 1943. Her family of mixed French, Spanish, African, and Chinese heritage was not a particularly musical one, but her grandmother still enrolled her in piano lessons at age four. León went on to study accounting and music in college, earning degrees in theory, piano performance, and music education (Spinazzola 2011). Although León was largely nonpolitical, US-Cuban political maneuvering following the 1959 revolution began to factor into her musical life.

León had some success performing in her home country in the 1960s but found her options limited. She wanted to continue her studies and pursue new musical opportunities abroad. About growing up in Cuba, she said, "If you live on an island you do a lot of staring at the horizon! I grew up only eight blocks from the sea, so that was very normal for me, to stare at the sea, always wondering what was on the other side" (Spinazzola 2011, 269). These feelings of confinement and her desire for new musical experiences led her to leave Cuba. She knew returning to the island would be extremely difficult, and the grandmother who initially set her on her musical path told her that if she left they would never see each other again. But León felt that leaving was the only way to further her musical education and pursue her career. In 1967 she took a plane to Miami as part of the Freedom Flights program, a collaborative immigration initiative operated by the US and Cuban governments. Although she initially intended to settle in Paris, circumstances led her from Miami to New York, where she has stayed.

Tania León had been making a name for herself in the art music circles of New York City in the 1970s, but Cuban authorities would not allow her music to be performed on the island. After President Carter lifted the travel ban she was allowed to visit her family in Cuba for the first time since her departure. During this trip, she listened to rumba with her father and witnessed a traditional *bembé* celebration; her father then encouraged her to incorporate the music of Cuba into her own work (Gidal 2010, 53). Upon returning to the United States, León corresponded with her father to plan her next trip, but he died in March 1980 before they could see one another again. She integrated elements of folkloric Cuban music in response to the overwhelming emotions stirred by returning to Cuba, reuniting with her family, and then losing her father (Iturralde 2007). Although her return to Cuba marked a turning point in her music, León has remained largely silent on US-Cuban politics and travel policies. She faced many challenges visiting family, and her ability to do so depended on who was in the White House. Despite her growing success as a composer in the United States, her music would still not be performed in Cuba. In a 1999 interview, León was asked how older Cubans would react to her as a female composer and conductor. She replied, "Well, let me tell you something. I have not had the chance to do that in Cuba. I have never performed in Cuba. Ever. You know, so I have no idea how this would be taken." When asked if her music has ever been performed in Cuba by anyone else, she answered, "I have no idea. I cannot tell you. I don't know."[26]

In October 2010, however, Tania León was invited to the Leo Brouwer Festival in Cuba as a featured composer. The changes instituted by the Obama administration in 2009 meant that León could fly to Havana for the festival without having to request a license. The festival was named for Cuban guitarist, conductor, and composer Leo Brouwer. He previously organized Cuba's primary guitar festival, and in 2009 Brouwer founded the chamber music festival that carries his name. The multi-day event takes place in various venues in Old Havana every October. Each year the festival has a different theme and features both Cuban and international artists. In 2010 the festival spotlighted Cuban female composers, and the committee selected two of León's pieces. The first was "Alma" ("Soul"), a composition for flute and piano from 2007, inspired by a bird's song and flight.[27] The second work was "Arenas d'un Tiempo" ("Sands of Time"), a 1992 piece for clarinet, cello, and piano inspired by a trip to Brazil. The composer brought her eighty-five-year-old mother, León's last surviving relative from that generation, to the event. This marked the first time that her mother could hear her daughter's music performed.[28]

While this visit illustrates the Cuban government's new openness to welcome back artists who left the island for careers abroad, tensions still persisted. The Leo Brouwer Festival and its participants were well covered in the Cuban media, but Tania León was frustrated to find that her name and references to her music were absent from all coverage.[29] The convention of not acknowledging expatriate artists in the media, however, is also changing. Since the revolutionary government took power, performers who left the country, whether for professional or political reasons, have been heavily censored by the Cuban Institute for Radio and Television. It has been rare for these musicians to even be mentioned in the media. In September 2013, however, the state-controlled Confederation of Cuban Workers newspaper, *Trabajadores*, published the names of all the Cuban artists who were nominated for Latin Grammys, including exiles.[30] As exiled musicians gained further acceptance in their native country, the ability to travel on a general license facilitated their ability to create relationships with audiences and colleagues on the island.

ACADEMIC TRAVEL AND EDUCATIONAL EXCHANGES

Advocates for the freedom to travel to Cuba grew frustrated with the Obama administration's slow movement and launched a legislative effort to lift the travel ban in 2010. The Democratic Party had majorities in the House of Representatives and the Senate at the time, but the legislation failed because of opposition to reform from within the party by Florida Democrats and Cuban American legislators. The White House neglected to weigh in on the issue and did not endorse or lobby for the legislation. The administration had already been planning to end the restrictions on academic and educational travel that were instituted under George W. Bush, but at the request of congressional Democrats, they waited until after the 2010 midterm elections. Late on a Friday afternoon before a holiday weekend in January 2011, the Obama administration quietly announced a series of policies that brought back Clinton-era "people-to-people" exchanges and made it easier for individuals to travel to Cuba (LeoGrande and Kornbluh, 380).

The new rules went into effect when the OFAC published them that April, allowing individuals to engage in various types of noncommercial, purposeful travel to Cuba without requesting a specific license. Instead they were permitted to travel under the auspices of a general license, which typically only required the traveler to have a letter documenting that their travel fit into one of the following categories:

(1) Participation in a structured educational program in Cuba as part of a course offered for credit by the sponsoring US academic institution;

(2) Noncommercial academic research in Cuba specifically related to Cuba and for the purpose of obtaining a graduate degree;

(3) Participation in a formal course of study at a Cuban academic institution, provided the formal course of study in Cuba will be accepted for credit toward the student's graduate or undergraduate degree;

(4) Teaching at a Cuban academic institution by an individual regularly employed in a teaching capacity at the sponsoring US academic institution, provided the teaching activities are related to an academic program at the Cuban institution and provided the duration of the teaching will be no shorter than ten weeks;

(5) Sponsorship, including the payment of a stipend or salary, of a Cuban scholar to teach or engage in other scholarly activity at the sponsoring US academic institution; or

(6) The organization of, and preparation for, activities described in (a) (1)-(5) above by members of the faculty and staff of the sponsoring US academic institution.[31]

The Berklee College of Music's Interarts Ensemble was one of the first university groups to travel to Cuba after these rule changes went into effect, when faculty member Neil Leonard brought the group to the 2011 Cubadisco International Fair. The Interarts Ensemble was awarded a Cubadisco International Prize for one of their albums and performed with various Cuban musicians during the ceremony. The trip was followed by Cuban musicians visiting Boston for performances at Berklee, and Leonard returned to Cuba for a performance in the Havana Jazz Festival.[32] My own trips to Cuba in 2011 and 2012 were justified under the general license for noncommercial academic research in pursuit of a graduate degree. My first trip, which involved taking percussion classes as part of the FolkCuba International Folklore Laboratories, also qualified as participation in a formal course of study. I spent nineteen days in Cuba on that trip, studying Afro-Cuban percussion with members of the Conjunto Folklórico Nacional, exploring and making contacts in Havana, and traveling outside the city for a couple days.

Studying percussion with members of the Conjunto Folklórico Nacional de Cuba allowed me to learn Afro-Cuban rhythms on conga and *batá*, the double-headed hourglass-shaped drums played in sets of three during Santería religious ceremonies. But working closely with and getting to know the other musicians in my class, both from Cuba and elsewhere, was the most rewarding part of the experience. The Conjunto Folklórico was formed in 1962 as part of the Teatro Nacional's Department of Folklore to act as an institution that could preserve Cuba's music and dance traditions while integrating them into the post-revolutionary national culture. By adapting Afro-Cuban religious musical traditions for the stage with modern theatrical aesthetics, the Conjunto Folklórico's dramatizations of rituals were the first of their kind (Hagedorn 2001, 136–41). They have since become a major part of the Cuban tourism industry, with various ensembles putting on staged folkloric performances throughout the country.[33]

The website for the Conjunto Folklórico describes the FolkCuba International Folklore Laboratories as "15 days of rhythm beginning on the third Monday in January and the first Monday in July [where] the most outstanding figures of the National Folklore Group of Cuba will impart the secrets of Cuban folk dances, with their African and Hispanic roots, and the magic sounds produced by Cuban percussion instruments."[34] That was about all of the information I had before showing up on the first Monday in July. I waited outside of the Conjunto Folklórico's building in the Vedado district of Havana, and it was apparent to me I was the only person who was not a native Spanish speaker. After we were ushered into the building and gathered on the wooden floor of the auditorium, everyone introduced himself or herself. The majority of participants were Cubans, but there were also visitors from Panama and Mexico, and they ranged from elementary school kids to middle-aged adults; most participants were in their late teens or early twenties. We sang some songs and then were asked to start dancing. At that point, one of the other participants and I realized we had been ushered into the dance class, not the percussion class. We explained the situation to the dance instructor, and she sent us to fill out our registration paperwork. The administrator then told us that the percussion instructor was not there and our lessons would not start until the next day.

Our instructor was Anier Alonso del Valle, a young and very talented member of the Conjunto Folklórico. We learned various rumba patterns and other Afro-Cuban rhythms on congas and *cajon*. When learning *batá*, we first learned the rhythms on *okonkolo*, the smallest of the three drums, but over the course of the lessons we memorized the patterns for twenty-one *orishas*, the deities in Santería religious practices, and learned to play them in the proper cycle. My experiences learning rhythms associated with the worship of Afro-Cuban deities confirmed Hagedorn's assertion that "folklore seems to exist without religion in the context of the FolkCuba workshops" (2001, 127). We learned many rhythms, but they were taught almost entirely without context. Anier had participated in traditional Santería ceremonies before and he could provide descriptions of the *orishas*, but he approached FolkCuba as a professional musician and percussion instructor. We moved very quickly from one rhythm to the next, only being told the name of its affiliated *orisha*. After two days, I started asking what the *orisha* represented when we learned a new rhythm, and Anier shared whether the deity was male or female and the elements or activities they represented. I learned much more about actual Santería practices from a young man named Leo I met on the street who invited me into his family's home, where his grandmother showed me the shrines for various *orishas* that they kept. Leo arranged for me to take some informal dance lessons taught by his girlfriend and brought me into neighborhoods far from the tourist areas and even to visit his sister in a Cuban hospital's maternity ward.

During part of my time in Cuba, I stayed in a *casa particular* in Vedado that was popular with academics visiting from the United States. It had three bedrooms that could be rented out, some of which were occupied by other visitors from US universities during my two weeks there. For two nights there was a group of faculty and administrators from the University of Georgia who were in Cuba to set up a study-abroad program, and near the end of my stay there was a New York University dance professor who stayed with Carlos while her students participated in a dance workshop. Following the US policy changes in 2011, numerous universities quickly set up programs in Cuba, many of which had a musical focus. As long as they were part of "a structured educational program in Cuba as part of a course offered for credit by the sponsoring US academic institution," university ensembles were able to perform in Cuba under these new rules.[35]

In addition to the 350,000 Cuban Americans who visited Cuba, the new policies allowed 73,500 US citizens without Cuban heritage to visit the island in 2011. That number increased to 98,000 in 2012. During the previous era of educational and cultural exchanges under President Clinton, the peak number of US visitors in Cuba annually was around 70,000 before dropping to an average of 30,000 under President George W. Bush.[36] While Obama's policies made it possible for many more individuals to legally travel between the United States and Cuba in 2011, only certain individuals could justify travel with the ease of a general license. Most musicians wishing to perform on the island still faced the challenges of a slow, confusing, and inconsistent bureaucracy.

VOICES FROM THE HEART, THE NATIONAL CHOIR OF CUBA, AND SPECIFIC LICENSES FOR CULTURAL EXCHANGE

Traveling to Cuba to participate in a concert or other musical event did not qualify for a general license on its own. Most musicians were instead forced to apply for a specific license that authorized travel to Cuba for public performances. 2011 OFAC regulations read:

> You may request a specific license authorizing certain travel-related and additional transactions incident to participation in a public performance, clinic, workshop, athletic or other competition, or exhibition in Cuba. The event must be open for attendance and, in relevant situations, participation by the Cuban public. All US profits from the event after costs must be donated to an independent nongovernmental organization in Cuba or a US-based charity with the objective, to the extent possible, of promoting people-to-people contacts or otherwise benefiting the Cuban people.[37]

After the administration announced the new policies in January 2011, many musicians were excited to visit Cuba. Over 3,400 applications for specific licenses were submitted to the OFAC in the first few months of 2011, but only a handful were granted by the end of the year.[38] In one example, a group of Irish American musicians intended to participate in Havana's second annual Celtic Festival in April 2011 but were denied their license just a week before the festival was to begin. The OFAC claimed the trip would go "beyond the scope of what was authorized" by citing an earlier set of guidelines from 2004.[39]

Other artists were more successful. In July 2012 a New Hampshire women's choir named Voices from the Heart visited Cuba as part of a cultural exchange with the National Choir of Cuba. They sang in Havana's CorHabana International Choir Festival as the only participating US group. After other international trips to Europe and Asia, the choir's director, Joanne Connolly, wanted to bring the ensemble somewhere more nearby, and she had heard about other musicians visiting Cuba after Obama became president. Cuba appealed to her musically, and she also hoped that it would be more affordable than their previous trips, but it was not.[40]

Getting their Specific License took two years of planning and coordinating with the help of Michael Eizenberg of the Educational Travel Alliance, a travel service provider licensed by the OFAC to make travel arrangements in Cuba for qualifying individuals and organizations.[41] Eizenberg oversaw the application process, which involved justifying the trip as a formal cultural exchange and providing documentation that certified all travelers were active members of the organization, identified the Cuban institutions with which they were working, predicted the number of audience members for whom they would perform, and described the opportunities for interaction with the Cuban people. Staff at the Educational Travel Alliance knew how to make their application successful, but the choir still grew frustrated with the process and not knowing what would be approved and when. According to Connolly: "We thought it was Michael, but it wasn't. It was Cuba. He really pushed. I think it's kind of his personal mission, but it did help us get our license. We wrote formal letters inviting the Cuban National Choir to the United States because he kept saying, 'That's true exchange, that's what we want.'"[42]

In order to make it a successful cultural exchange, Connolly traveled to Cuba ahead of the choir in March 2012. She went with a group from Boston's Bentley College on a short trip that was also organized by Eizenberg. At a formal dinner Connolly met Digna Guerra, who directs the National

Choir of Cuba, and took the opportunity to invite her to the United States. A month later, Guerra was in New Hampshire, where she spent five days visiting possible venues for her choir's part of the exchange. Her time in the United States also allowed her to teach Voices from the Heart arrangements of the Cuban songs "El Bodiguero" and "Guantanamera."

The group had no guarantee their trip would happen until less than two months before their departure, when their license application was approved. In their six formal concerts and more than a dozen informal sings, the choir members regularly interacted with Cuban musicians and audiences. Their first performance took place on the plane to Havana when they sang the Cuban national anthem "La Bayamesa" in three-part harmony, bringing tears to the eyes of their Cuban American flight attendants. They performed in the Museo Nacional de la Revolución with a children's choir and sang to elderly Cubans at a senior center in Old Havana. On July 3 the choir performed at the home of the US Interests Section's Chief of Mission in honor of US Independence Day. There they sang both national anthems for a mixed US and Cuban audience.[43] They visited Cienfuegos for two days before returning to Havana. In addition to Connolly's arrangement of "La Bayamesa," Voices from the Heart regularly performed the works "Finlandia," a song calling for peace between nations, and a song for *Yemaya*, the *orisha* of water and motherhood in Santería.

The cultural exchange was completed when Digna Guerra brought Coro de Entrevoces, a twenty-person group made up of members from the National Chorus, to New England in November 2012. Coro de Entrevoces began their tour in Portsmouth, which was followed by performances in Boston and on Cape Cod. Michael Eizenberg organized their visit and said that the Cuban performers were very excited about the exchange. They had traveled internationally many times, but this was their first time in the United States.[44] For many of the singers, the trip was a lifetime dream come true.

Connolly explained that she would like to return to Cuba one day but without the complications of travel licenses and coordinating such a large group. Obtaining a Specific License for cultural exchange was possible, but the process was unpredictable and stressful. Would-be-travelers were required to organize many aspects of their trips and to spend a significant amount of money before knowing whether or not their license would be issued. Voices from the Heart wisely worked with Michael Eizenberg and the Educational Travel Alliance to plan their exchange, but even then there was a significant amount of uncertainty surrounding their trip and license application.

99 PROBLEMS: PEOPLE-TO-PEOPLE LICENSES AND JAY-Z'S CUBA TRAVEL

The 2011 policy changes also permitted travel providers to organize cultural exchange tours that were open to anyone. After applying for and receiving a specific license to host "people-to-people" tours, these travel providers could bring any US citizens to Cuba if the trip itineraries met the criteria for cultural and educational exchange. The new regulations permitted more airports to schedule charter flights to Cuba. Previously travelers could only fly out of John F. Kennedy International Airport, Los Angeles International Airport, and Miami International Airport; an additional thirteen airports were authorized in 2011 to accommodate flights between the United States and Cuba. These reforms were meant to increase contact between US and Cuban citizens with the goal of what an administration official described as "helping strengthen Cuban civil society and, frankly, making Cuban people less dependent on the Cuban state."[45] The people-to-people programs, which existed under President Clinton and were reauthorized by Obama, were meant to encourage interaction between US and Cuban citizens through structured itineraries. Because musical performances and festivals take place in Havana and across Cuba frequently, many people-to-people travelers attend musical events as part of their organized trip. Some companies like Insight Cuba and the Cross Cultural Journey Foundation specifically designed trips around festivals such as the Havana Jazz Festival.

The relevant section in the Cuban Assets Control Regulations stated:

> OFAC may issue a specific license to an organization that sponsors and organizes programs to promote people-to-people contact authorizing the organization and individuals traveling under its auspices to engage in educational exchanges not involving academic study pursuant to a degree program. In general, licenses issued pursuant to this policy will be valid for one year and will contain no limitation on the number of trips that can be taken.[46]

Organizations interested in applying for one of these people-to-people licenses were required to provide detailed examples of their activities in Cuba and explain how those activities would result in meaningful interaction between US travelers and the Cuban people. Applicants were also required to include a certification stating that each traveler would have a full-time schedule of educational exchange activities resulting in the previously mentioned "meaningful interaction."

An estimated fifty thousand people traveled from the United States to Cuba between 2011 and summer 2012, when the initial round of people-to-people licenses started to expire.[47] From the first to the second year, the license application went from only six pages long to over one hundred pages, and by fall 2012 only a fraction of renewals had been approved by the OFAC. Many tour operators were forced to cancel trips and refund registered participants when renewed licenses were not issued before the departure date. When tour operators inquired as to their status, the explanations for delays included a backlog of paperwork and staffing issues.[48] These issues, however, were an intentional result of political posturing. The renewal delays followed a December 15, 2011, speech by Florida senator Marco Rubio in which he railed against the itineraries of these trips because they included activities like dancing. Senator Rubio claimed that the people-to-people activities amounted to nothing more than tourism that supplied money to a dictatorial regime and bordered on indoctrination.[49]

For months following his speech, Rubio held up the Senate confirmation of Assistant Secretary of State Roberta Jacobsen until reaching a quid pro quo with the White House requiring stricter guidelines for people-to-people trips. License renewals followed in October. Insight Cuba, one of the more prominent people-to-people travel providers, had to lay off twenty-two people and cancel one hundred fifty trips because of the delay.[50] After becoming acquainted with the new, more cumbersome application, organizations once again began organizing trips that could legally take any US citizens to Cuba with ease. People-to-people trips, however, were often expensive and typically cost between $2,500 and $3,000 before airfare for a five-day trip. For example, the 2013 Havana Jazz Festival tour from the Cross Cultural Journey Foundation cost $2,995 for five days in a double room, not including airfare. While the people-to-people trip gave participants an opportunity to experience Cuban music, it did not come cheaply.[51]

For popular musicians Beyoncé Knowles-Carter and Shawn "Jay-Z" Carter, however, money was no object. The two stars traveled to Havana with their family from April 3 to 6, 2013, for their fifth wedding anniversary. Neither musician performed in Cuba, so their trip was not a musical exchange, but it illustrates another legal pathway musicians used to visit Cuba in the Obama years. Most significantly, the attention and controversy surrounding the couple's travel to Cuba had repercussions that lasted long after the trip ended. Jay-Z and Beyoncé's arrival quickly received media coverage in both

Cuba and the United States as pictures surfaced of the rapper walking around the streets of Havana smoking cigars, and the photos prompted many people to ask how and why the celebrity couple was able to visit the island. The two performers had previously been guests at the White House and donated to President Obama's political campaigns, which fueled speculation that the president helped the Carters get a travel license. South Florida Republican representatives Ileana Ros-Lehtinen and Mario Diaz-Balart penned a letter to the director of the OFAC describing the oppressiveness of the Castro regime and the legal restrictions on tourism in Cuba before inquiring:

> We write to express concern and to request information regarding the highly publicized trip by US musicians Beyoncé Knowles-Carter (Beyoncé) and Shawn Carter (Jay-Z) to Cuba. We would like to respectfully request, within all applicable rules and guidelines, information regarding the type of license that Beyoncé and Jay-Z received, for what purpose, and who approved such travel.[52]

It was revealed that the Carters traveled on a people-to-people license belonging to the Sir John Soane Museum Foundation based in New York.

While in Cuba, the celebrity couple met with a dance group, a children's theater company, a singer, and visited an arts institute. These interactions meet the cultural and educational elements required for a people-to-people trip, but Cuban American legislators pounced on Jay-Z and Beyoncé's visit as proof that these exchanges were a front for tourism. In turn, they called for an end to the people-to-people license category. Ros-Lehtinen released a statement:

> If the tourist activities undertaken by Beyoncé and Jay-Z in Cuba are classified as an educational exchange trip, then it is clear that the Obama Administration is not serious about denying the Castro regime an economic lifeline that US tourism will extend to it. That was a wedding anniversary vacation that was not even disguised as a cultural program. As more human rights activists engage in hunger strikes, I don't think they will see any evidence of how this scam endeavor will help them become independent of the regime.[53]

Senator Rubio also entered the debate, saying that Jay-Z needed to "get informed" about Cuba, and that the artist should have met with some of the people who were being oppressed and persecuted. Popular Miami rapper

Pitbull responded with a song that defended the Carters against Rubio, raising the question, "Would they have messed with Mr. Carter if he was white?" (Abreu 2015, 225). Jay-Z himself addressed the trip with a track released online entitled "Open Letter" where he criticized politicians and pointed out the hypocrisy of US-Cuban policy. He rapped:

> Wanna give me jail time and fine
> Fine, let me commit a real crime....
> I'm in Cuba, I love Cubans.
> This communist talk is so confusing
> When it's from China, the very mic I'm using.[54]

Although Jay-Z named Obama in the song, the president only joked about the incident during the 2013 White House Correspondents' Association Dinner, when he referenced the rapper's hit song "99 Problems" in his remarks, saying, "This whole controversy about Jay-Z going to Cuba—it's unbelievable. I've got 99 problems and now Jay-Z is one."[55]

The controversy and ensuing media frenzy was called "Beyoncé-gate" in the *Atlantic*, and it ultimately brought much more mainstream media attention to US-Cuban travel regulations than there had been previously. The politicians who turned the Carters' trip into a controversy sought to weaken people-to-people travel and return to tighter travel restrictions, but they had the opposite effect. The majority of newspaper articles and op-eds on the topic were in favor of expanding travel and explained how anyone can go on a people-to-people trip. According to Tom Popper, president of Insight Cuba, "It's had a huge impact. Everything from our call center to our website to our blog to our Facebook page just lit up. People were Googling it and curious. The debate got heightened, and also people's awareness of this kind of tour was heightened."[56] Despite the protests of some South Florida politicians, people-to-people travel continued and the number of US citizens legally visiting Cuba continued to grow.

THE PATH TO NORMALIZATION

As "Beyoncé-gate" was raising public awareness about Cuba travel policies in April 2013, the Obama administration began in secret to pursue more significant steps to transform the US-Cuban relationship. Benjamin J. Rhodes, a top Obama aide, and Ricardo Zuniga, a Western Hemisphere official for the National Security Council, bypassed diplomatic channels while sending a message to Cuban officials to begin secret talks. Shortly after being reelected, Obama tasked the staffers with establishing a back channel to Havana that would allow for a much more transformative Cuba policy in his second term. Beginning in June 2013, the two aides quietly traveled to Canada to meet with Cuban officials, and the secret talks continued over the next eighteen months.

While talks between the United States and Cuba took place outside of the public's view, musical diplomacy between the two countries continued to be an important public forum for US-Cuban interaction. The executive actions that began in 2009 allowed for increased musical connections between the two countries, and cultural exchanges helped lay the groundwork for the process of normalizing diplomatic relations. After President Obama signaled that rules governing Cuba travel would be changing in 2009 and again in 2011, individuals and institutions flooded the OFAC with requests for travel licenses. The issuing of licenses that followed was both inconsistent and unpredictable, and the categories for travel separated US citizens into groups who were treated unequally. The office's failure to keep up also demonstrated that the restrictions did not reflect the will of the US public. It became legally possible for musicians to make cultural exchanges, but the legal framework for US policy toward Cuba continued to make travel uncertain and unreliable.

Anthropologists who study globalization have increasingly stressed that transnational economic and cultural forces are not universal and do not move throughout the world equally (Macleod 2002; Tsing 2005; Rockefeller 2011). These ideas can be applied to the US-Cuban relationship and the erratic movement of individuals between the two countries. Even after the Obama regulations went into effect, there was not a flow of music and musicians between the United States and Cuba. However, each successful legal trip and even the friction related to failed exchanges increased the potential for future US-Cuban interactions. The controversy of Jay-Z and Beyoncé's trip raised the awareness for and boosted participation in people-to-people travel. When Juanes initially announced his Peace Without Borders concert in Havana, he received strong negative feedback from the Cuban exile community. But because the overall response in Miami after the concert was positive, his performance cleared the path for other South Florida musicians to visit Cuba. Most musicians and fans of Cuban music have been forced to navigate complex regulations and bureaucracy to establish musical connections, but each successful trip raised the awareness of legal travel possibilities.

Tania León has said, "The artist is always ahead of the social transitions and transformations in her culture" (Iturralde 2007, 232). While she was speaking about changing compositional approaches, this comment can also be read in the context of the US-Cuban relationship. León was one of the first exiled composers to be invited back for a performance in Cuba during the Barack Obama and Raúl Castro era. Before the 2010 Leo Brouwer Chamber Music Festival, León's music had not been programmed in Cuba. Since that time, her music was featured in an international conference at the University of Havana in November 2013 entitled "Breaking the Taboo: Women Musicians in Traditionally Male-Dominated Fields," where guitarist Ana Maria Rosado presented León's works for guitar.[57] The reception of US performers in Cuba and the number of Cuban performers taking advantage of cultural exchange visas to perform in the United States demonstrated that the aspirations for increased musical interaction went both ways. The acceptance and enthusiasm for these performers by the public also suggested that there was a potential opening for political normalization.

3

THE POLITICS OF CUBAN MUSIC IN THE UNITED STATES

On October 9, 1999, Los Van Van, one of Cuba's most popular dance bands, visited Miami for the first time and were met by an aggressive, confrontational press and protests of over four thousand people. Concertgoers walked between protestors on each side of the street who were held back by barriers and police. Some protestors threw cans and bottles at people entering the concert while yelling insults including *"traidora"* (traitor) and *"dialoguera,"* the epithet coined in the exile community for anyone supporting negotiations with Cuba.[1] The scene was captured on film for a concert documentary that has since become popular in Cuba.[2] The opening scene depicts the Miami exile community as a violent mob and reinforces the picture that has been promoted by the Cuban government.

Juan Formell formed Los Van Van in 1969 when the Cuban regime was intent on institutionalizing the revolution through art and music. At a time when North American popular music was under attack by Cuban authorities for being imperialist, Formell formed a band that incorporated elements of rock and roll into Cuban dance music and paved the way for the popularity of Cuban timba in the 1980s and 1990s.[3] Los Van Van came to be one of Cuba's most popular bands and in turn became associated with the Cuban regime. Miami's Cuban American mayor Joe Carollo called them "the official Communist band of Fidel Castro" and tried to cancel the 1999 performance, which forced the ACLU to intervene.[4] Even though the concert was allowed to go on, the protests discouraged the band from returning to South Florida. They did not have the opportunity to come back to the United States until the Obama administration, and Formell credited Juanes and the Peace Without Borders concert for changing his mind about returning to Miami in 2010. Once again, protestors rallied outside of Los Van Van's return concert, but the demonstration was small and the number of concert attendees greatly outnumbered the picketers. During their performance, two recent exiles who had been major stars in Cuba, Issac Delgado and Manolín "El Médico de la Salsa" ("The Salsa Doctor"), joined Los Van Van on stage. The success of such a performance would have been unimaginable even a few years earlier. When asked about political intentions, Juan Formell said, "We came here to do music, just music. We didn't come to the US to do any kind of politics or ideology. If you ask me a political question, I'll answer you. I'm not mute, but this is not about sharing an idea or an ideology. You can think one way. I can think another. But we're talking about music."[5]

Cuban musicians who have performed in the United States demonstrate that the desire for further US-Cuban engagement comes from musicians in both nations, but politics informs these performances in complex ways even as performers try to publicly distance themselves from specific policy stances. An analysis of multiple events that featured Cuban music highlights how the US-Cuban international relationship is colored and shaped by regional politics within the United States. The Miami and South Florida region in particular is examined because of its importance to US national policy toward Cuba and its centrality to the popular music industry in Latin America. Regional issues can be further explored through differences between festivals in Miami and New York City. The chapter concludes with an in-depth analysis of the first US tour of the National Symphony Orchestra of Cuba in fall 2012, which included twenty-one performances in cities across the Midwest, along the East Coast, and throughout Florida. These performances and their reception illustrate that there is a desire for further US-Cuban cultural interaction, but there is also still resistance. Despite what musicians say and intend, it is impossible for these performances to completely avoid politics.

MIAMI, EXILE IDEOLOGY, AND THE LATIN MUSIC INDUSTRY

In December 2010 the Miami City Commission passed a resolution asking Congress to end cultural exchanges with Cuba, and other city commissions in South Florida followed suit. The Cuban population that transformed Miami's demographic, economic, and political makeup after the revolution has profoundly impacted US policy toward Cuba. Since the 1980s Miami has also grown to become the most powerful city in the Latin American popular music industry, which complicates the relationship between music and international relations. The exile experience and Miami's cultural and geographic distance from the rest of the country fostered pervasive ideologies that impacted the music and politics of the region. During the Obama presidency, however, the gradual transformation of ideological attitudes in the region became apparent.

Following the success of Fidel Castro and his 26th of July Movement, large numbers of Cubans deemed to be enemies of the revolution were executed, jailed, or punished. Individuals left their land and property behind to save their lives. Between 1959 and 1964, over 270,000 individuals migrated to the United States, and more than half of them settled in Miami-Dade County (Chun and Grenier 2004, 2). Immigration slowed in the 1970s, but by the end of that decade South Florida's Cuban American population was the wealthiest Hispanic constituency in the United States. Cuban immigrants made inroads into both the financial and political arenas of South Florida, allowing them to economically surpass many other immigrant groups in the country. The 1980s brought Cuban power in Miami to new heights through another population boom and new political allegiances. Cuban voting blocs were established in Congress and state legislatures, while organizations like the Cuban American National Foundation, the Latin Builders Association, and the Latin Chamber of Commerce furthered the economic and political status of Cuban Americans. Miami's entrepreneurial and business successes took place in relative geographic isolation because of the city's location at the end of a peninsular state. As a result, South Florida's Cuban exile community functioned largely in fiscal and social seclusion, which encouraged the entrenchment of Cuban culture in the region while promoting ethnic solidarity and slowing acculturation (Bosin 2004, 77–79).

Sociologists Alejandro Portes and Alex Stepick describe Miami as a city defined by waves of immigration where its residents have, in many ways, reproduced the institutions and social structures from their native countries within the United States. By the early 1990s, the rise of Cuban elites in Miami's power structure resulted in a city unlike others in the American urban landscape where the tensions and conflicts between different generations and immigrant groups along the lines of race, language, politics, and economics resulted in "acculturation in reverse" (Portes and Stepick 1993). Instead of assimilation into broader US culture, Miami fostered a bicultural society where residents are comfortable living within their own heritage (or that of their parents and grandparents) while simultaneously being fluent and comfortable in the heritage and culture of their adopted land. Despite the rise of Cuban American leaders in South Florida, Jorge Duany, director of the Cuban Research Institute at Florida International University, points out that there is still significant difference with regard to socioeconomic status and political ideology within the Cuban American community. The Mariel boatlift, which increased Miami's Cuban population by 20 percent, brought a group that had less education and fewer occupational skills than the exiles who arrived in the 1960s. The *marielitos* and arrivals with subsequent post-Soviet migrations looked more like traditional labor migrants and do not fit the narrative of Cuban immigrants as a privileged and prosperous homogeneous group (Duany 1999, 97–100).

Mariel was ended by President Carter days before the 1980 presidential election, and his handling of the crisis along with his other policies toward Cuba helped shape South Florida politics for the decades that followed. Many in the Cuban American exile community saw Carter's actions as capitulating to the Castro government, which pushed many South Florida voters toward the Republican Party. Strong support for Republicans who expressed hawkish positions toward Cuba and Castro continued through the 1990s. By the early 2000s, 69 percent of Cuban immigrants were registered as Republicans, and Cuban American leaders had taken control of the local Republican Party in Miami, creating a platform to bring their politics to the state and national level (Chun and Grenier 2004, 6; Portes and Armony 2018, 12).

Attempts to encourage regime change in Cuba and publicly express disapproval of the Castro government impacted Miami's local music scene and the city's place of influence in the Latin music industry. In 1996 Miami-Dade County passed a series of ordinances that collectively became known as the "Cuba Affidavit." These ordinances banned the county from entering into any contracts with firms doing business directly or indirectly with Cuba, and they blocked musical performances, film screenings, and art exhibits by artists from the island (Bosin 2004).

Miami's central role in the Latin music industry and the complicated relationship between music and anti-Castro politics in South Florida are exemplified by Gloria and Emilio Estefan. Gloria Estefan's father was a bodyguard for the Batista family who fled to the United States with sixteen-month-old Gloria after the revolution. In 1977 she began recording with the Miami Sound Machine and soon married the band's leader, Emilio Estefan Jr., who left Havana in his teens. The band played a crucial role in the transformation of Latin popular music and the development of the Latin pop genre. The group's first three albums were in Spanish, and they combined some Cuban percussion and dance rhythms with soft rock and pop. Miami Sound Machine developed a significant following in South Florida and throughout Latin America, and in 1985 they gained crossover success on the mainstream pop charts with their second English album, *Primitive Love*. The album contained a combination of up-tempo dance songs and syrupy romantic ballads, but it did not downplay the band's Cuban roots. This new approach with a stronger Latin tinge is manifested on the album's hit track "Conga," which became a major crossover success. The song's combination of electronic dance beats with Latin percussion made it very appealing to audiences by giving it both a modern and exotic sound. The song was fun and accessible "salsa-lite," and it appeared simultaneously on the Dance, Latin, R&B, and Pop *Billboard* charts (Party 2008, 66). Before crossing over, it would be difficult to categorize Miami Sound Machine as a "Latin" band; they performed US pop music with Spanish lyrics. According to Pérez Firmat, "At first [Miami Sound Machine] was a hispano-phone soft-rock group; later it became an anglophone soft-salsa group" (2012, 117). With *Primitive Love* the Estefans established a formula for mixing mainstream American pop with elements of Latin dance music and English lyrics, and this formula has been used ever since by Spanish-language artists looking to cross over into the broader US market. Miami's Cuban exile community avoided traditional acculturation in favor of biculturalism, and Miami Sound Machine also adopted a bicultural approach to maximize their popularity and profits. Their success fortified Miami's position as a central hub for the greater Latin American popular music industry.

Major record labels sought a Latin American headquarters offering political and economic stability, and they placed their main offices in Miami instead of a city in a Latin American country. The city is centrally located to offer easy travel between Latin American capitals and other important markets; it sits between Los Angeles and Madrid and between New York and Buenos Aires. Music executives have also claimed that Miami is a "neutral" place that can avoid the national resentments and rivalries associated with other Latin American cities. One music executive explained, "If you're based in Argentina, the Mexicans are going to think you're an Argentine operation, and vice versa" (Party 2008, 66). According to Richard Arroyo, the first managing director of MTV Latino, Miami was like "an entertainment Switzerland."[6] As a result, hit songs recorded in Miami could launch international careers reaching nearly all of the Western hemisphere and much of Europe.[7] Getting a musician from their home city to Miami and back in order to record an album was usually simple, as long as they were not coming from Cuba. The four major record labels, Sony, Universal, WMG, and EMI, all built a base of operations in Miami, and they consider Latin America to be one big market. By the mid-1990s, a boom in Latin American entertainment media in music, film, and television propelled Miami to the position of the third-largest production zone in the United States, behind Los Angeles and New York.[8]

The Estefans have been central figures in Miami's rise to musical prominence while also being outspoken members of the Cuban exile community. In 1999 the National Academy of Recording Arts and Sciences selected Miami as the location for the first Latin Grammy Awards show. They changed the location days before the event, however, following threats of violence and legal action, as the event would have been in violation of the 1996 Cuba Affidavit. As a result, Miami lost an estimated forty million dollars in potential revenue. When asked about the conundrum, Emilio Estefan stated that he would not "support a dictator, or music that comes from the dictator's house." If Cuban musicians were going to participate in the Latin Grammys, Estefan said he would not try to stop it but he also would not support it because "I don't support dictators" (Bosin 2004, 96). As central figures in the Latin music industry, the support of Gloria and Emilio Estefan was important to the success of the Latin Grammys. The awards eventually arrived in South Florida in 2003, and Juanes was the big winner of the night.

Six years later, when Juanes announced plans for his Peace Without Borders concert in Havana, the Estefans and many others in the Miami exile community criticized him. He initially asked Gloria and Emilio Estefan to accompany him, but they both declined and Emilio encouraged Juanes to cancel the performance.[9] When such powerful voices in the Latin music industry criticized the performance it caused other artists to reconsider, and some acts who initially expressed interest, including Ricky Martin and Enrique Iglesias, backed out of the concert. Before the Juanes concert was held, however, Gloria Estefan lent some support saying, "I hope he accomplishes what he's trying to do."[10]

The Cuban community continues to be prominent in South Florida music and politics, but Miami's demographics have been changing since the late 1980s with large numbers of non-Cuban immigrants arriving in the city. Miami now includes significant numbers of Colombians, Argentines, Haitians, and Brazilians in addition to Cubans. This has led some to call Miami a post-Cuban city that has instead developed a generalized transnational Latin identity (Party 2008, 69). These demographic changes are coinciding with the aging of the first generation of Cuban exiles. Now younger Cuban Americans and Cubans born after the revolution are more interested in visiting and having a relationship with the island. The fact that Juanes was able to perform in Cuba without damaging his career signals the beginning of a change in attitudes in Miami. The Cuban Study Group, an organization of Cuban American business leaders that lobbies for US-Cuban engagement, released a statement championing Juanes's initiative and declaring that Miami is changing. The statement continued, "It is time to give openness, reconciliation and dialogue the chance they deserve. . . . These results should encourage policy-makers to take steps to facilitate more of these exchanges in an effort to break down the barriers that separate the Cuban people."[11] The changing reactions to Cuban performers in Miami are further evidence of the city's transformation and the emerging diversity of opinions about Cuba.

CUBAN MUSIC FESTIVALS AND TRANSFORMATION IN MIAMI

Juan Formell and Los Van Van planned to play South Florida again less than a year after their successful 2010 performance as the headliners of a music festival in April 2011. The Fuego Cuban Music Festival was scheduled to take place at the Homestead-Miami International Speedway, a venue operated by the city of Homestead. Organizers MIA Resorts, Inc., and Fuego Entertainment billed the event as "The Cuban Woodstock" and the "First Cuban Music Festival in the United States" with the tagline "*Se parte de la historia*" ("Be a part of history"). Hugo Cancio, the president and CEO of Fuego Entertainment, said they chose Homestead over Miami to avoid directly provoking the Cuban American community, but controversy erupted when it was discovered that the festival was going to feature a number of musical acts from Cuba, including Los Van Van. Miami-Dade County Commissioner and former Mayor of Homestead Lynda Bell appeared on the Spanish-language radio station Radio Caracol to do an interview and announced she would do everything within her power to stop the concert, and she contacted Speedway officials who promised her it would be canceled. In the interview she stated, "We understand free speech and will defend free speech, but not when public facilities and public funds are being utilized."[12]

Days later Speedway officials canceled the event citing the risk of controversy and protests. They claimed they were not told the event would feature Cuban musicians, so they sued MIA Resorts for breach of contract and fraud. They also denied speaking to Commissioner Bell. MIA countersued for their damaged reputation and business losses. Documents presented during trial showed that Speedway officials had approved promotional materials advertising a Cuban music festival. In 2012 a jury ordered Speedway officials to pay $531,371 in damages to MIA and determined that the venue's managers defamed the production company by saying they lied about presenting Cuban acts.[13] The event also prompted an investigation by the American Civil Liberties Union (ACLU) into potential First Amendment violations. John de Leon, president of the Greater Miami chapter of the ACLU, stated, "The First Amendment prohibits the government from shutting down concerts or events they disagree with. It's unconscionable that a public official would attempt to thwart people's ability to attend a lawful cultural event in this community."[14] Bell, however, issued a statement denying any part in the cancellation of the festival.

Despite the controversy surrounding the Fuego Cuban Music Festival, later events featuring artists from Cuba faced little opposition. The Global Cuba Fest in Miami Beach brings together numerous Cuban musicians from the island and the exile community each year. In 2000 Ever Chavez immigrated to Miami from Cuba, where he had produced events for the Teatro El Público and Trianón Theater in Havana. Wanting to hear more contemporary Cuban music in Miami, he founded a nonprofit called FUNDarte to present Cuban music, and in 2008 he partnered with Miami Light Project for the first Global Cuba Fest.[15] The first few years of the festival featured Cuban artists living in South Florida and elsewhere in North America. But by its fourth year the event was coming much closer to fulfilling its purpose, which, Chavez claims, is uniting the global landscape of contemporary Cuban music from within the island and the diaspora on a single stage.

The 2012 Global Cuba Fest took place on April 1 in Miami Beach with an evening concert that featured Roberto Carcassés and Interactivo in their first US performance. Interactivo mixes traditional Cuban rhythms like *danzón* and *son* with jazz and rock; their performance during the festival also featured other performers from Cuba including singer Melvis Santa, guitarist and vocalist William Vivanco, and singer Francis del Río. Telmary Diaz, a Cuban rapper and spoken-word artist who spends time between Havana and Toronto, also joined them on stage. In 2013, the festival expanded to a multi-day event featuring more artists from Cuba. It kicked off with a concert by Cuban singer Ivette Cepeda and her band Reflexion and was followed by a series of concerts during the weekend of March 15 to 17. Each subsequent festival has also featured Cuban performers from the island as well as those living in Miami, New York, and Spain. Unlike many previous concerts that stirred controversy and led to protests from the exile community, the Global Cuba Fest was met with little criticism. According to festival organizer Ever Chavez it was because they avoided politics and intentionally worked with nonpolitical artists who do not promote any specific ideology on stage.[16] In contrast,

Emilio Izquierdo, an active member of the anti-Castro exile community who organized protests against Pablo Milanés in 2011, claimed that the Global Cuba Fest had no resistance because Miami's Cuban community largely did not know who the musicians were.[17] Unlike Los Van Van, most of the performers from Cuba at the Global Cuba Fest were young, rising stars who would not be known by those who left Cuba before the twenty-first century.

Standing in contrast to the Global Cuba Fest, which is meant to present contemporary Cuban music and bring together performers from the island and the diaspora, the annual Cuba Nostalgia festival is designed to celebrate pre-Castro Cuba and does not feature any artists currently residing on the island. Cuba Nostalgia started in 1999 and has combined live music, visual art, and food to allow Miami's Cuban immigrants that came to the United States in the early years of the revolution to remember the Cuba they left behind. The event transforms the Miami-Dade County Fair Expo Center into a prerevolutionary Cuba with a massive map of Havana covering the floor, a replica storefront of the once iconic El Encanto department store, and a recreation of the Malecón where individuals can have their pictures taken.[18] The festival also features a full lineup of live music with a focus on prerevolutionary Cuban genres like *danzón, son,* cha cha cha, *guaracha,* bolero, and mambo performed by South Florida Cuban American musicians. Beyond allowing older Cuban Americans to recall their past, Cuba Nostalgia is designed to educate younger generations and create nostalgia for the pre-Castro period that never existed in their lifetimes.

These festivals and concerts and the reactions to them are indications of a transformation in attitudes toward Cuba in South Florida. These changes have been documented by the FIU Cuba Poll, a research project first conducted in 1991 through Florida International University's Cuban Research Institute to measure the views of Cuban Americans about US policy options toward Cuba. In 1997, 77 percent of individuals said that travel to Cuba for any purpose other than visiting relatives should not be allowed; in 2011 57 percent favored lifting all restrictions on travel. That number rose to 75 percent among those who arrived in South Florida after 1994. For the first time since the poll began, a majority of people favored ending the embargo and 65 percent favored establishing diplomatic ties with Cuba.[19] Individuals in South Florida can experience these attitudinal transformations through increasingly common musical performances featuring Cuban artists. The political and economic power structure in South Florida, however, lags behind in its acceptance of these concerts and festivals, and the region remains largely in the hands of pro-embargo, anti-Castro politicians and community leaders.

CUBA IN NEW YORK AND THE ¡SÍ CUBA! FESTIVAL

Cuban music events outside of South Florida have generally avoided controversy simply by being away from the center of Cuban American political activity. While they have different purposes from festivals in the Miami area, they have their own challenges as well. Cuban American musicians and promoters are typically involved in the conception and organization of these events, but they either have a wider target demographic or seek to draw an audience based around a specific interest. By the nature of their location, these events are under less political scrutiny than those in Miami, but participating musicians and organizers still make a point to maintain their nonpolitical intentions.

New York was the foremost US city to feature professional Cuban musicians in the first half of the twentieth century. New York developed a significant Cuban American population that predated the revolution, and as a result, anti-Castro attitudes are less pronounced than in Florida. Even before the relaxation of travel restrictions under Barack Obama, New York City was the site for Cuban music festivals. When Tania León worked with the American Composers Orchestra, she helped conceive and run the Sonidos de Las Américas (Sounds of the Americas) concert series to promote and share music by Latin American composers who were rarely programmed in North American concerts. The series included orchestra and chamber music performances, symposia, master classes, public forums, and radio broadcasts. Each year the event focused on the music of a different nation, and the first five featured music from Mexico, Venezuela, Brazil, Puerto Rico, and Argentina, respectively. The sixth festival, which took place in March 1999, was devoted to the music of Cuba.

Clinton-era regulations made it possible to invite Cuban composers and musicians to the United States. Although the event was in New York, it still garnered attention and stoked controversy among some Cuban American groups who spoke against its happening. León explained:

> Fortunately, by the time the whole thing finished, the entire community recognized that this was a very specifically historical event because this hadn't happened for 40 years. There were people that didn't see each other in forty years and hadn't talked to each other for forty years and for the first time they were in front of each other composer to composer, two Cuban composers, one that remained and another one that left, who used to be very close, and they didn't see each other again until this moment.[20]

By bringing together composers, the Sonidos de las Américas concerts carried on the tradition started by the Pan-American Association of Composers earlier in the twentieth century. As a festival organized by a Cuban expatriate, it intentionally aimed to reunite members of Cuba's diasporic musical community. The Global Cuba Fest was designed to do the same thing almost a decade later. The Cuba-themed event was the last of the Sonidos de las Américas that León organized for the American Composers Orchestra. New York City did not have another major festival featuring Cuban artists living on the island until after Obama was elected.

The ¡Sí Cuba! Festival lasted from March until June 2011 and took place in multiple venues throughout the city. The idea for the event came about in 2009 after the State Department started issuing visas to Cuban artists. A number of New York institutions and venues including the World Music Institute, the Americas Society, Carnegie Hall, the Brooklyn Academy of Music (BAM), and others planned independent Cuban events, but promoters came together to collectively brand these performances, exhibitions, and screenings as a citywide celebration of Cuban art and music. Karen Brooks Hopkins, president of BAM and a primary organizer of ¡Sí Cuba! thought of the festival after returning from a trip to Havana and discovering how many events were already in place that could be promoted on a grander scale. With the help of other institutions, the festival acted as an organizational and promotional umbrella.[21] Over 125 Cuban artists came to New York to participate, representing a diverse array of musical genres along with dance, literature, film, and visual art. Some of the better-known musical acts participating in the festival included Los Muñequitos de Matanzas, the Septeto Nacional, the Ballet Nacional de Cuba, and the Creole Choir of Cuba.

While the festival was successful, there were challenges getting musicians from Cuba to New York and responding to political criticism of the festival. Some artists were unable to get permission to leave the island to participate, and hip-hop artists in particular were underrepresented in the festival lineup because many of them are critical of the Cuban government and address taboo topics with their lyrics. As a result, members of Havana's underground hip-hop community were not allowed to leave the country. Telmary Diaz, who was residing in Canada, was the only Cuban rapper at the festival. Considering so many Cuban artists were in attendance, political controversy was at a minimum. Cuban musician and outspoken critic of the Castro government Paquito D'Rivera expressed his disapproval of the festival and argued that everyone in the festival had been authorized to leave Cuba by the government and were therefore sent by Castro.[22] The limited criticism did not deter musicians or audiences, and there were initially plans to try to repeat the success of ¡Si Cuba! with a follow-up festival in Los Angeles; it never came to fruition.

¡Sí Cuba! did, however, lead to additional Cuban events in New York City. The Brooklyn Academy of Music hosted Red Hot + Cuba on December 1, 2012, which featured twenty-four musicians, most of whom were from Havana. Andres Levín, who is from Venezuela but frequently collaborates with Cuban musicians, led the performers. The concert took place on World AIDS Day and benefited the AIDS awareness organization Red Hot. The intention of the concert was to raise money for AIDS relief and awareness, but US-Cuban politics reared their head when singer David Torrens told the audience that borders were humanity's "most selfish invention" before singing "*Ni de Aquí ni de Allá*" ("Neither from Here nor There").[23] Fall 2012 also saw the Voices from Latin America Festival presented by Carnegie Hall and featuring Chucho Valdés as a performer and festival artistic advisor. Like ¡Sí Cuba!, Voices from Latin America took place over a number of weeks at multiple venues throughout the city featuring Cuban and Cuban American performers, but its scope was expanded to also include musicians from Mexico, Brazil, and Venezuela.[24] These events and the enthusiasm for the Cuban performers appearing in them reshaped New York City into a cultural space once again driving US-Cuban engagement.

THE NATIONAL SYMPHONY ORCHESTRA OF CUBA'S FIRST US TOUR

One of the most significant cultural exchanges to take place as the United States moved toward a policy of engagement with Cuba was the National Symphony Orchestra of Cuba's cross-country tour in October and November 2012. The orchestra's performances brought Cuban musicians face to face with US audiences in a wide variety of communities, many of which did not have significant Cuban American populations. The reactions to this extended cultural exchange and the positive receptions the orchestra received in one city after another illustrated the broader desire for further US-Cuban interaction. Numerous complications arose as part of organizing something as complex as an international tour, and questions about politics could not be avoided despite the orchestra's stated intent.

The National Symphony Orchestra of Cuba was formed in Havana in October 1960, when the revolutionary government began establishing new centers of music, film, theatre, and literary production. It emerged partly from the remnants of the prerevolutionary Havana Philharmonic Orchestra, but its budget was doubled and performers were offered substantially higher salaries (Moore 2006, 82). Fidel Castro extolled the National Symphony Orchestra as a success of the Cuban Revolution in his 1961 "Words to Intellectuals" speech, where he stated:

> What are the rights of revolutionary or non-revolutionary writers and artists? Within the Revolution, everything. Against the Revolution, no rights at all. . . . We would like to point out certain aspects in which progress has already been made and which should be the occasion for encouragement for all of us. For example, there has been the success achieved with the symphony orchestra, which has been reconstructed and totally reintegrated, and which has attained high levels not only artistically, but also revolutionarily, because 50 members of the symphony orchestra are already militiamen.[25]

Artists, including orchestral musicians, were encouraged to join Cuba's National Revolutionary Militia in the early 1960s. All artistic works were also supposed to be in support of the revolution, so the argument that Cuban musicians are representatives of the Castro regime is not without merit. Over the years, the National Symphony Orchestra of Cuba has engaged in cultural diplomacy around the world. The orchestra has introduced and promoted Cuban and Latin American music to international audiences, and the group has toured throughout Europe and in Russia, Mexico, Nicaragua, Peru, and Argentina. Yet the ensemble was unable to visit their neighboring country just ninety miles to the north until 2012.

The first organizational steps for this tour were taken shortly after President Obama announced the easing of travel restrictions, which encouraged the Tampa-based Florida Orchestra's board members to reach out to the Cuban orchestra and initiate a multi-year exchange. The first phase took place in September 2011, when a wind quintet from the Florida Orchestra traveled to Havana to perform with Cuban wind musicians. This marked the first time since 1999 that a professional American orchestra had sent musicians to Cuba, and only the second time for such an exchange since the 1959 revolution.[26] The following May the Cuban orchestra's conductor, Enrique Pérez Mesa, came to Tampa. What began as a collaboration and exchange between two organizations quickly became a larger endeavor as additional parties worked to bring the orchestra across the country for a series of performances.

Tour organizer Leonid Fleishaker of World Touring Entertainment grew up in Leningrad and as a young violin student became a fan of Cuban musicians when they came to study in the Soviet Union. Since immigrating to the United States, Fleishaker has organized tours for numerous groups from the former Communist Bloc including the Red Star Red Army Chorus, Moscow City Ballet, and Lezginka Dance Company of Daghestan. Fleishaker worked with Eric Amada of Arts Management Associates, a touring and production company that maintained close relationships with many of the venues where the orchestra would play and who had previously organized international tours for ensembles from China and elsewhere.[27] The participation of individuals like Fleishaker and Amada was key to this endeavor's success. It would have been nearly impossible for the orchestra to organize something like this alone, as travel policies have hindered the development of contacts in the United States and communication between the two countries is expensive and inconsistent. However, as political changes led to increased interest in Cuba, the potential profits of the tour encouraged Fleishaker and Amada get involved. The final key player in bringing the National Symphony Orchestra of Cuba to the United States was Ignacio Herrera, a Cuban pianist now living in Minnesota with a strong personal mission to bring the two countries closer together through music.

Ignacio "Nachito" Herrera joined the orchestra as the featured pianist throughout the tour. The Cuba native and resident of White Bear Lake, Minnesota, played with the National Symphony in 1978 at the age of twelve when he gained a reputation as a piano prodigy for his performance of Rachmaninoff's Concerto No. 2 in Havana. Herrera originally came from Artemisa, a town about sixty kilometers southwest of Havana, and received formal musical training with keyboard masters including Ruben Gonzalez, Jorge Gomez Labrana, and Frank Fernandez. He was the musical director at Havana's Tropicana Club before joining the group Cubanismo as lead pianist and arranger, which allowed him to tour internationally, including performances in the United States in the late 1990s. Herrera received an artist-in-residence visa to act as the music director for the play *Los Rumbaleros* in St. Paul, Minnesota, in 2001. When the World Trade Center and Pentagon were attacked on September 11, Herrera and his wife decided it was best he stay in the United States. He was convinced that if he went back to Cuba he would not be able to return. Because of preferential immigration policies for Cubans, Herrera was able to remain in the country after his visa expired and obtain a green card. His family joined him over a year later.

Despite the differences in temperature and culture between Havana and Minnesota, the Herrera family has made a home in the American Midwest. "I love Minnesota," Nachito explained. "I love New York. I love San Francisco. But we embrace Midwestern roots that are like us—the family getting together on weekends, going to church on Sundays."[28] Herrera is a regular fixture at the Dakota Jazz Club in St. Paul and he teaches university students in the area. He also regularly works with the Minnesota Youth Symphony. After hearing the news about the potential to bring the National Symphony Orchestra of Cuba to the United States, Nachito and Aurora Herrera quickly joined the effort. The policies that permitted Cuban emigrants to visit their native country allowed Herrera to visit Havana in January 2012 to finalize plans for the tour, choose repertoire, and begin rehearsing with the orchestra.

When the tour began in Kansas City, Missouri, Herrera was with them from their arrival through their stops along the East Coast and into the South. Herrera made a point to travel on the bus with the Cuban orchestra musicians and to stay in the same places as they crossed the country. He explained:

> I tried to be part of the tour traveling with them all the time, actually giving them support if they want to buy something or they want to go somewhere. Obviously, they didn't speak English and things like that so I definitely wanted to be with them twenty-four seven because I wanted to be able to capture the whole different opinion of how they feel about this country. They were extremely happy. They all definitely want to come back.[29]

Herrera also arranged a number of the pieces that he performed with the orchestra, and he served as a translator during onstage forums and interactions with the public.

TOUR LOCATIONS AND REPERTOIRE

Like many other performers who have participated in cultural exchanges between the United States and Cuba, the touring musicians went out of their way to avoid any discussion of politics. Despite the apolitical claims of participants from both countries, however, the tour was an act of musical diplomacy that emphasized the history of US-Cuban musical interaction and underscored transnational commonalities. The tour began when seventy-seven members of the National Symphony Orchestra of Cuba, including directors and tour managers, left Havana on October 15, 2012, to fly to Miami, and then on to Kansas City. Eric Amada had first contacted Clark Morris, the executive and artistic director of Kansas City's Harriman-Jewell Performing Arts Series, about the opportunity to present the Cuban orchestra almost two years prior to the tour commencing. Amada and the other tour organizers chose Kansas City to be the site of the opening concert because they felt that the audience would be welcoming, and the orchestra would be able to perform in the brand-new, $400-million Kauffman Center for the Performing Arts in downtown Kansas City. Upon arriving, French horn player Dania Perez realized that her instrument's lead pipe had been crushed and the bell severely damaged while going through Cuban security. In an act of goodwill, a brass instrument shop owner in Kansas City fully repaired the horn and returned it less than five hours later free of charge. The repair job would normally have run around $400.[30] Additionally, Kansas City Strings provided all of the cellos and basses for the tour, because transporting them from Cuba would have been too difficult and costly. This spirit of friendship and cooperation between host cities and venues, audiences, and musicians was consistent throughout the tour.

After opening night, the orchestra played concerts in Illinois and Iowa before traveling to the East Coast. A performance in Toronto was initially scheduled while the orchestra was in the Northeast, but the Department of Homeland Security would not grant performers the multiple-entry visas that would have been required for a Canadian detour. In the final days of October while the orchestra was touring the East Coast, they were forced to contend with Hurricane Sandy. They played at Kean University in Union, New Jersey, the day before the storm hit and were able to perform an afternoon concert in Danville, Virginia, the next day. The following concert in Newport News, Virginia, however, was canceled as the region was battling wind, flooding, and the encroachment of freezing weather. The tour culminated in West Palm Beach just days after the reelection of President Barack Obama.

While in Florida the orchestra had a brief residency in the Tampa Bay area. They gave master classes for students at the University of South Florida, performed a chamber music concert at the Cuban Club of Tampa in historic Ybor City with members of the Florida Orchestra, and then gave a full performance in St. Petersburg as part of their ongoing cultural exchange. Tampa has a significant Cuban American population, but many Cuban immigrants arrived in the early twentieth century before the Cuban Revolution.

As a result, anti-Castro politics are much less pronounced in Tampa than in Miami. Tampa politicians and leaders have in fact been making efforts to expand trade and connections with Cuba. US Representative Kathy Castor, who represents the area, commented about the exchanges with the Florida Orchestra and the National Symphony Orchestra of Cuba:

> The Florida Orchestra's cultural exchange with Cuba is a remarkable new milestone for the Tampa Bay community and travel and trade with the island nation. The new exchange is another meaningful step that follows the easing of travel restrictions and the designation of Tampa International Airport as entry/exit point to Cuba. I am confident Floridians will have more opportunities to visit Cuba and share traditions across borders.[31]

In contrast, there were no tour performances in Miami. Producers and tour organizers said that they did not intentionally avoid Miami and there was no political reason for not playing there. Fleishaker explained that they were unable to find an appropriate venue and a date that would work.[32] Aurora Herrera, on the other hand, said that the politics of Miami did create complications, if not for the tour then for Nachito's career and cultural exchanges in general. She told the *Twin Cities Pioneer Press*: "The radio stations in Miami won't play [Nachito's] music because of this, and I think that's wrong and stupid. It was never our intention to turn this tour into a political statement. China has a communist system, yet it doesn't interfere with trade and cultural exchanges here. Why China and not Cuba? There's no reason for it."[33]

As the orchestra traveled across the country, they intended to move audiences with their music. Nachito Herrera said that the pieces selected for the tour would act as a "musical voyage that takes the audience and musicians across space and time," and Clark Morris described the selections as being able to showcase the orchestra while speaking to musical commonalities between Cuba and the United States.[34] When the Kansas City audience was caught by surprise with an unannounced performance of the "Star Spangled Banner," they stood up as quickly as they could and started sitting down at its conclusion. They quickly realized the next piece was also unlisted, and although unfamiliar to most in the audience, its soldierly melody and rhythm suggested it was the Cuban national anthem, so they respectfully stood up once again.[35] For the rest of the tour, each concert opened with the US national anthem and "La Bayamesa," the Cuban national anthem, which was composed in 1867 during Cuba's struggle for independence from Spain.

The first piece listed in the program for each performance of the tour was Gershwin's *Cuban Overture*, which he composed as the result of a vacation he took to Cuba in 1932, when Latin music marketed as rumba was booming in the United States. Gershwin wrote about his trip in a letter to George Palay:

> I spent two hysterical weeks in Havana where no sleep was had, but the quality of fun made up for that . . . Cuba was most interesting to me, especially for its small dance orchestras, who play [the] most intricate rhythms most naturally. I hope to go back every winter, if it is possible, as the warm climate seems to be just the thing my system requires for relaxing purposes. (Pollack 2006, 534)

Gershwin's experiences and interactions with Cuban musicians inspired his *Cuban Overture*, originally entitled *Rumba*. The piece quotes the song "Echale Salsita," which was popular in Cuba during his trip, and incorporates various Cuban rhythms and instruments rare in symphonic pieces prior to Varèse's *Ionisation* and Roldán's *Ritmicas*, both of which had premiered earlier that decade. Gershwin specified in his score that the percussion including "Cuban sticks" (claves), bongo, gourd, and maracas be placed right in front of the conductor's stand, but the National Symphony Orchestra of Cuba did not do this on the tour. Instead the percussionists played the parts behind the orchestra with the rest of the section, as the instruments do not have the novelty they did in 1932. Gershwin elected to change the title from *Rumba* to *Cuban Overture* after its premiere because he felt the original title misled listeners into expecting something like a Tin Pan Alley rumba; this was decidedly not a dance piece but an orchestral work exhibiting technical complexity and advanced compositional techniques (Pollack 2006, 535–39). Gershwin's most famous piece, *Rhapsody in Blue*, was also a regular feature on the orchestra's tour, and it allowed Herrera to display his virtuosity and flexibility as a pianist. It was the fusion of jazz and the concert hall in this 1924 work that initially brought Gershwin fame and made him one of the United States of America's most iconic composers.

Gershwin's *Rhapsody* was part of an earlier US-Cuban musical exchange when Cuban composer and pianist Ernesto Lecuona premiered it in Havana in 1928 (Pollack 2006, 105). Music by Lecuona, who has been called "the Gershwin of Cuba," was heard in all but one of the concerts on the orchestra's tour. Lecuona composed "La Comparsa" for piano at age seventeen in 1912, and Afro-Cuban influences can be found in the slow piece's ostinato bass

(Moore 1997, 77). Lecuona left Cuba soon after the revolutionary government accused him of embezzlement and dissolved the royalty-collecting organization he founded, stating that art should be offered freely to the people without fees that go to a single composer (Moore 2006, 75). He settled in West Tampa and opposed the revolution until his death at age sixty-eight in 1963. Despite being an exile and opposing the Castro government, Lecuona has continued to be revered in Cuba. According to Herrera, all piano students at Cuban conservatories continue to play his music. In addition to "La Comparsa," which was arranged for symphony orchestra in 2004, the tour also included Herrera's *Tribute to Lecuona*.

The National Symphony Orchestra of Cuba also performed compositions by two other Cuban composers. Guido López-Gavilán, one of Nachito Herrera's former teachers in Cuba, composed *Guaguancó* and toured with the orchestra as a guest conductor. *Guaguancó* is based on the traditional Afro-Cuban rumba guaguancó, a style typically performed with conga drums, hand percussion, and vocalists for a sexually charged couples dance. López-Gavilán recreated this traditional rumba in an orchestral arrangement. The vocal lines are emulated with a call-and-response melody that moves throughout the orchestra, and the interlocking rhythms normally found in the conga drums are played on the string instruments, first through pizzicato playing and then by having the bassists and cellists use their hands to drum on the bodies of their instruments. Another Cuban piece, Jorge López Marín's danzón "El Médico de Pianos" (The Piano Doctor), was written to thank American piano tuner and repairman Benjamin Treuhaft after he fixed Marín's piano during a trip to Cuba in the 1990s. Treuhaft repaired old pianos, including many made in the Soviet Union that had atrophied in Cuba's tropical climate. He subsequently founded the Send a Piana to Havana project to donate quality pianos to Cuban students.[36]

In addition to Gershwin and Cuban composers, performances also featured European Romantic composers. During the question-and-answer session after the concert in Kansas City, someone asked, "I understand why you chose the Gershwin, but why Mendelssohn?" The orchestra's director responded that he chose Mendelssohn's Symphony No. 4 to show audiences their range and grasp of the European masters. After working with the intense rhythms of Cuban composers and Gershwin, he wanted to find something more mellow and romantic but still dynamic and engaging, so he chose Mendelssohn. Other pieces included Mendelssohn's Violin Concerto in E minor, Schubert's Symphony No. 5, and Herrera once again performed Rachmaninoff's Piano Concerto No. 2.

Beethoven's Symphony No. 5 was performed twelve times, making Beethoven the third most performed composer on the tour. The opening of this symphony contains the most famous motive in Western music, so this piece supported the orchestra's desire to display their command of the Romantic repertoire. Additionally, Beethoven's music has been called transcendent and even ethical, so his symphonies have figured in numerous US-Cuban musical interactions. The idea of Beethoven's music as having a moral core gained traction in the early twentieth century. Prominent German music critic Paul Bekker wrote about the ethics of Beethoven in that the music is related to ideals of freedom, and after the centenary of Beethoven's death in 1927 articles described the celebratory events as having united the world (Buch 2003, 178; Nielsen 2018). Following a 2011 tour of Cuba by the Harvard-Radcliffe Orchestra, the orchestra's director of development said: "The highlight of the weeklong tour was our performance of Beethoven's Symphony No. 9 . . . Presenting this incredibly significant work as a joint concert certainly left a deep impression of Beethoven's message—that brotherhood and love are universal—in the heart of Old Havana."[37] If, as music scholars have argued, Beethoven's music "finds the one spirit in us all" and "is a presentiment of coming social harmony," then it is a fitting work in a musical program that attempts to unite people from two estranged countries (Broyles 2011, 56).

These musical selections combined the familiar with the unfamiliar, which appealed to regular symphony attendees but also attracted new audiences to performance halls throughout the tour. Before the Kansas City performance, Clark Morris of the Harriman-Jewell Series said: "I think it's a very special night. Many of our audience members are very seasoned concertgoers, but they have so infrequently heard Cuban musicians, so [this is] a new experience for them."[38] Throughout the tour, the excitement of seeing a group from Cuba perform in the United States for the first time attracted new and diverse audiences to concert halls. In a review of the orchestra's concert in Allentown, Pennsylvania, the critic wrote: "The concert at Symphony Hall was well-attended, although there were seats for more. My sense was that the enthusiastic audience consisted of a number of people who were new to orchestral concerts—the applause after every movement, although hardly a serious matter—was a clue."[39] By reaching new audiences and creating personal experiences through music, the National Symphony Orchestra of Cuba facilitated conversations about the US-Cuban relationship and motivated some previously disinterested individuals to support further US-Cuban musical and political engagement.

THE DISENGAGEMENT OF POLITICS IN US–CUBAN MUSICAL INTERACTIONS

Even though Cuban performers distanced themselves from any overtly political stance when visiting the United States, the challenges in arranging these cultural exchanges, including where performances took place and what reactions they inspired, exposed a range of attitudes and realities about the US-Cuban relationship. Claims of nonpolitical intentions were helpful in facilitating these exchanges and a degree of depoliticization was required. Politics, however, could not be avoided despite performers' intentions; audiences interpreted performances as political statements, musicians were asked directly about politics, and protesters confronted concert attendees directly.

The National Symphony Orchestra of Cuba experienced this firsthand when their performances were used by audience members to both show support for and protest against the Cuban government. At the end of the concert in the Bronx, a small contingent of attendees stood up in support of the Cuban revolution chanting "*Cuba, sí, bloqueo, no*," and "*¡Viva Cuba, viva Fidel!*" There were no performances in Miami, where the possibility for political demonstrations and controversy was highest, but the orchestra was confronted by protesters while in Florida.[40] At the final performance in West Palm Beach, a group gathered outside the venue to protest the continued imprisonment of American Alan Gross, who had been in a Cuban prison for three years at the time.[41] Because of the US government's policy of disengagement with Cuba, there had been no official negotiations for Gross's release. While the protest called for Gross's release by the Cuban government, it was also a critique of US policy toward Cuba and the inaction of both the president and Congress in securing Gross's freedom. The local synagogue organizing the demonstration notified the staff at the Kravis Center for the Performing Arts in advance, so they were not surprised by the protest. Additionally, to alleviate any potential anger among their patrons, the Kravis Center altered their policies for subscribers to allow individuals to exchange their tickets to the Cuban orchestra performance for another show not included in the regular subscription series. Sharon McDaniel, who was involved with organizing the performances for the Kravis Center, said that negative reactions were considered before scheduling the orchestra, but they also received some positive feedback from members of the Cuban community in West Palm Beach. The performances went on, and the orchestra received enthusiastic responses from the audience in the concert hall.

Like the tour organizers and performance hall directors, the orchestra hoped to avoid political distractions while in the United States and continued to maintain their nonpolitical intentions. Yet their musical selections could be understood as a call for renewing the US-Cuban musical relationship. Many pieces selected were composed as the result of US-Cuban interactions that stretched from the 1930s to the 1990s. When asked about politics in a forum with the audience after the Kansas City concert, Herrera all but confirmed the goal of encouraging further musical engagement while also reaffirming attempts to keep the tour apolitical. He explained:

> I have the Doctor in Music degree. I don't have a Doctoral in Politics degree or something like that. I like to talk about it sometimes, but I don't think it is the intention of this tour.... I definitely hope it's not the last time [to have the orchestra in the United States], and I will keep working hard to keep promoting Cuban music in the United States.

Another audience member then asked him if the tour was meant to coincide with the fiftieth anniversary of the Cuban Missile Crisis, and Herrera replied that their intention was to never have the orchestra involved in any political situations. He stressed that he was not born when the Cuban Missile Crisis occurred and concluded by saying, "Let's move forward, let's just forget about what happened, and let's keep doing performances and promoting the music of Cuba." The audience in Kansas City was very receptive to Herrera's statement, and they responded with enthusiastic applause.

Andy Gomez, a senior fellow at the University of Miami's Institute for Cuban and Cuban-American Studies, explained that the instinct to reflexively paint any visit by an artist from the island as negative and controversial has subsided. Musicians know that playing explicitly revolutionary songs and actively making political arguments would be counterproductive. As a result, the people-to-people and cultural exchanges that took place during President Obama's first term were able to break down some barriers despite the continuing opposition of some Cuban Americans. To those individuals, Gomez appeals: "Forget about the government. Don't talk about Fidel, don't talk about Raúl. We need to talk about the people."[42]

Those members of the Miami exile community, however, are actively working to keep current and future generations from forgetting their history and the surrounding politics, which is demonstrated by events like the Cuba Nostalgia festival. Ninoska Pérez Castellón, a prominent anti-Castro talk show host on Miami's Radio Mambí and founding member of the Cuban Liberty Council, described the orchestra's tour as an attempt to soften the image of the Cuban dictatorship. He argued that celebrations of arts and culture only obfuscate the reality of Cuba, which he equated with the plight of dissident groups like the Ladies in White, who have been jailed for demanding the release of political prisoners.[43] Those who were forced to leave their country cannot simply forget the hardships they faced or ignore the abuses that continue to be committed in Cuba. Musicians from the island are not guilty of preventing free speech, attacking protestors, or jailing political dissidents, but they are often seen as representatives of a government that is responsible for those human rights violations. The National Symphony Orchestra of Cuba now occupies a different position from the one it did in the early years of the revolution when Castro championed the ensemble as an example of revolutionary policies at work, but because of Cuba's political and economic system they are affiliated with the government through the Ministry of Culture. Most exchanges with Cuban musicians still require coordination with officials in the Cuban government, and as a result they can be construed as lending support to the Castro regime. Individuals opposed to US political diplomacy with Cuba may oppose musical diplomacy for the same reasons.

Those who want to aid the Cuban people but oppose cultural exchanges regard participating musicians first and foremost as representatives of the Castro government while largely discounting them as Cuban people deserving support. When asked about his own intentions and how these exchanges impact the musicians, Nachito Herrera told me:

> Right now, more than any kind of political situation, I'm more focused on establishing a bridge between musicians from my country and musicians from the US because no matter what I always like to defend the idea that music is just what? It's music. And I think musicians from here definitely deserve to play there and of course musicians from my country deserve to play here. Why not play at the orchestra hall in Minneapolis, why not Lincoln Center in New York?[44]

The statements regarding the nonpolitical nature of the National Symphony Orchestra of Cuba's tour of the United States should also be accepted as sincere. The musicians wanted audiences to judge their performances based upon the skill and musicianship presented and not for what the performances meant in the context of US-Cuban relations. The political implications of such a nonpolitical stance, however, should not be ignored. Decades earlier a group of artists in the late Soviet Union intentionally adopted an apolitical stance, which had a destabilizing effect on late socialism. By refusing to see themselves in political terms of support or opposition, these artists created a space that the state could not easily define or understand (Yurchak 2008).

Musicians in the National Symphony Orchestra of Cuba did not previously have the option to adopt a nonpolitical stance in this way. Although musicologists have argued that music is always political, musicians' claims that their compositions or performances are nonpolitical should be respected as genuine and sincere. Their nonpolitical musical performances are best interpreted as an expression of what Yurchak has termed a politics of indistinction, which is neither a traditional politics of resistance nor tacit support and acceptance of the status quo (2008, 212–13).[45] For the National Symphony Orchestra of Cuba, a nonpolitical stance facilitated the US tour by allowing venues and audience members to participate without feeling like they were supporting the Castro government. In turn, this stance encouraged further US-Cuban musical engagement. At the time of the tour the United States and Cuba did not have formal diplomatic relations, and the ability for musicians to travel between the two countries was difficult and inconsistent. The nonpolitical nature of the performances illustrated that political barriers to musical exchange were unnecessary and outdated. The musical selections underscored this idea by emphasizing the history of US-Cuban musical interaction.

CONCLUSION

The uneven and discontinuous nature of musical interactions between the United States and Cuba arises from local and national issues as much as international political tensions. Cuban artists have experienced strikingly different receptions when performing in Miami compared to elsewhere. Yet that too is changing. The growing acceptance of musicians from Cuba in Miami is a sign of larger political changes in the region. The 2012 US elections took place on November 6 while the National Symphony Orchestra of Cuba was on the last leg of its tour in Florida. That night Barack Obama won nearly half the Cuban American vote in the state, a record high for a Democrat. Mitt Romney, the Republican presidential candidate, took a stance on Cuba that was typical for his party and promised to strengthen travel restrictions and be tough on Castro. Despite efforts including Spanish radio ads, Romney failed to make significant inroads with the South Florida Hispanic community, and the percentage of the Cuban American vote he received was a historic low for a Republican presidential candidate. The 2012 election also saw voters elect Congressman Joe Garcia, a Cuban American Democrat representing Florida's twenty-sixth Congressional district who supported Obama's Cuban travel reforms.

The political and demographic changes in South Florida and amongst Cuban Americans across the country have in turn encouraged more Cuban musicians to perform in the Sunshine State as protests and scandals like the cancellation of the Fuego Cuban Music Festival became increasingly rare. Events based around Cuban music bring communities together, but the politics of programming Cuban artists have also exposed rifts in the Cuban American community. The primary criticism of Cuban musicians from Los Van Van to the National Symphony Orchestra of Cuba is that they are a part of the Castro government. Going to enjoy their concerts is perceived by some in the Cuban American exile community as showing acceptance for a totalitarian regime and its actions. Juan Formell of Los Van Van responded to comments and questions about political intent on their first trip to Miami: "I am not part of any political party, not at the city or the state or the national level. Like all musicians who live in Cuba, we are part of the Ministry of Culture, but we don't come here representing the Ministry of Culture, or the government, or as any kind of ambassadors. We come here as artists, as musicians, to play."[46]

For these musicians, performing in the United States is an end goal in itself. Nachito Herrera said that only a couple of the orchestra members who went on the US tour had ever been in the country before. It was seventy-six-year-old tuba player Remberto Depestre De La Torre's first time in the United States. In his lifetime, this musician had seen many different phases of the US-Cuban relationship, so it was a powerful experience for him to finally visit and see so much of the country. The musicians were all happy with their experience and wanted another opportunity to play in the United States. The personal meaning in these events was much stronger for the participants than the political contexts in which they occurred, and their personal experiences created new musical experiences for audiences.

These musical experiences could improve the possibility for movement toward increased musical interaction and political normalization. As was shown by the success of the ¡Sí Cuba! Festival and the orchestra's tour, US audiences had a significant interest in hearing Cuban musicians perform. When members of the National Symphony Orchestra of Cuba declared that they were disinterested in promoting any political position or ideology, they created a space outside of simple political classifications that improved the possibility for movement toward increased musical interaction and political normalization. In turn, the number of people in the audience, the excitement on behalf of the presenters, and the comments and questions during pre- and post-concert events showed a strong desire for further US-Cuban engagement and musical interaction.

4

JAZZ AS INTERCULTURAL DIALOGUE AT THE HAVANA JAZZ PLAZA FESTIVAL

On the evening of Friday, December 21, 2012, I was in the *jardines* of the Teatro Mella (the Mella Theatre's gardens) in the Vedado district of Havana. International travelers visiting for the Havana Jazz Plaza Festival mingled with Cuban locals in the packed outdoor venue. During daylight hours, the *jardines* open every afternoon and vendors sell a small selection of food and beverages including beer and liquor, making it a popular place for people to congregate on warm days. While it typically does not cost anything to enter the gardens, a ticketing table blocked the entrance during the jazz festival in the evenings. Individuals were required to purchase a ticket or show their festival pass. A large mural illustrating the staging of a play by Bertolt Brecht adorned the back wall of the gardens above the stage, which was illuminated at night by multicolored spotlights hanging from trees. With no other performances at 6:00 p.m. during the Friday, Saturday, and Sunday of the festival, the outdoor space became a popular standing-room only spot for festivalgoers to have a few drinks and enjoy a performance before going to a mainstage performance inside the Mella or walking to one of the other venues.

On stage, Canadian jazz saxophonist Jane Bunnett was performing with the Cuban fusion group Sintesis. The ensemble, which formed in the late 1970s, combines jazz and funk with elements of Afro-Cuban rumba and songs for Santería *orishas*. They started with a song for Eleguá, then moved through other *orishas* including Ogun, Iye, and Obatala. Ele Valdés Oropesa, the group's lead singer and keyboard player, incorporated the names of *orishas* into her vocal improvisations and danced in place while moving her arms to reference the traditional dances associated with each deity. Throughout these different songs, Jane Bunnett played soprano saxophone and sang along. The high-energy outdoor performance was one of the most engaging musical fusions I witnessed at the festival.

Partway through the performance, a middle-aged white man jumped on stage next to Bunnett with a flugelhorn. He performed two songs with Sintesis before taking a bow and stepping back into the crowd. When he walked past me, we struck up a conversation, and he introduced himself as Jane Bunnett's husband, Larry Cramer. He and his wife were leading a festival tour for a Toronto radio station to celebrate thirty years of Canadian-Cuban jazz partnerships. The couple has been visiting Cuba regularly since 1982. Unlike the travelers at the festival from the United States, the Canadians faced little difficulty getting to Cuba and did not need to justify the purpose of their travel. Bunnett and Cramer, however, believe that their Cuban connections cost them a contract with a major record label in 1996 when anti-Castro groups threatened some of their US performances with Cuban musicians. They ultimately moved to a different label and have since recorded multiple times in Cuba.[1]

While Cramer was telling me about the radio station trip and Cuban jazz in Canada, a peanut vendor walked past us. Cramer stopped the man and bought all of his peanut-filled paper tubes, much to the pleasure of the vendor. Before walking away, Cramer invited me to a special jam session on Sunday at the Melía Cohiba hotel and then wandered into the crowd, singing "El Manisero" ("The Peanut Vendor") and handing out peanuts to some of his fellow Canadians on the tour. Two days later, I made my way to the Vedado hotel in the afternoon. Not knowing where in the hotel the performance would be, I wandered around until I heard music and followed it into the cigar bar. The room was jam-packed, as most of the people from the Toronto radio tour were there. Cramer and Bunnett were on the small stage at the far end of the room with a group of other musicians, and Cramer was acting as the host by inviting musicians to the stage and introducing them. Guests included Bobby Carcassés and Guillermo Rubalcaba, a pianist who played with the Buena Vista Social Club. The deep-rooted friendship between the Canadian and Cuban musicians was apparent from their interactions on stage. The Canadian–Cuban musical relationship had grown through thirty years of direct human interactions and collaborations, and it came to life during that relaxed and easygoing jam session.

The challenges that US musicians faced to participate in the Havana Jazz Plaza Festival, however, made many of their experiences anything but relaxed and easygoing. The policy changes instituted by the Obama administration made it possible for them to perform in the festival without running afoul of the law, but they were forced to improvise and adapt their plans to be active participants in the US-Cuban musical relationship. The International Havana Jazz Plaza Festival has promoted jazz as a form of intercultural and improvisational dialogue between the United States and Cuba for decades. An understanding of the festival as it exists today requires an investigation of jazz history in postrevolutionary Cuba and of some of the country's major jazz personalities who contributed directly to the development of the festival. An analysis of the 2012 festival's programming and design shows how the event set the stage for musicians from the United States to simultaneously navigate US-Cuban relations and engage in intercultural musical dialogue. Higher profile musicians and festival fixtures Chucho Valdés and Arturo O'Farrill provide additional examples of Latin jazz icons who actively engage in musical diplomacy and redefine jazz in the process.

JAZZ AFTER THE REVOLUTION

Jazz was an important element in the US-Cuban musical discourse from the music's origins through the 1950s, as discussed in chapter 1. Chucho Valdés, the current director of the Havana Jazz Plaza Festival recalled these connections to *Down Beat* magazine in a 2013 interview:

> Before Afro-Cuban jazz, before Chano Pozo and Mario Bauzá, there was another phase between Cuban music and American music. Jelly Roll Morton felt like there was a "Latin tinge." ... We have this thing in Cuba called the habanera. It is in the contradanza. In New Orleans, there was another thing called ragtime. When you hear habanera and ragtime, you feel there is something that is very similar. The ragtime and habanera are family.[2]

He went on to describe the Cuban roots of trumpeter Manuel Perez, who helped pioneer jazz in New Orleans and then returned to Cuba to play with musicians in Santiago. This history of jazz as presented by Valdés demonstrates how Cuban musicians understand and perform jazz as their own music, and not as a genre that is being borrowed from the United States. Cuban music contributed to the origins of jazz, and musicians performed jazz in Cuba since the genre's earliest days.

Jazz continued to expand as a bridge between the United States and Cuba through the 1950s. The Oscar-nominated 2010 animated film *Chico y Rita* is set during this time period and tells the fictional story of a Cuban pianist and a singer who travel from Havana to New York City and encounter numerous historical musicians. After Rita is discovered singing in a Havana club, she is brought to the United States to pursue a career as a singer and actress. Her on-again, off-again lover Chico leaves Cuba to find her, and he connects with Cuban percussionist Chano Pozo in New York. After another dalliance in the city, Rita leaves for California and Chico joins Dizzy Gillespie's band on tour. Chico is arrested during a bar raid and charged with drug possession, resulting in his deportation back to Cuba in early 1959 just after Castro takes power. While he initially tries to continue his musical career, he realizes that will be impossible when he is informed that his performances have been canceled because "jazz is considered imperialist" and "the enemy's music." If he wants to keep working, he is told he will have to join the socialist party in power following the revolution.[3] Bebo Valdés, who supplies the music Chico performs in the film and was one of Cuba's best pianists, composers, and arrangers in the 1950s, left the country after facing these same challenges. The new Cuban government created many obstacles for jazz musicians while sometimes being outright hostile to them, leading many jazz musicians to leave. In addition to Cuban authorities suppressing jazz on the island, the embargo and travel ban also prevented US jazz musicians from reaching the island, straining the connection that jazz provided between the two countries.

    Cuba still had many jazz lovers, although it became difficult for them to study, perform, and listen to the music. One problem for jazz musicians was the shortage of records, which are central to any young performer's jazz education. Musicians were forced to make deals with foreign acquaintances and sailors who visited Cuba. They could also find jazz on the US government's Voice of America radio broadcasts. The Cuban government tried to jam the signal, but the station's *Jazz Hour* program hosted by Willis Conover gave young jazz aficionados in Cuba a taste of what musicians were doing in the United States. Valdés said, "It was through that program, in 1963, that I first heard the John Coltrane Quartet. After a gap of three years, I thought it was like science fiction."[4] The Cuban government's official rejection of jazz in the 1960s occurred at a time when the government was also denying black Cubans the freedom to mobilize. In 1959 and 1960, the new government was committed to combating racial inequality, but the backlash to desegregation and other race-based policies by white professionals led Castro to abandon future racial-equality efforts. In 1962 the government closed independent black social clubs, where many young black dance band musicians learned their artistic trade from family and friends. Additionally, the government curtailed the practice of art forms that were associated with an Afro-Cuban or black identity and suppressed attempts to bring awareness to racism on the island (Moore 2006, 173–74). Jazz was associated with the civil rights movement in the United States, and its racial connotations likely contributed to why the Cuban government prohibited the genre in the 1960s.

While the government was not supportive of jazz, Cuba's jazz musicians continued to perform in a number of venues including Havana's famous cabarets, which were still open at the time. Leonardo Acosta recalled that Saturday jam sessions at the ICAIC (Instituto Cubano del Arte y la Industria Cinematográficos) were the hub of Havana's jazz scene in the mid-1960s. Performers at those sessions included numerous musicians who would go on to become big names in Cuba, such as Acosta, Paquito D'Rivera, Chucho Valdés, Bobby Carcassés, and others. Jazz gained minimal official support in 1967 when the Consejo Nacional de Cultura founded a jazz ensemble called the Orquesta Cubana de Música Moderna. The group combined musicians from multiple generations and exposed young stars like Valdés, D'Rivera, Arturo Sandoval, Juan Pablo Torres, and drummer Enrique Plá to the national spotlight; some of these musicians gained international exposure when the ensemble performed in international festivals like the Jazz Jamboree in Poland. But bureaucratic decision-making kept the ensemble from reaching its musical potential, and it eventually became a house band for the state recording studio (Acosta 2003, 197–202).

Just as government cultural institutions were beginning to accept jazz, the music fell victim to a nationwide "revolutionary offensive" in March 1968. The government closed all cabarets except one reserved for visiting foreign delegations, and soon bars, small clubs, and other aspects of nightlife that supported live music were also shuttered. The purpose of the revolutionary offensive was to support the government's agricultural efforts by mobilizing workers to contribute to the sugar harvest, but its end result hurt overall economic activity. Musical life was especially hard hit because the offensive coincided with a hardening of socialist policies that saw all small businesses nationalized, including bars and clubs. By the end of the decade those venues were allowed to reopen, but most never did. Cabarets and popular dance music all but disappeared from public social life by the early 1970s, and approximately 40 percent of popular entertainers had nowhere to perform (Moore 2006, 112). Cultural life in most regions and neighborhoods took decades to recover.

When venues for jazz performers were shut down, some of the country's most talented jazz musicians found themselves turning to more official channels for their livelihood. As part of the Consejo Nacional de Cultura jazz commission, Armando Romeu, Paquito D'Rivera, Rafael Somavilla, Horacio Hernández, and Leonardo Acosta were charged with organizing a series of concerts at different locales. Early venues included a synagogue, the Casa de la Cultura in Vedado, and the Amadeo Roldán Theater in old Havana (Acosta 2003, 205). Leo Brouwer formed the Grupo de Experimentación Sonora (Sonic Experimentation Group) in 1969, and it also provided an outlet for a number of Cuban jazz musicians. Brouwer's ensemble provided musicians with opportunities to engage with what was happening elsewhere in the world and contributed to the education of numerous young musicians.

The group Irakere, founded in 1973 by Chucho Valdés, made musical experimentation and jazz synonymous in the 1970s. Son of famous jazz pianist Bebo Valdés, Chucho started playing piano at age three. He went to hear his father perform at the Tropicana, where he also heard Woody Herman, Glenn Miller, Ray Brown, Buddy Rich, Nat King Cole, Roy Haynes, and other major jazz artists of the day. Valdés recalled these influences:

> I loved jazz as a kid. This was a big impression on me. My dad would say, "Now we're going to hear Nat King Cole, now we're going to hear Sarah Vaughan. . . . Learn how to play the blues, learn how to play some of their rhythms." I had that kind of school at home. I couldn't have had it any closer. And then he sent me to play classical music, so I had classical music training, and of course the Afro-Cuban music. That's why, when I write, all these things come out.[5]

These influences emerged in the musical synthesis of Irakere. All but one of the eight founders of Irakere had been members of the Orquesta Cubana de Música Moderna. In 1973 some were still members of the orchestra and others were stationed outside of Havana in the military, which created bureaucratic obstacles for Valdés as he tried to form the ensemble. After some time and effort, however, the group came together.

Cultural officials initially regarded Irakere's music with significant skepticism because of their unconventional stylistic choices such as using *batá* drums and Yoruba chants in their jazz arrangements. The virtuosity of the performers brought the group notoriety, and soon they were celebrated for their experimental choices. They played danceable tunes, their own versions of popular international hits, and more traditional jazz arrangements. Irakere performed in some European jazz festivals before 1977, but the arrival of the jazz cruise from the United States that year provided the connections and exposure that would bring the group international acclaim. In 1978 they played the Newport Jazz Festival in the United States and the Montreux Jazz Festival in Switzerland, the latter of which was recorded and released as their first album outside of Cuba. They again performed with US musicians during the Havana Jam festival in 1979, after which they toured the United States as an opening band for Stephen Stills and received a Grammy for best Latin album. International exposure and acclaim also made these musicians aware of career opportunities they could not access while living in Cuba. Paquito D'Rivera was the first Irakere musician to leave the country; Arturo Sandoval started his own group but then left for the United States himself. Over time, Irakere's growing international popularity played a key role in the acceptance and institutionalization of jazz in Cuba.

HISTORY OF THE HAVANA JAZZ PLAZA FESTIVAL

By 1979 singer and multi-instrumentalist Bobby Carcassés had grown tired of the limited opportunities for live jazz in Havana, so he organized a series of concerts in the theater and outdoor plaza of the Casa de la Cultura; the following year that concert series became the first Jazz Plaza Festival. Carcassés was born in 1938 in Jamaica where his father served as a Cuban diplomat. He did not come from a musical family and received little formal training but demonstrated musical talent at a young age. Initially a singer, Carcassés also took up piano, bass, percussion, and flugelhorn, and he started performing with the famous variety shows at the Tropicana club, where he heard some of the best jazz players from the United States and Cuba. Following the revolution, Carcassés argued for the importance of jazz by pointing out its many Cuban influences and promoted it as an inherently revolutionary music because of its roots in oppressed African American communities in the United States.[6]

Carcassés was director of the Casa de la Cultura when he decided to turn the series of jazz concerts into a festival in 1980. The initial festival did not have any official support, so Paquito D'Rivera thought it was unlikely to succeed but still helped with the planning.[7] Carcassés recruited many of his friends, among them jazz musicians from multiple generations, to organize and perform in the first festival (Acosta 2003, 236). The free event was successful thanks in part to Irakere's ability to draw a large, enthusiastic audience. The number of groups increased year after year, and the festival expanded into additional venues. Retired jazz musicians who had not performed publicly since the early years of the revolution brought out their instruments to participate. Like many jazz festivals around the world, the Havana festival's lineup expanded beyond straightforward jazz to include other popular genres, and contemporary dance bands like Los Van Van became regular participants.[8]

When the festival gained prestige and started to attract international talent, government authorities removed Carcassés and the initial organizing group from their positions overseeing the event. Government officials took control of Havana Jazz Plaza because they decided that an international festival needed to be organized from a higher office in the revolutionary government. A number of the original jazz musicians who created the festival stayed on as advisors but had no real decision-making power. According to Leonardo Acosta, this caused numerous problems. Organizers began charging for admission to the originally free festival, but as the cost went up, the quality went down. The number of venues increased, but they were spread out across the city and Havana's poor transportation system made it difficult for visitors to travel between them. The venues also suffered from a lack of pianos and functioning amplification equipment (Acosta 2003, 238). After attempts at rapid commercial expansion failed to increase the appeal of the festival, officials decided that a famous Cuban performer should be designated as the festival director. In an attempt to draw high-profile jazz musicians from around the world, the government first appointed Arturo Sandoval to this position. He was followed by Gonzalo Rubalcaba and Chucho Valdés, who has served as festival director since 1996. Positioning a prominent Cuban musician as the face of the festival has been successful in lending prestige to the event as a whole.

Throughout the 1980s and 1990s, the Havana Jazz Plaza Festival secured participation from many of the world's top jazz musicians including those from the United States. Dizzy Gillespie was the first US artist to appear as a festival headliner when he came to Havana in 1985, which was captured in the documentary film *A Night in Havana*. Dizzy's presence at the festival marked a significant step forward for the event in terms of artistic quality, participation, and international interest; when he returned in 1986 he brought bassist Charlie Haden's ensemble with him. Haden's performance with Cuban pianist Gonzalo Rubalcaba led to invitations for Rubalcaba to perform overseas, and years of collaboration between the two musicians followed.[9] Other major performers from the United States in the late 1980s and 1990s included Joe Lovano, Ray Anderson, Don Pullen, Roy Hargrove, and Max Roach. The festival also attracted nonmusician attendees from the United States, many of whom traveled to Cuba illegally.[10]

When tourism became a central part of the Cuban economy in the Special Period, the country's financial challenges extended to the jazz festival. The US dollar became an accepted monetary note, and prices for the festival were set in both foreign and national currencies (Acosta 2003, 238). This caused confusion and frustration for foreigners who lived on the island who now had to pay more than their Cuban friends to attend, and many Cubans could not afford to buy drinks from festival bars that would only take foreign currency. In the late 1990s, the festival went from being an annual to a biennial festival, until the mid-2000s when it returned to a yearly schedule. While there have been many transformations since the festival's debut in 1980, it continues to be a major draw for jazz aficionados around the world, and the number of US participants rose when Obama relaxed the travel ban.

Festivals have been subjects of academic inquiry for the last century, but the fields of anthropology and folklore have long focused on festivals as liminal spaces or ritualized transgressions (Stoeltje 1992). The analysis of modern popular festivals, however, must be placed in international contexts of globalization, tourism, and contemporary socioeconomic processes. The Havana Jazz Plaza Festival was one of many international festivals to emerge in what David Picard and Mike Robinson have described as a post-1960s festival boom throughout the world (2006, 2). This boom, they claim, relates to communities reasserting their identities in response to feelings of cultural dislocation caused by rapid structural change, social mobility, and globalization processes. In the Cuban context, the Havana Jazz Plaza Festival was a way for Cuban jazz musicians to reclaim jazz as a Cuban musical genre. Unlike many other cultural actors around the world who use festivals to reassert local identities in response to outside economic and cultural forces, Cuban musicians were responding to their own government's cultural policies. The jazz festival helped jazz music regain official acceptance on the island, and the festival has since experienced regular transformation as global pressures, economic forces, and communicative networks have directed it internally and externally. My trip to the festival in 2012 proved to me that its artistic quality remains high even as transformations within Cuba and in the US-Cuban relationship impact the event.

JAZZ PLAZA 2012: JAZZ ON ALL STRINGS

The 28th Havana Jazz Plaza Festival began on Thursday, December 20 and ran through Sunday, December 23, 2012. While the New Year is a bigger celebration in Cuba than Christmas, there were still many restaurants with

Christmas trees and shops featuring snowmen and Santa Claus in the window. A few festival performances included renditions of classic Christmas songs. Although it was common to see young Cubans wearing fashionable scarves around their necks, the weather was generally warm and comfortable. The festival took place in the Vedado district of Havana, which is situated west of Habana Vieja (Old Havana) and the densely populated Habana Centro (Central Havana). Vedado, in contrast, has a more suburban layout with slightly more space between buildings and significantly more trees and lawns than the city's historic areas. Many of the homes and buildings in Vedado were built between the 1920s and 1950s, when US investment was on the rise. In addition to being a residential district with approximately 175,000 residents, Vedado is also a commercial hub with numerous hotels, entertainment venues, and a few skyscrapers.

Unlike the older parts of the city, Vedado is situated as an easy-to-navigate grid, and much of the construction is in an Art Deco style reminiscent of some buildings in New York and Miami. Because the population is less dense than in Centro Habana there are fewer *jineteros*, the street hustlers looking to make a quick profit from foreigners often by running a scam, pimping, or just hanging around long enough to get some free drinks or a meal. While some festival performances still had people approaching concertgoers to sell bootleg CDs and DVDs, they were friendly and not too aggressive. The greatest danger one faces walking around Vedado is from the city's dilapidated infrastructure, which requires pedestrians to be aware of potholes, open manholes, crumbling balconies, and exposed electrical cables.

The theme of the 28th festival was "El Jazz en Todas las Cuerdas" (Jazz on All Strings). As such it featured more string performers and ensembles than many other jazz festivals, but the theme did not dominate programming. The 2012 festival also featured a special concert and presentation for Cuban women in jazz. Up until a week before the festival, the lineup had not yet been released, and most advertisements for festival tours only mentioned Chucho Valdés. The final list of musicians included performers from Cuba, the United States, Norway, Mexico, Spain, Uruguay, Germany, Brazil, Argentina, and Canada. Vedado's Hotel Meliá Cohiba was the primary tourist hub during the festival. Constructed in 1994 as a partnership between the Cuban government and Spain's Meliá hotel chain, the twenty-two-story building towers above other buildings in the area. There are now twenty-six Meliá hotels in Cuba. As one of the few buildings constructed along Havana's famous Malecón seawall during the Special Period, the Meliá Cohiba does not feel like other Cuban hotels. It was designed to appeal to American and European businesspeople and has wi-fi throughout the hotel, in-room hot tubs, and an attached shopping center. The hotel bars served as performance venues, and it was the only place to purchase festival passes. The Paradiso cultural tourism organization sold passes at a table outside the hotel gift shop. When I went to purchase my pass, however, the salesperson informed me that he would not accept the convertible pesos (CUCs) that I had with me. Passes could only be purchased for US$160 or 130 euros. After coming back with US currency, I was given a laminated pass on a lanyard, a festival poster, and a printed program. When handing me the program, the salesperson crossed out multiple performers including Roy Hargrove, Roberta Cambarini, and Xiomara Laugart, and corrected the times for the Teatro Mella performances by writing over the printed times. I assumed an all-access pass would be the most economical way to attend festival events but was wrong. Some events were free to get into, others only cost five CUC for foreigners (approximately $5 US) and twenty national pesos for Cubans (approximately $1), and festival events overlapped so it was impossible to go to everything.

The printed program listed the eight Cuban sponsors of the event with small logos underneath the schedule. In printed order they included: Ciego Montero, the primary bottled water and soft-drink distributor in Cuba that is now partly owned and operated by Nestlé; the Casas de Cultural Consejo Nacional (National Council for Houses of Culture), which provides music education to children and other cultural programming nationwide in neighborhood casas de cultura; the Consejo Nacional de las Artes Escénicas (National Council of Performing Arts), which oversees various dance and theatre organizations including some performance venues; Internacional Cubana de Tabacos S.A. (Cuban International Tobaccos), a joint Cuban-Spanish cigar venture; Paradiso, the Cuban tourism agency that focuses on cultural tourism; the Fondo Cubano de Bienes Culturales (The Cuban Fund for Cultural Goods), which promotes the marketing and production of visual and applied arts; the Instituto Cubano de la Música, the organization that directly oversees the jazz festival as well as policies governing the performance and distribution of music in the country; and the Centro Nacional de Música Popular, an institution within the Instituto Cubano de la Música that promotes and represents professional musicians on the state roster. The largest sponsor ad, however, for Chivas Regal Scotch Whisky, took up the full back page of the program. Beneath the picture of the bottle, some text said, "*Donde hay amigos hay verdadera riqueza*" (Where there are friends there are true riches). The irony of the festival being sponsored by a scotch as opposed to a rum like Habana Club was not lost on me or other attendees, as multiple people commented and joked about it. It does, however, speak to the international nature of the event.

The festival performances began on Thursday night, but a colloquium was held at the Casa del ALBA Cultural in the morning and afternoon on Thursday and Friday. ALBA refers to La Alianza Bolivariana para los Pueblos de Nuestra América (The Bolivarian Alliance for the Peoples of Our America) and is a transnational initiative started by Venezuela and Cuba in 2004 for "the defense of Latin American and Caribbean culture and identity of the peoples of the region."[11] Multiple partner countries have since joined the ALBA initiative, but the only physical "*casas*" in the network are in Havana and Caracas. They are meant to be intellectual centers for hosting lectures and debates, promoting Latin American and Caribbean arts and culture, and facilitating projects that require the participation of multiple countries. The Casa del ALBA in Havana is a well-maintained two-story colonial-style building painted yellow that opened in 2009. It sits along the Línea, one of the main streets and thoroughfares in Vedado, and it is across and down the street from the festival main stage at the Teatro Mella. ALBA's outdoor courtyard hosts musical performances in the afternoons, and there is visual art on display throughout the building. The exhibition on view during the jazz festival featured various artistic representations of the iconic Che Guevara photo taken by Alberto Korda. The colloquium included multiple sessions in the second-floor lecture hall with musicians and musicologists speaking on topics ranging from the relationship between traditional Cuban genres and jazz to upcoming websites and publications dedicated to Cuban jazz. The best part of the colloquium, however, was the opportunity to see and hear some amazing Cuban musicians in a small, intimate venue. These included Bobby Carcassés, violinist Omar Puente Fiffe, the string duo of Jorge Reyes and William Roblejo, and Pancho Amat, who is one of the best contemporary *tres* players in Cuba.

The festival's main performances were scheduled for 9:00 p.m. at the Teatro Mella and the Casa de Cultura de Plaza; late night performances followed at 11:00 p.m. at the club in the basement of the Teatro Bertolt Brecht and the bar of the Hotel Melía Cohiba. Additional venues hosted concerts in the afternoon and early evening on Friday, Saturday, and Sunday. These included 6:00 p.m. performances in the gardens outside the Mella, 7:00 p.m. concerts in the theatre of the Bertolt Brecht, and on Saturday and Sunday 4:00 p.m. concerts in the Mella. Despite the schedule and its last-minute changes, none of the performances started on time and many ran late, unintentionally causing performances to overlap. Thankfully, the venues were not far from each other and it was only a five- to ten-minute walk to get from the Mella to any of the others.

The Mella Theatre is named after Julio Antonio Mella, who founded the Cuban Communist party in the 1920s. It maintains the Art Deco style from its original construction as a movie theatre in the 1950s; the outside is green with orange accents and sports a light-up marquee. While the Mella is newer than many other buildings in Havana, its aging infrastructure became apparent when clumps of dust and sparks from a spotlight fell from the ceiling over the stage during concerts. When I saw sparks falling on the second night of the festival, I noted the lack of fire exits in the building; thankfully they were not needed. The Mella is a fitting home for the jazz festival as it hosted the first postrevolutionary interaction between Cuban and US musicians when the jazz cruise came into Havana in 1977. It is now a site for numerous festivals and other large-scale performances. The almost 1,500-seat theatre was still not large enough for the Chucho Valdés performance on Thursday night, which attracted many Cubans and foreign visitors. The oversold concert had people sitting on the floor and in the aisles.

The Casa de Cultura de Plaza was the primary outdoor venue, where concerts scheduled for 9:00 p.m. started late and ran until 1:00 a.m. or later. This Casa de Cultura is in the area of Vedado known as the plaza district and had previously been the Lyceum and Lawn Tennis Club before the revolution. In 1980 it served as the original home of the Havana Jazz Plaza Festival. In addition to the outdoor performance space, the Casa also includes a two-story building with an art gallery and multiple rooms used for art and music classes. It was typical for people to go to the earlier concert at the Mella and then walk the five blocks west and one block north to the Casa de Cultura to listen and dance late into the night. The performances here included a broader selection of music, ranging from groups easily classified as jazz to a variety of Cuban dance bands like NG La Banda and Will Campa. The popular music, later concert times, and open gate without a ticket taker at the Case de Cultura attracted younger and more local crowds than many of the other festival concerts. The fact that it was outdoors also drew additional attendees who simply followed the amplified music that could be heard from blocks away.

Despite the multiple venues, the festival's footprint in Havana was relatively small. The *Granma* newspaper listed festival events daily, and there were a few televised news stories about some of the performers. Yet even inside of the Melía Cohiba lobby there were no signs about the festival other than at the table selling passes. Someone visiting Havana, but not specifically for the festival, could easily go about their week without realizing that a major international jazz festival was happening. I interacted with numerous Cubans and international travelers who were unaware of the jazz festival until I asked them about it or until they stumbled upon a performance.

By contrast, the US visitors I spoke to had planned their trip specifically around the jazz festival. Isaac Peña, a performer at the festival from Austin, Texas, was caught off guard by the presence of US attendees. He told me, "I was actually surprised when we went to the Chucho Valdés concert and I was like, 'Oh, there's a ton of Americans here.' I mean it was the first time that I was hearing American English all over the place."[12] Many of the US travelers had come with an organized tour from Cuba Explorer Tours, a Canadian company that has offered a jazz festival tour every year since 2005 and specializes in helping US citizens navigate travel restrictions. There were over ninety people on the tour, which was enough to fill two busses, and they were easy to spot during concerts because they sat in one large group in reserved seats. The Cuba Explorer Tours itinerary included many scheduled activities similar to a people-to-people tour, but the US citizens on it were using a variety of general licenses.

One couple from New Jersey came on a license for visiting family, but they went with the organized tour to simplify arrangements and to attend the festival. The young woman was born in the United States but her mother emigrated from Cuba and her grandmother still lived there. Because this was their first time in Cuba they were extending their trip after the organized tour ended to visit Trinidad and other small towns, and to spend more time with her grandmother. Many of the US travelers were staying on after the festival to engage in other activities and visit other parts of the country. At a Friday evening concert, I spoke with a retired lawyer who previously worked in the music industry, which she used to justify the trip as professional research. Following the festival, she and her sister were also traveling to Trinidad.[13] Another group from Michigan was able to justify travel using a religious license. The day before the festival, they visited a church outside of Havana and donated some supplies to the congregation. The rest of their time was spent attending festival events.[14] There were also a number of smaller organized tours and groups who planned their own trips either legally or illegally.

Visitors from the United States were drawn to the festival for various reasons, including an interest in jazz. The Havana Jazz Plaza Festival was especially attractive to visitors from the United States because it was a limited event in which they felt they could "experience Cuba before it changes." Both festival attendees and participating musicians from the United States expressed this attitude. As President Obama's policies created greater legal opportunities for US citizens to visit Cuba and the Cuban government announced modifications to the island's economy, visitors feared that soon the old cars would disappear from Havana's roadways and that North American chain restaurants would start appearing. Barbara Kirshenblatt-Gimblett (1998, 59) describes a festival as a form of environmental performance in which tourists can access in a concentrated form what they would normally try to locate in the diffuse culture they are visiting. While this makes Cuban festivals particularly attractive to individuals who feel they have a limited amount of time to experience a country they have previously been unable to visit, festivals also risk giving the impression that intercultural encounter occurs while people are at play. When travelers have a full itinerary for their time in Havana and use a charter bus to go from their hotel to performances, they risk not knowing the country more broadly. In a country where issues of conflict and marginalization are already underrepresented in official state media, the presentation of Cuban culture through festival staging can further suppress tensions in Cuban society by making them invisible to international visitors. In attracting these and other tourists from around the world, Cuban festivals also commodify the island's musical culture, presenting it in a way that visitors can understand. By seeking this one-stop Cuba experience, visitors make themselves active participants in the commodification process. Instead of being passive consumers of the festival product, they drive change by injecting foreign funds into the economy, supporting the tourism industry on the island, and sharing their experiences with others on travel forums and review sites.

US MUSICIANS AT JAZZ PLAZA 2012

The festival showcased a wide variety of music, and that extended to the musicians representing the United States, which had the most performers of any country other than Cuba. The US musicians had different cultural backgrounds, ages, and skill levels. They played different types of jazz and some did not consider themselves to be jazz musicians at all. The six musical acts from the United States included Nachito Herrera, pianist Arturo O'Farrill, saxophonist Jimmy Sommers, the Friends University Jazz Band, the Will Magid Quartet, and Trio Los Vigilantes. While the latter three groups are not widely recognized performers or big names in Latin jazz, their experiences are telling representations of what musicians who aspired to perform in a

Cuban festival during the Obama era endured and encountered. A closer analysis of these three groups of relatively young musicians, the music they performed, and their stories of getting to the island illustrate how this festival, in particular, has created transnational connections between the United States and Cuba.

The ensemble from Friends University, a private Christian college in Wichita, Kansas, played the most traditional jazz at the festival. Under the leadership of director Lisa Hittle, nineteen students came to Havana to perform in the Jazz Plaza Festival. Hittle said that visiting Cuba had been on her bucket list for many years, and she chose to pursue it after learning that Texas Christian University's jazz ensemble played the festival in 2010. TCU's trip took place just before the streamlined regulations for educational institutions were announced, and the ensemble was required to travel on a Specific License. Shortly before the group was scheduled to leave, however, the OFAC questioned the validity of the university's licensing category, and the trip was nearly canceled. It was not until several Texas Congressional members got involved that final confirmation was received ten days before the band's departure for Havana.[15] Despite those challenges, TCU's director told Hittle that it was one of the greatest trips his band ever took and encouraged her to proceed.[16]

In December 2011 she joined an organized Havana Jazz Festival tour through Toronto-based Authentic Cuba Tours in order to arrange for Friends University to participate. With the help of the staff at Authentic Cuba Tours, she arranged a meeting with a festival official and secured an invitation for the band. Throughout 2012 the band held fundraisers and learned about Cuban music and history; to prepare, they watched Jane Bunnett's 2000 documentary *Cuban Odyssey: Spirits of Havana*, in which the saxophonist and her husband travel throughout the Cuban capital playing music with old and new friends. Hittle again turned to Authentic Cuba Tours to help organize their trip, which qualified for a general license, and the tour company set up an additional trip for twenty Wichita residents who were able to obtain licenses on their own.

On Friday night at the Mella Theatre, the host introduced the band as "Los Amigos Jazz Band de Universidad de Kansas." Before they started, Hittle addressed the audience and had one of the trumpet players translate into Spanish to explain that they would be playing the big band music that celebrated their US heritage. Based on her time at the festival the previous year, the band's director knew that most of the music at the festival was either Latin in nature or variations of free and fusion styles. So she decided that instead of trying to do that, they would do what they did best and pay tribute to American big band music. They opened with Benny Herman's 1948 "Sidewalks of Cuba," the only piece in their set with any reference to the island, and continued to play selections by artists like Stan Kenton, Woody Herman, Duke Ellington, and Cole Porter; they received a largely positive response from the audience. Cuban percussion professor Luis Gonzalez joined the band on vibraphone for three songs partway through their set. Hittle had not met Luis before the band arrived, and she first contacted him because the band needed to use a set of vibes in their performances. The band sent their equipment needs to the jazz festival through the staff at Authentic Cuba Travel and initially had trouble locating a vibraphone. She eventually received Luis's information, and the band developed a great rapport with the percussionist. They spent much of their time in Havana with him and visited the Instituto Superior de Arte, where he teaches, to deliver a gift of music supplies, including reeds and drumsticks, to the institute's students. The band's second performance was scheduled for Saturday night as the opening act in the 7:00 p.m. concert at the Bertolt Brecht, but the performance was delayed after strong winds knocked down power lines outside Havana, causing a blackout at the theatre and delaying setup. After the power was restored, there was a second delay as the band waited for music stands to be dropped off because the Bertolt Brecht did not have its own. The concert was able to start just after 8:00, and the band got a big response from the audience that largely consisted of the tour group from Wichita. A tourist from Munich who sat next to me in the concert leaned over to say, "It looks like they're playing for a home crowd."

While their trip only gave them five days in Cuba, the band was able to experience numerous activities outside the festival. In addition to visiting the Instituto Superior de Arte they also toured Old Havana and the Museo de la Revolución. They spent time visiting a retirement home and learning to dance with some of the residents. That experience culminated in an informal birthday party for one of the band members. A Wichita television news crew followed the band and captured much of the trip; the footage eventually aired in a thirty-minute special hosted by a local news anchor.[17] All of the students have expressed their desire to return, and while the university was initially reluctant to approve it, this trip opened the door to additional experiences. In September 2014 Hittle and Friends University hosted Jane Bunnett and the Cuban group Maqueque on campus and in 2017 brought them back to perform with the university ensemble. Hittle also intends to bring her ensemble back to the jazz festival again.

Unlike most of the students from Friends University, Will Magid has traveled extensively as a musician. The young genre-bending trumpeter and multi-instrumentalist combines jazz, electronic dance music, and diverse musical influences from around the globe. Magid, who now performs under the name Balkan Bump, has played on several continents, but the 2012 Jazz Plaza Festival represented the first time he performed in Cuba. His appearance in Havana came about after Conner Gorry, a US expatriate living in and writing about Cuba, visited her friend in San Francisco; that friend was Magid's manager. When Gorry heard Magid's group and witnessed their energetic rapport with the audience, she decided to try and get them on the lineup for the next jazz festival and to coordinate their trip. Magid gave her some copies of his CD to present to festival organizers, and a few months before the festival they received a formal invitation to perform. As a professional musician with a degree in ethnomusicology, Magid's travel qualified for a general license for professional research.

The Will Magid Four's lineup for the festival included bass, guitar, and drums backing Magid on trumpet, sampler, and synthesizer. When the musicians arrived in Havana, Gorry met them and served as a guide for their five-day residency in the city. Describing the festival experience, Gorry explained:

> I wasn't too worried when a few days before the opening of the festival the schedule wasn't finalized, the band didn't have the proper equipment and we had no assurance that Will's rig could be properly accommodated/set up. Jazz Festival organizers were super gracious, as only Cubans can be under so much pressure, and we were pleased with the results, though the guys wanted to play many more (and longer) gigs than they were able within the structure of the Festival.[18]

The group's first performance was on Thursday night at the Casa de Cultura and was scheduled against the oversold Chucho Valdés concert at the Mella, which meant their set was not well attended. The bass player introduced the group in Spanish and explained that their music was for dancing and invited the seated audience members to get up when the music moved them. After a slow and ambient introduction with little sense of rhythm that did not seem to fit the claim of dance music, Magid cued the group in for an upbeat, groove-based tune. By the second piece, people's heads were clearly bouncing along with the music and a few people outside the seating area started to dance. The third song featured vocals by Magid and one verse in Spanish that he read off of a piece of paper, which the audience appreciated and applauded. Throughout their last two songs the energy continued to build as the music toggled between jazz, electronic dance music, and psychedelic jam rock. However, just when the audience was growing and really starting to get into their music, the set was over and Magid thanked the audience in Spanish before leaving the stage.

After leaving the stage, the band hung out for the rest of the evening's performances headlined by Wil Campa's flamboyant salsa ensemble. Campa's set began with a video narrated by a deep voiced announcer, smoke, lasers, and a choreographed introduction of the band as they entered in matching outfits. By this point there was a lot of dancing in the crowd, which had grown much larger than it was for the Will Magid Four. By 1:00 a.m., when the music ended and the American band members were going back to their *casa particular*, the bassist realized his instrument was missing. Conner Gorry felt somewhat responsible for not explaining that risk and how thefts spike in Cuba at the end of the year. While standing around trying to decide what to do and how they would perform again in two days absent a key instrument, Wil Campa and his wife overheard their story and responded by graciously offering to lend them a bass.[19]

Will Magid's performance on Saturday night was in the Bertolt Brecht; it started late because of the power issues and delays in Friends University's sound check. The quartet played third, after Friends University and Jorge Aragón's trio. Once again, their audience was very small, as the US contingent from Kansas left when Friends University was done and many of the Cuban listeners left after Jorge Aragón. The people traveling with Magid's band were there along with a group of six young women the band members had met earlier on the trip. Beyond that there were about ten other people in the room, including myself. Partway through the band's second song, there was another power outage. "Thank you, have a great night!" Magid jokingly yelled to the audience who then encouraged them to keep playing. The bassist stepped backstage and came back with the upright bass that Friends University had used. Magid and the bass player gathered around the drum set as the guitarist held up a cell phone to give them a little bit of light, and they started playing a rendition of "The St. James Infirmary Blues," which was originally made famous by Louis Armstrong. Magid moved to the front of the dark stage for the vocal part and a trumpet solo when the lights came back on, and they kept playing as the electric guitar player was able to join them again. Throughout their next three songs, the infectious dance beat brought a dozen dancers to their feet. When the Will Magid Four performed the Eastern European–influenced "Balkan Suite," the German friend I made just before the concert leaned over and said, "This is strange to be hearing the type of music I listen to in Munich, here in Havana, being played by a band from California." When they were seemingly done, the band got a great response and played an arrangement of Fela Kuti's "Zombi" as an encore. The band's high-energy and intercultural set inspired many people from the small but enthusiastic audience to talk with Magid and have a picture taken with him at the end of the concert.

Will Magid was supposed to perform one other gig on the ElectroBus, a converted bus that becomes a mobile dance party as it drives through Havana in the early hours of the morning. The bus, organized by Cuban DJ duo I.A. Electrónica, had only been on the road once before and was scheduled to depart at midnight on Friday featuring Magid as a DJ. However, for reasons that the musicians did not entirely understand, the government prohibited the ElectroBus from going out that night. Magid was most looking forward to the ElectroBus gig because it was an underground event organized by young people, and he wanted to play with people closer to his own age. He was disappointed in the audiences for the festival performances, which were fairly small and included a lot of international tourists rather than Cubans; the ElectroBus would have been different. It also would have allowed him to share more of what interests him musically. He bemoaned:

> It was a jazz festival, so I have a ton of harder electronic music, even flirting with dubstep and really grimy, funky electronic dance music that I might only have hinted at in my sets. That was more because of the context of the jazz festival than the fact that it was in Cuba. I kind of avoid playing jazz festivals because of how institutionalized the genre's become.[20]

On the other hand, Magid was still very grateful to those who organized the festival and for the opportunity to perform. He received multiple invitations to perform in Havana again, and he hopes to return when he does not have to pay for his trip out of pocket and can perform with young Cuban musicians. The Will Magid Four were only in Cuba for five days, but even with all their challenges they say the trip was not long enough.

Of the US musicians at the 2012 Jazz Plaza Festival, the group that was farthest from jazz and had the most trouble getting to Cuba was Trio Los Vigilantes from Austin, Texas. Under the direction of Isaac Peña, who sings baritone and plays *requinto*, Trio Los Vigilantes performs boleros from the mid-twentieth century and earlier.[21] The bolero is a romantic and danceable song style typically performed at a slow tempo and accompanied by strings. It was cultivated in Cuba at the turn of the twentieth century by singer-composers like Sindo Garay and Pepe Sánchez. It became popular throughout Latin America by the 1920s, and in Mexico bolero groups commonly sang with smooth, three-part harmonies accompanied by guitar, which became the standard international style (Manuel 2006, 42). Trio Los Vigilantes, which consists of Peña, Luis Ángel Ibañez on guitar and baritone vocals, and John Pointer on cello and tenor vocals, often perform their arrangements with a string quartet. The group was formed in the late 1990s and is dedicated to reviving the bolero; they primarily perform songs from the genre's mid-century golden age when Peña's father had his own trio in southern Texas. As professional musicians studying the bolero and its history, they were able to justify their trip as professional research for a general license but chose to fly through Mexico.

The trio had been invited to the jazz festival each year since 2010, but 2012 was the first year they accepted. They were connected to the festival through a friend who brought US citizens to Cuba on people-to-people tours in the late 1990s and early 2000s and knew someone on the festival committee. They submitted their music to her and received their official festival invitation in late October. In order to help pay for their trip, the trio set up an account with PayPal as an online fundraising tool and were able to raise nearly two thousand dollars. But two weeks before the festival, the account was suspended when PayPal staff discovered that it was being used to facilitate travel to Cuba. The musicians tried to explain that their travel was for a legal, licensed purpose and therefore the PayPal account was not in violation of any embargo-related financial restrictions, but they were unable to access the funds until after the trip. The trio booked their flight to Havana from Monterrey, Mexico, which was more affordable than flying through Miami because they could drive to Monterrey. However, after arriving at the Mexico border the night before their flight, Mexican border authorities told them that they could not drive their car into the interior of the country. The last bus of the night from the border to Monterrey had already left, so their only viable option to still make their flight the next morning was a $250 cab ride. Despite the increasing costs, the trio decided they had already come too far to turn around.

When they landed in Havana after seventeen hours of travel, they had a short amount of time to find and hire a string quartet to accompany their festival performances. Peña had previously explained to their festival contact that they would need a string quartet, but he was told to work that out once they arrived. The trio first visited one of the art schools expecting university players but instead found students in their early to mid-teens. They then reached out to a government office that organizes orchestral music in the Amadeo Roldán Theatre. After giving a CD to an administrator, showing her they had written arrangements and were willing to pay the group, she put them in contact with some musicians from the National Symphony Orchestra of Cuba who perform as a quartet called Puras Cuerdas (Pure Strings). The quartet agreed to do two rehearsals and the two festival performances for $200.

The group's first performance was in the Jardines del Mella at 6:00 p.m. on the Saturday of the festival, and their second performance was Sunday night at the Bertolt Brecht. The dark, intimate space for Sunday's concert seemed fitting for the trio's sound; they performed first that night and were followed by Miguelito Nuñez from Cuba, Shanti Lo from Botswana, and Carlos Averhoff Jr. from Cuba. The audience was larger and had more Cubans in attendance than were at the previous night's concert at the Brecht, which featured Friends University and Will Magid. Several older Cubans sang along with the trio's boleros from their seats. The band expected some of the older individuals to remember a few songs they played, but overall they were surprised by how much old music they heard while in Havana. The group did not alter their sets much from what they would typically play in Texas. They had considered playing their arrangement of Compay Segundo's "Chan Chan," popularized by the *Buena Vista Social Club* album and covered by Trio Los Vigilantes on a 1999 album. However, when they asked their guide if audiences would be interested in hearing an American group perform it, he said no. After a couple of days in Cuba they realized why. Every day they heard renditions of "Chan Chan" and "Cuarto de Tula," another song from the *Buena Vista Social Club*, and "Guantanamera." So the trio left out what Cuban hits they had in their repertoire and did their usual set of traditional boleros along with an arrangement of "Because" by the Beatles. Before the group was able to perform all of the pieces they had prepared, however, they were cut off because the hall manager said their thirty minutes were up.

Upon returning to the United States, Trio Los Vigilantes had to recover not only their sleep patterns but their finances. The musicians went into debt to finance the trip, so after resolving their PayPal issue they held another event to make some money back by giving a performance while sharing photos and videos from the trip with fans. The Austin musicians faced many difficulties getting to Cuba, frustrations with the festival itself, and the almost obligatory waterborne stomach sickness that US visitors I spoke to had to deal with. Yet they still hope to come back to Cuba to one day participate in the annual bolero festival.

Beyond improvisation and the use of some standard instrumentation, trying to characterize jazz in the context of the Havana Jazz Plaza Festival becomes a challenge in itself as the festival brings together big band jazz with Latin and experimental jazz alongside traditional Cuban genres. Musicians from Cuba and abroad perform varied styles of music that illustrate the international nature of both the event and jazz as a musical genre. Latin jazz itself emerged through intercultural music making and can be considered on a stylistic continuum that bridges jazz with traditional Caribbean and Latin American musics (Washburne 2012, 91). Both ends of this continuum and the Latin jazz that connects them were present and performed at the 2012 Havana Jazz Plaza Festival.

Many musicians at the festival aligned with the category of Latin jazz and bridged traditional Cuban and Latin American genres with jazz. Chucho Valdés performed with his band the Afro-Cuban Messengers (a name referencing Art Blakey and the Jazz Messengers) as well as a number of guest musicians during the oversold opening concert at the Mella on Thursday night. Valdés describes his ensemble as atypical. With various percussion instruments including drum set, congas, and *batá* drums, Valdés emphasizes polyrhythms that draw from Afro-Cuban traditional music and also incorporates vocals in the West African Yoruba language. Additional instruments, including piano, bass, saxophone, and trumpet, are common to jazz ensembles. In many ways, Valdés is continuing the musical experimentation and fusions that he started when he formed Irakere. Sintesis similarly combined jazz and popular dance music with afro-Cuban musical traditions. While musicians like Valdés, Sintesis, and others represented the middle space, the festival also had the other two ends of the spectrum with jazz in traditional, modern, and experimental forms alongside various types of traditional Latin and Cuban music. Friends University played the most standard style of big band jazz that is found in educational institutions all over the United States. Many of the other ensembles were set up as small jazz combos who played modern jazz with a focus on individual instrumental solos. Most of these groups came from Latin American countries, but the style of jazz they played would not be considered Latin jazz. The traditional musics included Cuban son and rumba found throughout Vedado during the festival; the boleros of Trio Los Vigilantes; Pancho Amat, who played the tres during the colloquium; and Grupo Abdón Alcaráz from Spain, who performed Andalusian flamenco. The Havana Jazz Plaza Festival is a physical and audible manifestation of the shared in-between space at the center of the Latin jazz continuum. The musical forces even extended beyond the Latin jazz continuum to incorporate Africa and Europe into the transnational dialogue between jazz, popular, art music, and various folk music traditions.

The forces at play in the festival were not only cultural but also political, especially for the US musicians who had to negotiate legal restrictions and overcome various challenges to experience Havana and participate in the festival dialogue. The US performers at the jazz festival who I spoke to were all forced to alter their plans at one point or another to deal with the circumstances of getting to and then performing in Cuba. Perhaps because they are used to improvising musically, they took their challenges in stride when they were either forced to wait for a situation to resolve itself or to push forward and find a new solution. Even with everything they had to contend with, they all want to visit Cuba again. Attending and playing in the Havana Jazz Plaza Festival is an expensive undertaking for visitors from the United States and other countries, but it is appealing because it is a prominent site for intercultural musical dialogue. The music that can be found throughout the Vedado district of Havana as part of the festival is as diverse as the number of nationalities present. Through jazz, those nations and cultures are able to speak to one another. As new musical sounds emerged from these dialogues, they reflected the new sociopolitical arrangements between the United States and Cuba.

ARTURO O'FARRILL AND CUBA: THE CONVERSATION CONTINUES

Of all the US performers at the Havana Jazz Plaza Festival, Arturo O'Farrill can most appropriately be considered a musical diplomat. In 2012 O'Farrill was an honored guest and performer for a reception at the home of US Interests Section Chief of Mission John Caulfield before performing at the Mella on Friday night of the festival.[22] In his concert, the pianist played with a fairly traditional small jazz ensemble including drum set, bass, trumpet, saxophone, and a percussionist who played congas and claves. Much of their music was based on Cuban dance styles, and they drew from the Latin jazz tunes Dizzy Gillespie had popularized. As the founder of the Afro Latin Jazz Orchestra and son of Cuban jazz composer Chico O'Farrill, Arturo O'Farrill has dedicated himself to emphasizing the role of Cuban music in jazz while also reestablishing the musical and political relationships between Cuba and the United States.

His father, Arturo "Chico" O'Farrill, was born in Cuba to an Irish father and German mother in 1921. Chico O'Farrill learned to play trumpet while at military school, where he was exposed to big band jazz, and later studied arranging with Cuban composer Felix Guerrero. The senior O'Farrill worked and played with various jazz ensembles in Havana until moving to New York City in 1948. Musicians like Machito and Dizzy Gillespie were already finding success combining Cuban music with jazz when Chico arrived, which helped him find steady work as an arranger for musicians like Benny Goodman and others. On December 21, 1950, Chico O'Farrill collaborated with Machito's band to record his piece *The Afro-Cuban Jazz Suite* with Charlie Parker, Buddy Rich, and Flip Phillips. This multi-movement work drew upon O'Farrill's formal training as a composer and arranger to bring classical ideas of harmonic development and contrasting themes into Latin jazz music. In 1955 O'Farrill returned to Cuba for two years before moving to Mexico City, where his son, Arturo O'Farrill Jr., was born in 1960. Chico O'Farrill and his family returned to New York City in 1965, where he worked as a freelance composer and arranger for television commercials and jazz bands for the next thirty years. His career underwent a resurgence beginning in 1995 when he released the album *Pure Emotion* and was featured in a Jazz at Lincoln Center program. Chico O'Farrill died at age seventy-nine in 2001. He had not been back to Cuba since 1958.[23]

Arturo O'Farrill followed in his father's footsteps as a musician, composer, and arranger. He studied piano and received his musical education from the Manhattan School of Music, Brooklyn College Conservatory, and the Aaron Copland School of Music at Queens College. In 1995, when his father's career was experiencing a renaissance, Arturo became the director of the Chico O'Farrill Afro Cuban Jazz Orchestra. After the Lincoln Center Jazz Orchestra found success performing Latin jazz concerts and collaborating with Arturo O'Farrill, Lincoln Center invited O'Farrill to lead a new band modeled after Wynton Marsalis's group and dedicated solely to Latin jazz. He named the new group Lincoln Center's Afro Latin Jazz Orchestra (ALJO), because O'Farrill felt that neither "Latin jazz" nor "Afro-Cuban" conveyed the music's diverse and global nature (Washburne 2012, 94–97); despite the ensemble's inclusive name, the majority of the band's music is rooted in Cuban musical traditions. The ALJO's tenure at Lincoln Center lasted from 2002 until 2007.

O'Farrill first visited Cuba in 2002, and he intended to return to the island with his band to play his father's music. However, the George W. Bush administration curtailed OFAC license opportunities before a performance could be scheduled. O'Farrill's dream was on hold until the Obama administration began to loosen travel restrictions, and in 2010 Chucho Valdés invited the bandleader to participate in the 26th Havana Jazz Plaza Festival. O'Farrill brought his sons and the band named after his father, the Chico O'Farrill Afro Cuban Jazz Orchestra, to participate in the festival. In addition to performing his father's *Afro-Cuban Jazz Suite* and other compositions in multiple concerts, Arturo O'Farrill also debuted a new composition entitled "Fathers and Sons: From Havana to New York And Back."[24] The visit to Cuba in 2010 also marked the beginning of an ongoing relationship between O'Farrill and the US Interests Section in Havana.

Hours after landing in Havana in 2010, O'Farrill and the rest of the band participated in a reception at the Cuban home of Charles Barclay, then the deputy chief of the United States Interests Section. During the event, the bandleader addressed the crowd in Barclay's living room: "I needed to complete a musical, spiritual, and cultural journey for my father. In some ways, the relationship between jazz and Afro-Cuban music has still not been understood. We've only begun to uncover the relationship between these two places."[25] O'Farrill actively worked to foster that relationship in the years that followed. He returned to participate in the Havana Jazz Plaza Festival annually, traveling with different musicians and premiering new compositions each year. He performed for events in conjunction with the US Interests Section and the chief of mission during his festival visits. These jazz receptions brought US citizens living in Cuba together with Cuban jazz aficionados to enjoy O'Farrill's music in a spirit of cooperation and a shared transnational interest in jazz. The Afro Latin Jazz Alliance, a not-for-profit organization created by Arturo O'Farrill in 2007 to produce performances for the Afro Latin Jazz Orchestra, initiated various cultural diplomacy initiatives to bring US and Cuban musicians together. The organization facilitated performances by Cuban jazz saxophonist Michel Herrera and Los Muñoquitos de Matanzas in New York City in May 2011 and also started work on the Chico O'Farrill School of Jazz, an educational music exchange with Cuba.[26]

In December 2014 the Afro Latin Jazz Alliance sent the full Afro Latin Jazz Orchestra to Cuba for the first time to participate in the 30th Havana Jazz Plaza Festival. In addition to festival performances, Arturo O'Farrill and some Cuban musicians played a reception at the residence of the US chief of mission and premiered a new composition entitled "24 Hours in a Dog's Life" with the MalPaso Dance Company featuring choreography by Cuban dancer, professor, and the company's founder Osnel Delgado. Most significantly, the trip brought O'Farrill, his sons, the ALJO, Cuban composers, and numerous guest performers together to record an album entitled *Cuba: The Conversation Continued*. In total fifty-eight individuals traveled to Cuba as part of the effort, including twenty-four musicians, twenty-one producers, five videographers, two photographers, and six staff from the Afro Latin Jazz Alliance. A press release from the Alliance on December 12, 2014, promoted the significance of the album's collaborative recording sessions and tied it to the organization's larger cultural diplomacy efforts:

> *Cuba: The Conversation Continued* sets forth a revolutionary new path where America and Cuba seek ways to reconcile, and realize they're really part of the same roots. Just as Cuban artists should learn the elements of American jazz, stateside musicians should have an opportunity to understand Cuban syncopations as a crucial component of jazz education. O'Farrill is a leading force in making sure this happens, and along the way, he's creating a common musical bond between the two countries.[27]

The US Interests Section's jazz reception took place on December 16, just after the musicians arrived in Cuba; the following day O'Farrill's efforts to forge and rekindle US-Cuban musical connections took on new relevance.

On December 17, 2014, Presidents Obama and Castro announced plans to reestablish diplomatic relations between the two countries. The US musicians watched President Obama's surprise statement live on television, during which he declared that Alan Gross and a US intelligence agent had been released by the Cuban government. In return, the United States was releasing three members of the Cuban Five who were still in prison. The United States and Cuba would both reestablish embassies in one another's countries, and policies would be enacted to increase travel and commerce. The Castro government also agreed to increase internet access on the island and to release a number of political prisoners, but President Obama said that ordinary Cubans still faced many barriers to freedom and that the United States would continue working to advance freedom and human rights on the island.[28] The announcement itself came after eighteen months of secret negotiations between Washington and Havana that were encouraged by Pope Francis.

That evening the Afro Latin Jazz Orchestra attended a celebration with their fellow Cuban musicians at the home of *tres* player Cotó, who dedicated the day to the brotherhood between Cuba and the United States. Cotó, whose real name is Juan de la Cruz Antomachi, told his guests that their two countries could become united as one through culture.[29] The spirit of transnational collaboration was encouraged by the political events and can be heard on the album, which producers retitled from *Cuba: The Conversation Continued* to *Cuba: The Conversation Continues* to reflect the present and future possibilities of US-Cuban engagement. The recording sessions took place from December 19 to 21 in Abdala Studios, which were opened in 1998 by Silvio Rodriguez.[30] Arturo O'Farrill contributed two compositions to the album. The other US composers on the album are Zack O'Farrill, Earl McIntyre, Dafnis Prieto, and Michele Rosewoman. It also features four Cuban composers: Alexis Bosch, Bobby Carcassés, Cotó, and Michel Herrera.

The centerpiece of the album is Arturo O'Farrill's *Afro Latin Jazz Suite*, which was commissioned by the Apollo Theater for the sixty-fifth anniversary of Chico O'Farrill's *Afro-Cuban Jazz Suite*. Like his father's piece, which featured Charlie Parker on alto saxophone, the *Afro Latin Jazz Suite* is a multi-movement work, featuring alto saxophonist Rudresh Mahanthappa. While not a member of the Afro Latin Jazz Orchestra, the second-generation Indian American is one of seventeen guest musicians included on the album. An analysis of the suite illustrates how the music performed and recorded at the Havana Jazz Plaza Festival is situated on a continuum that connects jazz and traditional musics and serves as a liminal space through which listeners can recontextualize jazz and Cuba's place in jazz historiography.[31] The first movement of the *Afro Latin Jazz Suite* is entitled "Mother Africa." The nearly ten-minute movement begins with a three-minute introduction that features Mahanthappa's virtuosic and Parker-like playing in unaccompanied solos interspersed with chords and orchestrated melodies played by the full ensemble. The cluster chords Arturo wrote for the introduction's climax and concluding cadence are drawn directly from the dominant and tonic opening chords used in his father's composition. Following the introduction, which concludes with thick jazz harmonies, the ensemble drops out to be replaced by a sparse ostinato pattern typical of West African traditional music. A bell pattern provides the musical timeline for a layered ostinato built through the addition of rhythmic voices beginning with djembes, a rhythmic piano line, bass, and then Mahanthappa on saxophone. When the saxophone, trumpet, and trombone sections come in, they each play brief melodic runs and rhythmic motifs that fit into and play off of the ongoing ostinato. The second half of the movement features an improvisatory saxophone solo before the bell pattern returns and the full ensemble provides a closing cadence using some of the same dense harmonies heard in the introduction but with a more conclusive final chord. This movement provides the piece's most direct connections to the past as it draws not only from Chico O'Farrill's 1950 work but also from the African roots of jazz.

The connection to jazz history continues in the second movement, which is subtitled "All of the Americas," as Arturo O'Farrill regularly stresses that jazz is not a North American but a Pan-American genre. In the opening section of this movement, Venezuelan-born percussionist Roberto Quintero provides an underlying rhythm on the maracas that is accompanied by a simple repeating pattern in the baritone saxophone. Additional reed and then brass instruments enter to create an increasingly polyphonic texture until the percussion pattern changes and the piece builds up again with new melodic fragments. Rudresh Mahanthappa is again the featured soloist, after which the rhythm section shifts once more to play an afro-Peruvian *festejo* rhythm before the movement concludes.[32] The liner notes describe the melodic lines as being drawn from Islamic Northern Africa while the accompanying drum patterns are from Central Africa. Their juxtaposition represents how these regional cultures were brought together in the Americas through the Atlantic slave trade, and the inclusion of the *festejo* can be heard as one of the distinctly American traditions that emerged from African roots.

The third movement is only a minute and a half long and is subtitled "Adagio." The slow and reflective section stands in sharp contrast to the high-energy movements that preceded it, and it recalls the unhurried "Canción" passage from the original *Afro-Cuban Jazz Suite*. The peaceful if somewhat pensive "Adagio" segues quickly into the chaos of the fourth and final movement, "What Now?" The movement opens with a solo saxophone and dissonant punches played by the rest of the wind instruments, and passages alluding to the second movement are played with a newfound sense of urgency. O'Farrill's ostinato piano then propels the music forward and provides the underlying harmonies for the movement, which includes solos by trumpet Jim Seeley and a return of Rudresh Mahanthappa's alto saxophone. According to the liner notes, "What was a Chico-Bird dialogue has become an Arturo-Rudresh conversation."[33] The piece concludes with a rising arpeggio that climaxes with fortissimo saxophones trilling over two sustained chords: a C major triad and a G-flat major triad with an added ninth. The dissonance created by these two chords at the end of the suite leaves the question of "What Now?" unanswered and unresolved.

The story told through the movements of the *Afro Latin Jazz Suite* can be heard as a meditation on the musical conversation between Cuba and the United States. In the first two movements, O'Farrill references the African traditions that were brought to both countries. Interaction with European and native musical practices facilitate the creation of new styles and genres, and jazz emerges and matures as a part of the discourse between New

Orleans, New York, and Havana. In the "Adagio," US and Cuban policies restrict that conversation following the Cuban Revolution. Then with very little warning, the conversation becomes lively again but the future is uncertain. Other tracks on the album evoke the US-Cuban musical conversation even more directly. The track "Blues Guaguancó" by Bobby Carcassés does this by bringing together two distinct musical traditions from the African diaspora that were separated by the Straits of Florida, and he incorporates Yoruba words and syllables into improvisatory scat singing over rumba rhythms. In "Second Line Soca (Brudda Singh)," guest singer Renée Manning helps to illustrate the relationship between New Orleans and Havana in a piece that includes rhythms and horn parts associated with the New Orleans brass band tradition while emphasizing Caribbean and Latin elements in the music. The album as a whole reflects not only this musical conversation but also O'Farrill's transatlantic understanding of jazz and his inclusive philosophy in creating the Afro Latin Jazz Orchestra.

The double LP was released in August 2015. The *Afro Latin Jazz Suite* won the Grammy Award for Best Instrumental Composition in 2015, and in 2016 the album won the Latin Grammy Award for Best Latin Jazz Album. While accepting his Latin Grammy, Arturo O'Farrill thanked the US and Cuban people as well as presidents Barack Obama and Raúl Castro for having the courage to change the world. Since recording *Cuba: The Conversation Continues* in Havana, O'Farrill has been a persistent voice in promoting US-Cuban musical exchange and political dialogue. He has remained an annual fixture at the Havana Jazz Plaza Festival and has helped numerous other US jazz musicians participate in the festival and visit Cuba for the first time.

CONCLUSION

Getting to the Havana Jazz Plaza Festival continued to be expensive and challenging for visitors from the United States even during most of the Obama administration, but it was attractive because musicians wanted to be part of the festival's intercultural musical dialogue. Participating musicians aspired to renew the once thriving musical relationship between Cuba and the United States, and their performances have been used to negotiate differences and find commonalities while creating connections between individuals on both sides of the Straits of Florida. The music that can be found throughout the Vedado district of Havana as part of the festival is as diverse as the number of nationalities present. Through jazz, those nations and cultures are able to speak to one another, and their performances illustrate the international nature of the event and jazz itself.

For a number of years after the revolution, jazz was marginalized and disparaged in Cuba. Many performers left, but a number of devoted jazz musicians and enthusiasts like Bobby Carcassés and Chucho Valdés continued to practice and promote jazz on the island. Carcassés started the festival, and now it has become a major international event attracting performers and tourists from around the world. When asked why he has been devoted to jazz throughout his life, Carcassés says he stays in Cuba to promote jazz because it is important not only as music but also a philosophy of freedom.[34] With the new opportunities for legal travel, US musicians and visitors flocked to the festival. As a result, they have become invested in US-Cuban politics and the musical dialogue between these estranged countries. New musical compositions emerged from artists like Arturo O'Farrill during the festival, and they suggested and precipitated new sociopolitical arrangements. After returning to the United States, these performers actively share their experiences and help others navigate the legal issues surrounding travel to Cuba, which creates more connections and strengthens existing ties. Following the major policy shift in US-Cuba relations announced on December 17, 2014, interest in Cuban music increased dramatically and more US citizens began arranging trips to the alluring and once forbidden island to experience its music firsthand.

5

NEW MUSICIANS AND TRAVELERS IN CUBA

Nachito Herrera appeared on stage with the National Symphony Orchestra of Cuba at the 2012 Havana Jazz Plaza Festival just one month after their US tour ended. The concert took place on Saturday afternoon during the festival in the Teatro Mella, but attendance seemed low; the balcony was practically empty. The orchestra played some of the same pieces that were part of their tour program, including *Rhapsody in Blue* and some of Herrera's arrangements that showcased his skills as a jazz pianist. But unlike the US tour, they played no works by nineteenth-century European composers and instead emphasized jazz throughout. A group of musicians going by the name of the Havana Jazz Social Club, made up of three trumpeters, a trombonist, saxophonist, flutist, bassist, drummer, conga player, and bongo player, came on stage and played with Herrera. After their first two pieces were enthusiastically received, a salsa-dancing couple in flashy matching outfits joined the musicians to entertain the audience. It was one of the largest stage shows of the festival, and the enthusiastic response from the crowd and calls for encores confirmed that the audience appreciated it.

Herrera played the jazz festival wearing the same "uniform" he wore for the opening performance of the US tour in Kansas City: a red guayabera shirt and a pair of shiny black and red dress shoes. Black and red are the colors of the *orisha* Eleguá, who is both a trickster and the guardian of the crossroads. In a typical *toque de santo*, the Santería religious celebration that culminates in a practitioner communing with an *orisha*, Eleguá is always the first to be acknowledged. As the protector of the crossroads, he can open the pathway allowing people to interact with the other deities. Nachito Herrera also stands at a crossroads. The festival program identified him as an artist from the United States, but he was born and grew up in Cuba. As a figure at the crossroads between the United States and Cuba, he has been able to open pathways to US-Cuban interaction. While both Barack Obama and Raúl Castro's administrations introduced policies to make US-Cuban cultural exchanges possible and to reestablish diplomatic relations, musicians still struggled to navigate those regulations and make a trip on their own. Typically, US musicians depend on someone like Nachito Herrera, someone at the transnational crossroads and whose connections in both countries can be drawn upon to facilitate musical exchange.

US-Cuban musical and social networks flourished in the late 1990s and early 2000s. When the Bush administration restricted travel in 2004, the ties that constituted those networks were severed. Policy changes that began in 2009 created opportunities for some of those networks to be reestablished and for new ones to form, and US-Cuban musical diplomacy efforts often rely on the personal social networks of well-connected individuals. A case study of the 2013 Cubadisco Festival and Nachito Herrera's role as a facilitator illustrates the importance of personal networks in enabling these exchanges. The 2015 visit by the Minnesota Orchestra demonstrates how networks between Minnesota and Cuba continued to grow and accelerate with political change. The difficulties of travel from the United States to Cuba and the fact that musicians cannot directly profit from their performances as part of an exchange also raise questions about the reasons people want to visit and perform on the island. Following the December 2014 announcement of normalizing relations, the allure of Cuba increased, motivating an increased number of US musicians to play concerts for the Cuban people. Their ability to legally visit Cuba, however, continued to depend upon their travel being "purposeful," while politicians and members of the exile community opposed to normalization derided any travel that resembled tourism. Yet the actual differences between purposeful travel and tourism are difficult to define. As increased travel and tourism to Cuba exposed and contributed to growing inequalities in the island's economy, a summary of US musicians' experiences also reveals the direct and indirect impact of these musical exchanges.

SOCIAL NETWORKS IN FACILITATING US-CUBAN MUSICAL EXCHANGE

Recording stars like Juanes, Kool and the Gang, and Wynton Marsalis have the influence and resources to hire professionals that can arrange their Cuba travel and handle any confusing logistical issues. The majority of US musicians that I spoke to in Cuba, however, did not have those resources; they were able to play on the island because of personal connections with other individuals. Many of these musicians had previously been interested in going to Cuba, but they were unsure about travel restrictions, how to actually get to the country, where to stay, and how to book a performance. They depended on others in their social networks to provide that information and facilitate performances in Cuba. Some musicians already had ties to individuals like that, even if they were removed by multiple degrees; others had to expand their networks to find someone with that information.

In one of the most commonly cited articles pertaining to the study of social networks, "The Strength of Weak Ties" (1973), Mark Granovetter asked a sampling of individuals where they found information about new job opportunities. In most cases, people gained information from a personal contact, but the most useful information came from a weak tie. Weak ties refer to indirect relations through intermediaries or individuals that are connected but have little contact. In the case of the job seeker, weak ties are outside the individual's direct social circle (Knoke and Yang 2008, 5; Prell 2012, 45). The ability of musicians from the United States to perform in international Cuban music festivals underscores the "strength of weak ties" argument.

Conner Gorry helped arrange for Will Magid to be invited to Cuba; their connection was a weak tie as they had no direct connection to one another until meeting through Magid's manager at a concert. Magid had been interested in visiting Cuba for some time, but it was Gorry who actually took the initiative because she wanted to bring more American popular music to the island. Gorry explained that rock music is greatly missed in Cuba: "I would definitely do it again and since first coming here in 1993 have dreamed of bringing rock and roll acts from the US to Cuba."[1] Trio Los Vigilantes made it to the Havana Jazz Plaza Festival because one of the band members was friends with someone who had organized trips to Cuba in the late 1990s, and he was able to secure their invitation to the festival. Even Arturo O'Farrill depended on weak ties for his initial invitation to the Havana Jazz Plaza Festival. Chucho Valdés played in New York City shortly after the Lincoln Center Jazz Orchestra's 2010 residency in Havana; Lincoln Center acted as the intermediary that connected O'Farrill with Valdés, who extended the festival invitation.

Other people, like Lisa Hittle of Friends University and Joanne Connolly of Voices from the Heart, hired outside help and actively took advantage of the few resources they had in their networks to enable a cultural exchange. After hearing that Texas Christian University's ensemble had played the jazz festival, Hittle used her connections to track down the director to ask him questions. The information she received led her to join an Authentic Cuban Tours trip to the island during the festival. The tour organizers put her in contact with festival officials, and she was able to arrange for Friends University to receive an invitation. Voices from the Heart's travel committee decided to investigate the possibility of a trip to Cuba and were eventually put in contact with Michael Eizenberg, who in turn set up a meeting between Connolly and Digna Guerra, director of the Cuban national choir. Through their connection, a formal cultural exchange was arranged and necessary travel licenses were obtained.

Benjamin Brinner's *Playing Across a Divide*, about musicians in Israel, explains the importance of social networks in the lives and careers of practicing musicians:

> Professional musicians are always enmeshed in larger sets of relationships as they join, create, and reshape networks relevant to their musical work. At all stages of their careers they navigate the links that bind them to others with related interests and needs in order, for instance, to find employment and partners for performances. Reputations, musical ideas, fads, and other intangibles flow along the same links, which extend to nonmusicians who act as producers, managers, critics, listeners, performers in other media, and so on. The network concept can usefully be extended further to include institutions such as schools, events such as festivals, venues such as particular clubs or concert halls, and artifacts such as recordings. (2009, 163)

Brinner's study explained how musicians bridged East-West and Israeli-Palestinian geographic, religious, and political divides. Beyond serving a similar function connecting the United States and Cuba, social networks highlight the cultural and political friction inherent to US-Cuban musical exchanges.

While not an extensive quantitative social network analysis, the following two case studies explain the importance of social networks in enabling US-Cuban musical diplomacy efforts and facilitating legal travel. Both Nachito Herrera and the concert touring company Classical Movements function as hubs in their exchange networks because they are central nodes through which many other individuals and institutions are related. They are also bridges in that they connect two otherwise separate networks of musicians and musical organizations, one in the United States and one in Cuba. In turn, these exchanges expand and strengthen the social networks that facilitate them while elevating the status of bridging individuals and organizations. Unlike many actors in social networks, Herrera and Classical Movements are committed to musical diplomacy and actively seek to create smoother musical pathways that connect Cuba and the United States.

MINNESOTA MUSICIANS AT CUBADISCO

Nachito and Aurora Herrera wanted to support music education in Minnesota and encourage musical exchanges with their native country, so they created the Nachito Herrera Foundation, which was officially incorporated in 2012. The foundation is described as a non-profit organization dedicated to fostering cultural and educational exchanges between the United States and Cuba. Their first opportunity to put the foundation into action came in 2013. After playing at the jazz festival, Herrera returned to Havana in January to begin recording an album with the National Symphony Orchestra along with the Havana Jazz Social Club. He then received an invitation to perform at the Cubadisco Festival in May where he would be introduced as one of the new artists on Cuba's EGREM record label. Seizing the opportunity, the Nachito Herrera Foundation helped bring eight musicians from Minnesota to Havana to perform with the orchestra at the festival.

This was another dream come true for Herrera. He described the process and his excitement:

> Right away my wife and I started working because it would be wonderful for the Foundation to invite students and professional musicians to work there with us. So after the first few months we were doing auditions for different students from the University of Minnesota and then from Hamline University, St. Thomas, St. Olaf, and finally we got a group of ten students to go.[2]

Some of the students who auditioned for the trip had previously played with Herrera as part of the Minnesota Youth Symphony. Melissa Deal grew up in Bloomington, Minnesota, a suburb of the Twin Cities, and was a freshman violinist at the University of Minnesota when she learned about the opportunity to perform in Cuba. Deal had met Herrera in high school when the pianist was a guest soloist with the youth symphony. At the time, Herrera told them about a program he was developing to take music students to Cuba, where they could learn about the culture through music. Nachito and

Aurora initially selected ten students to come with them to Cubadisco. To make the trip possible, Nachito and Aurora partnered with a travel provider that was authorized to organize Cuba travel and obtain OFAC licenses. After determining who could qualify for a general license and attempting to obtain Specific Licenses for the rest of the musicians, only five of the ten students were able to participate. Three professional singers from the Twin Cities, Norah Long, Bruce Henry, and Maurice Jacox, also joined the students.[3]

While many of the participating musicians were told about the trip earlier in the year and had plenty of time for preparation, licenses could not be finalized to confirm the trip until three weeks before they left. Herrera organized a benefit concert with some of the participating musicians to fund travel expenses just two weeks before leaving for Cuba. With such a quick turnaround, the participating musicians were just trying to keep up; many doubted that the trip would actually happen.[4] Despite the challenges of obtaining licenses and finalizing plans at the last minute, the benefit concert raised enough money, and the eight musicians flew to Havana to participate in Cubadisco.

Cubadisco is a combination of an awards show, music festival, and academic symposium with award presentations and concerts televised live throughout the country. The annual festival is designed to celebrate the Cuban recording industry, so it attracts sales representatives and people in the music business from around the world. As such, it is an opportunity for EGREM, the state record label, to sell Cuban artists and records for distribution in new markets. Each year Cubadisco has a different theme, honorees, and featured musical genres. In 2013 the event lasted from May 17 to May 26 and emphasized young artists and concert music. The opening gala took place at the Teatro Nacional and featured the National Symphony Orchestra and guest artists including Herrera and many of the musicians he had brought with him.

The concert was promoted as a showcase of traditional North American music. The performers did not know if this theme was already planned or was added to incorporate the professional singers from Minnesota, but it allowed each of them to perform with the Cuban symphony on the festival's main stage. Norah Long did some American musical theatre arrangements; Bruce Henry performed gospel; and Maurice Jacox sang jazz and R&B. Norah Long primarily performs musical theater in the Twin Cities area. She was surprised that she was only contacted in March for the May festival, when in her experience events of that size typically start scheduling acts up to twelve months in advance. Long and Herrera had never performed together before the trip, but they shared many mutual colleagues and met a few times to discuss ideas for the festival before traveling to Havana. They discussed what music to play but did not make any final decisions until she could speak with the conductor in Havana, requiring her to bring full orchestral parts and scores for five pieces to share with the orchestra just days before the performance. Because the charter airline limited passengers to a total of forty-two pounds of luggage, she had to sacrifice articles of clothing and other belongings to bring all the sheet music with her.[5]

Long traveled separately from the rest of the Minnesota contingent because she had a gig in the Twin Cities, which forced her to miss the beginning of the festival. Once she arrived on the island, her performance schedule for the festival was altered. Her Thursday night concert was pushed to Friday and then was canceled altogether, and she was never given a clear explanation of why. As a result, she ended up performing only once at Cubadisco. There she sang favorites from her musical theater repertoire, including a medley of "The Cockeyed Optimist," "Singin' in the Rain," "A Spoonful of Sugar," and "Make Someone Happy," which she had performed accompanied by a quartet the previous month for a benefit concert in Minnesota. When she found out she was going to Cuba, she took the medley to composer and arranger Robert Elhai, who created a full orchestral arrangement in one week to be premiered at Cubadisco. "I wasn't quite sure whether the audience would be that interested in it or enjoy it very much, but they were genuinely appreciative and they seemed to really enjoy it," she said. "I just sort of gave myself permission, like Nachito said, to be me and to bring my experiences from our musical culture down there with me."[6]

The student musicians from Minnesota joined the orchestra for two concerts that featured Cuban stars like the Buena Vista Social Club's Omara Portuondo. Melissa Deal was the only one of the Minnesota students to perform a solo for the festival; she played Saint-Saens' "Rondo Capriccioso" in the Teatro Nacional. She and the other students were unaware of how important the festival was to the Cuban music industry. During rehearsals, they met numerous performers like Portuondo and only later found out how famous she was. Deal's biggest surprise, however, was how welcoming everyone was to her and the other students: "In an instant we were like their family. I mean, this is the national orchestra, and they invited us to come stay at their homes the next time we returned."[7]

Herrera played a second performance at the festival, and he was also busy recording with the National Symphony Orchestra while on the island. He did not get to spend a significant amount of time with the musicians from

Minnesota during their trip, so Aurora Herrera took the students to the Santería museum and other attractions when they were not at Cubadisco. The Nachito Herrera Foundation hired a guide to drive the musicians around Havana, and they were able to visit the beach one day. The musicians participated in additional musical endeavors outside the festival by joining Herrera in a recording session, visiting a conservatory to play with other students, and attending a variety of performances and dance clubs.

The musicians enjoyed their experiences in Cuba, including the people they met, and all said they would like to return either as performers or tourists. The connections they made added new contacts to their social networks that could facilitate any return trips to Cuba. Their performances and interactions also strengthened existing ties. Norah Long recalled that Aurora Herrera suggested future collaborations with the Cuban orchestra such as recording an album or performing with them when they returned to the United States. Long told me, however, that she was unsure if that would happen: "I learned when I was down there, don't count chickens before they hatch."[8] Despite her skepticism about these continuing efforts, she and other musicians did perform in concerts with Herrera in the Twin Cities after they returned from Cubadisco. In June 2013 Herrera accompanied Deal in a recital at the University of Minnesota School of Music. They also continued to play together at the Dakota Jazz Club.[9]

Herrera was a beneficiary of the additional contacts and ties created by the exchange. Organizing the trip increased the pianist's prominence in both the United States and Cuba; increased status is not uncommon for someone who is at the intersection of two networks. During Cubadisco he met another guest artist, violinist Jorge Saade of Ecuador, and discussed potential collaborations that would extend beyond the United States and Cuba. Herrera's work with the University of Minnesota students provided him with additional contacts with the university; after returning to the Twin Cities he began discussing how he could help other groups of student musicians perform in Cuba. The Nachito Herrera Foundation's first cultural exchange increased the potential for ongoing collaboration between Herrera and the university.

In the network connecting Minnesota and Cuba, Herrera is simultaneously a musical actor and an articulator, able to "manage musicians' connections to networks such as the festival circuit" while also "positioned at a cut point in or between networks, with control over which music to broadcast, record, or present on stage" (Brinner 2009, 175). As the Nachito Herrera Foundation continued to organize cultural exchanges, his importance in this network increased with the addition of more actors and ties. Herrera helped bring the Havana Jazz Social Club to Minnesota the following year, and the Foundation has participated in a variety of different trips to Cuba for musicians and nonmusicians alike. As Brinner concluded in his research: "Networks are rarely static. They expand or contract as new members join and links are formed or people leave or break off connections. Networks change not only due to these internal dynamics, but also in relation to their sociocultural environments" (206). The ability of this network to continue expanding depends not only on the sociocultural environment but also on the political one. As the US-Cuban political relationship changed, new social networks formed out of old ones, and a new network connecting Minnesotan and Cuban musicians gained prominence.

Following the December 2014 announcement that the United States and Cuba would begin to reestablish diplomatic relations, US media attention and public interest in Cuba reached levels not seen in decades. In turn, more individuals and musical groups explored the possibility of visiting the island. The announcement triggered what National Public Radio called "an orchestral race" as board members, administrators, and performers from major US orchestras jockeyed to be the first such ensemble to play a concert in Cuba following the newly renewed diplomatic relations. No major orchestras from the United States had performed on the island since the Milwaukee Symphony Orchestra visited in 1999.[10] The Minnesota Orchestra won the race by calling on the resources and expertise of Classical Movements, the musical touring company and travel service provider that the orchestra had worked with before. The orchestra also drew upon its own history and touted the fact that the group (when it was known as the Minneapolis Symphony Orchestra) visited Cuba in 1929 for its first international tour.[11]

The decision to visit Cuba in 2015 came just a year after the Minnesota Orchestra had ended a fifteen-month lockout, then the longest work stoppage for an orchestra in US history. After announcing budget deficits, the orchestra's board presented a proposal to cut performers' salaries up to forty percent that was rejected by the musicians. The resulting lockout began in October 2012 and lasted through the entire 2012–13 season. The first five months of the 2013–14 season also saw no performances, until the musicians announced a settlement in January 2014.[12] Later that year, Kevin Smith, who had previously led the Minnesota Opera for twenty-five years, took over the Minnesota Orchestra as president and CEO.[13] Smith was the driving force behind the trip to Cuba, which he began seriously pursuing in January 2015. The visit to Cuba would not only be a valuable public relations win for the orchestra after the lockout, but it would also allow the musicians and administration to test their newly reaffirmed relationship as they worked together to organize an international trip in a matter of months.

International tours for orchestras are typically planned years in advance, but the staff at the Minnesota Orchestra worked with Classical Movements to organize the trip to Cuba in 110 days. Classical Movements emphasizes their more than twenty years of cultural diplomacy efforts on their website, spotlighting that they have worked in over 140 countries and produce over 200 concerts globally every year.[14] The company had organized Cuba travel for musicians beginning in 1996, when travel licenses were made available under the Clinton Administration. The staff at Classical Movements developed many valuable contacts on the island, but they ceased providing travel services to Cuba when the Bush administration tightened the travel ban. The company began applying for travel licenses as soon as the Obama administration announced their availability. In 2010 Classical Movements facilitated the Harvard-Radcliffe Orchestra's trip to the island, and they received the largest Specific License the OFAC had ever issued to bring 210 members of the Yale Alumni Chorus to Cuba for a ten-day tour. Over subsequent years, the company's staff worked to reestablish relationships with the Cuban Ministry of Culture and the island's musical and tourism institutions; Classical Movements has since become the leading concert tour company in the world in bringing performing artists to the island. Neeta Helms, the founder and president of Classical Movements, credits her company's success to having won the trust of the Cuban government: "This is always a process. To this day there are so many interests, and we crossed so many bridges with the foreign ministry. Everyone always has an agenda, and we have to make sure that everyone is happy."[15]

Within weeks of being approached with the idea, staff at Classical Movements secured an invitation to Cubadisco for the Minnesota Orchestra. It was largely coincidental that the orchestra's time in Cuba coincided with the Cubadisco festival, but it made for an excellent performance opportunity; the positive impression left by Minnesota musicians at the festival two years earlier also helped. The changes to travel restrictions that coincided with the December 2014 announcement allowed the orchestra to travel on a general license and avoid the extended OFAC application process.[16] With such a quick turnaround, the orchestra did not have time for an extended fundraising effort to pay for the trip. According to Smith, they had forty-eight hours to come up with the nearly one million dollars to secure their spot at Cubadisco and ensure no other US orchestras would take their place. They turned to board member Marilyn Carlson Nelson, a former CEO of the Carlson hotel and travel company, and her husband Glen, who agreed to underwrite the full cost of the trip.[17]

The musicians left the Twin Cities on Wednesday, May 13, along with seven staff members from Classical Movements, more than the company had ever sent on a single tour. Because the Minneapolis-St. Paul International Airport was not already approved to provide flights to Cuba, Classical Movements helped the airport request and receive a waiver from US Customs and Border Patrol to accommodate the first-ever direct flight from Minneapolis to Havana. They also had to secure permission for the largest plane ever to make the flight from the United States to Havana's José Martí Airport. They needed a plane that could not only hold all the musicians, staff, and members of the media traveling to Cuba but also fit their instruments, equipment for a live radio broadcast of the performances, and the orchestra's acoustical shell.[18] Once they arrived, the Minnesota musicians were treated to a welcome reception at the Hotel Nacional arranged by Classical Movements, which included a performance by the Cuban singers Coro Entrevoces.

The orchestra played two concerts at the Teatro Nacional as part of Cubadisco. On Friday evening, they performed an all-Beethoven set in honor of the all-Beethoven concert that the Minneapolis Symphony Orchestra played on the island in 1929. The pieces included Beethoven's Symphony No. 3, "Eroica," which was on the 1929 program. They also performed the Egmont Overture and Beethoven's Choral Fantasy with the Cuban National Choir. Classical Movements staff helped select the Choral Fantasy, as they were in communication with both the Cuban and Minnesotan musicians and worked to find a piece that could be played together. On Saturday, May 16, the Minnesota Orchestra opened their concert with unlisted performances of both "La Bayamesa" and "The Star-Spangled Banner." The first piece listed on the program was Cuban composer Alejandro Caturla's *Danzon*, which the orchestra played at the suggestion of Classical Movements.[19] The remainder of the concert had a theme of star-crossed lovers, featuring Bernstein's "Symphonic Dances from *West Side Story*" and Prokofiev's *Romeo and Juliet* suite. The concerts were broadcast live by Minnesota Public Radio and simulcast by public radio stations throughout the United States.[20] During their five-day trip to Havana, the orchestra's musicians also visited music students at the Escuela Nacional de Arte, rehearsed with the Cuban youth orchestra, and jammed with Orquesta Aragón in the Hotel Melía Cohiba's Habana Café. While the exchange was arranged to celebrate the renewed diplomatic relations between the United States and Cuba, at the time of the Minnesota Orchestra's visit, the US Interests Section in Cuba had not yet become an embassy; there was still no standard communication between US officials and the Cuban Ministry of Culture. As a result, Classical Movements had to do all the negotiating without the aid of US officials on everything from travel arrangements to permissions for the international radio broadcasts.[21]

A mapping of the social network that facilitated the Minnesota Orchestra's travel to Cuba further demonstrates the value of network nodes that act as bridges and articulators. Unlike the 2013 network that centered on Nachito Herrera, who largely instigated and facilitated the exchange and network formation, the 2015 network resulted from the Minnesota Orchestra administration seeking out a well-connected bridging institution in the form of Classical Movements. Both Herrera and Classical Movements worked to hide or lessen the friction arising within their networks during these exchanges. This friction arose from last-minute decisions and changes made by Cubadisco organizers, a lack of communication infrastructure connecting Cuba and the United States, and legal barriers to travel. Both the OFAC and Cuban government institutions are parts of these networks, even if they are hidden from most of the participating actors. Despite the inherent challenges, the impact of the Minnesota Orchestra's travel to and performances in Cuba resulted in an expansion and strengthening of the network.

The Associated Press referred to the Minnesota Orchestra's Cuban performances as representative of the orchestra's revival following its near-death from the lockout, and both performers and administration cited the trip as significant in rebuilding their relationship with each other.[22] At the end of 2015, the Minnesota Orchestra closed its fiscal year with a meager surplus, a significant improvement over the deficits of previous years. The orchestra's musicians also dissolved the nonprofit organization they formed during the lockout and donated $250,000 of the nonprofit's remaining holdings to support the Minnesota Orchestra's community and educational programming.[23] In September 2016 Marilyn Carlson Nelson, the board member who funded the orchestra's visit to Cuba, was elected to be the board's chairwoman; the Cuba exchange was cited as a success story and sign of her commitment to the organization.[24] Cuban musicians also saw benefits from this exchange. Their networks expanded to include additional resources, and follow-up initiatives brought some of the younger Cuban musicians who performed with the Minnesota Orchestra to the United States for a residency.

Classical Movements cited the trip to Cuba as a major success and used it to expand their business as a travel service provider. On July 5, 2015, Coro Entrevoces visited Minneapolis for a concert with the Minnesota Orchestra that reciprocated the exchange begun earlier in the year. Classical Movements arranged the Cuban choir's US tour, which included the Minneapolis concert. In the Classical Movements annual newsletter, *Pax Musica*, which spotlights stories from the touring year, they featured the Minnesota Orchestra performances on the front page: "Making headlines around the world, Classical Movements arranged the Minnesota Orchestra's historic tour to Cuba in May, building the entire operation from the ground up in just 110 days, and affirming its place as the top concert touring company for travel to Cuba." The article concluded, "The arrival in Havana of a major American orchestra, one of the first cultural exchanges following the restoration of diplomatic relations between the US and Cuba, speaks volumes about the power of cultural diplomacy through music."[25]

An expanded view of both Minnesota-Cuba networks shows that they are connected through multiple ties. They are connected directly through Herrera who has performed with the Minnesota Orchestra and through Cubadisco, the Cuban institutions involved with both exchanges, and the US Department of Treasury's Office of Foreign Assets Control. The networks are also linked by music professionals in Minneapolis that bridge Herrera's network and the Minnesota Orchestra. Taking a wider viewpoint demonstrates that a great number of US-Cuban musical exchanges during the Obama era were connected through various travel providers, bridging individuals, and Cuban performance venues and institutions. This network's expansion was all but guaranteed following the December 2014 announcement about US-Cuban policy changes, which increased the strong desire and curiosity that many US individuals have in visiting Cuba.

THE ALLURE OF CUBA: PILGRIMAGE, TOURISM, AND PURPOSEFUL TRAVEL

More than fifty years of an embargo and travel ban have made Cuba a mysterious place in the US popular consciousness, and much of the marketing rhetoric for travel packages, such as referring to Cuba as the "forbidden island," reinforces those images. Even the marketing of Cuban music has used these techniques. For example, the 1991 record *Cuba Classics 2: Dancing with the Enemy*, which was produced by Ned Sublette, had these provocative questions written prominently on the packaging: "Are politics our enemy? Are governments our enemy? Can music be our enemy? Can communists have a good time? Can we have a good time? Is a music communist? Can it be capitalist? Do you enjoy it more either way?"[26] The fact that people from the United States have been unable to legally tour Cuba for decades has increased the allure of the island and made many individuals even more interested in visiting.

Music has often played an important role in the appeal of Cuba in the popular imagination. Even before the revolution and embargo, songs like Irving Berlin's 1920 song "(I'll See You in) Cuba" celebrated the island with the opening lines "Not so far from here / There's a very lively atmosphere / Everybody's going there this year / And there's a reason." It then described Cuba's party-like, alcohol-fueled ambiance at a time when alcohol was prohibited in the United States. While many US Americans freely visited Cuba prior to the revolution, music helped define the nation in the minds of those who could not visit the island; music's role became even more prominent once the travel ban went into effect.

Even after the Obama administration created opportunities for US-Cuban musical exchange, the musicians from the United States who played in concerts and music festivals on the island could not be paid for their performances because of economic regulations. OFAC rules require any profits to be given away to a charitable organization, but it is rare for US musicians to be paid at all by Cuban institutions.[27] While donors funded travel to Cubadisco for the Minnesota musicians, many other performers spent a substantial amount of their own money getting to Cuba. As a result, these trips can become a significant financial liability for working musicians. An international festival performance can be added to a musician's résumé, but a performance there is unlikely to significantly increase a musician's profile because Cuba's cultural events rarely make it into the US press. Instead, musicians and other individuals from the United States often are drawn to Cuba for other reasons. When I asked Isaac Peña of Trio Los Vigilantes why they went to the festival, he explained, "The festival doesn't pay. Obviously, people need to want to go there, otherwise they're not going to lure someone. In a way, Cuba is kind of taboo. It's kind of like this forbidden thing that you want to experience."[28]

During the original 1977 jazz cruise, Arnold Jay Smith documented the trip for *Down Beat*; he spoke to some of the passengers, including a NASA engineer who played the vibraphone. The engineer wanted to sign up for the voyage when it was first announced solely for the music, but his wife vetoed it because of financial considerations. That changed after Havana was added to the itinerary. "Cuba cinched it for us," he said. "Imagine all of these great sounds and being among the first Americans allowed back into Cuba! We couldn't resist."[29] This couple was drawn to Cuba not only for the music, but also because it had been off limits to them. This attitude continues to motivate travelers from the United States into the present. Individuals may travel out of a desire to discover a place they know little about or to see a country they have long heard stories of and can finally visit. Travel also became a means for US citizens to express goodwill toward the Cuban people. Whether out of curiosity to visit somewhere seemingly forbidden or to attend a specific musical event and gain a new understanding of the music and culture, getting to Cuba often involves numerous challenges. Because of the ordeals involved, musical travel to Cuba often takes on a quality of pilgrimage.

Pilgrimage has traditionally been understood in a religious context as a journey to a holy place as an act of spiritual devotion in order to obtain some spiritual benefit. The definition has been expanded to include modern, secular travel to a site with the potential to affect the pilgrim in a personally meaningful or moral way. Determining what qualifies as a pilgrimage, however, is difficult because motivations vary and are defined internally. An individual's aspirations for increased US-Cuban musical interaction becomes a pilgrimage when he or she travels to the island to pay homage to great artists and music, reflects upon the complicated and often unpleasant histories of the United States and Cuba, and seeks an internal transformation through musical experience.[30] Victor and Edith Turner describe how a pilgrim voluntarily undergoes a transformational process and occupies a liminal space outside of normal social classifications. Many of the liminal attributes characteristic of pilgrimage and coming-of-age rituals also apply to the secular pilgrimage of US musicians to Cuba. As the Turners explain, these attributes include:

> Release from mundane structure; homogenization of status; . . . communitas; ordeal; reflection on the meaning of basic religious and cultural values; movement itself, a symbol of communitas, which changes with time, as against stasis, which represents structure; individuality posed against the institutionalized milieu; and so forth. (Turner and Turner 1978, 34)

The Turners also refer to pilgrimage centers as faraway places that are often hazardous or difficult to reach. Geographically, Cuba is not far from the United States of America, but it is difficult to visit and outside the norm of places that individuals from the United States regularly travel. The minimal internet access and unreliable telecommunications services connecting the island to the United States further contribute to the perception of Cuba as a faraway place.

The Turners' concept of *communitas*, which is a phenomenon of bonding and community that combines qualities of lowliness, sacredness, homogeneity, and comradeship, is central to understanding US-Cuban travel as pilgrimage (Turner and Turner 1978, 250). Many of the performers who visit Cuba as a type of pilgrimage experience this phenomenon with their bandmates and with the locals they meet on the island. For example, when the Friends University students visited a senior home and danced with the people living there, some of the residents learned that it was the birthday of one of the students. Andre Reyes, a pianist with the band, described what happened next in the TV documentary about their trip:

> They ended up giving him a gift; they didn't even know who he was and they gave him a birthday present. He was outside crying, and I was outside crying. Just to be that close to people in that small two-hour span and to realize that you actually care about these people, love these people. That day really changed me probably the most out of all the days we were there.[31]

Communitas can occur as a result of any of the three types of secular pilgrimage named by Davidson and Gitilitz (2002): pilgrimages intended to secure identity; political pilgrimages; and popular pilgrimages like those to celebrity shrines.

A pilgrimage of the type that secures or confirms one's identity can take varying forms when one travels to Cuba. A trip for this purpose is particularly appealing to young Cuban Americans who have never been to the country that their parents or grandparents came from. At the 2012 Havana Jazz Plaza Festival, the couple from New Jersey who were part of the Cuba Explorer Tours trip were visiting a relative and hoping to gain a better understanding of their heritage. When discussing my research with Cuban American friends of mine from Miami, they expressed desires to make a similar pilgrimage. "I would love to go," one friend told me, "but my grandfather would kill me if he ever found out I did." These generational differences within the exile community are reshaping Miami politics. Many people from the older generations who left Cuba in the 1960s swear they will not visit Cuba until the revolutionary government is gone; many of their grandchildren, however, want to see and experience the country that they have heard about for their entire lives.

Chi Saito, a Japanese guitar player based in California, participated in the FolkCuba percussion workshop with me in 2011. He and I were the only non-Cubans in the class that summer, and we bonded because Chi spoke English but no Spanish so I did my best to serve as a translator. This trip to Cuba served as a pilgrimage both to secure Chi's identity as a musician and to cure a personal affliction, which are commonly desired pilgrimage outcomes (Turner and Turner 1978, 12–13). Chi was in Los Angeles when a major earthquake hit Japan on March 11, 2011. He was anguished over the events and the media's coverage of the aftermath, and he needed to get away for the sake of his own mental and emotional wellbeing. He had some disposable income at the time and was interested in studying either Romani or Cuban music, but he was unsure where to go to find Romani musicians. He found out about FolkCuba when he started researching a trip to Cuba. During a layover in Cancún, he met some Japanese tourists who recommended a *casa particular* that catered specifically to Japanese visitors. His experiences in Cuba reaffirmed and renewed him as a musician. Although he owned a pair of congas for ten years prior to visiting Cuba, he lacked the musical knowledge and technical skills to make hand percussion a part of his professional performance repertoire. After visiting Cuba, however, he has continued to study the music, added congas into his live performances, and brought interlocking rhythms found in Afro-Cuban music into his guitar compositions.[32]

Other individuals may be drawn to Cuba for political pilgrimage. Those with left-leaning ideologies traveled to Cuba for such a purpose during the Cold War.[33] Most US-to-Cuba travelers today, however, visit Cuba more out of a sense of political reconciliation between nations than out of support for the Castro government. Many musicians I spoke with visited the Museo de la Revolución while in Havana, but visiting the museum was not a way for them to support the revolution. Instead it allowed people from the United States to reflect upon the history of the schism between the two nations.

Popular pilgrimage can draw people to Cuban music festivals and other musically significant locations, such as the childhood homes of musicians, historic venues, and regions where musical genres originated. Festivals present a time for fans of Cuban music to demonstrate their support and to connect with the music in a way that cannot be done in the United States. The immense popularity of the Buena Vista Social Club inspires many people to try and visit the actual club and bar in Havana. *Jineteros*, the street hustlers who try to get money from tourists, are aware of this and often approach foreigners offering to take them to the original Buena Vista Social Club bar.

This is really just an attempt to get some free drinks or food out of them, because the Buena Vista Social Club as a location no longer exists. Nevertheless, on two occasions during my Cuba trips, individuals brought me to different bars and told me we were in the real Buena Vista Social Club.

Not all people from the United States visiting Cuba to take in a musical performance are on a pilgrimage. Many want to visit Cuba as tourists, but the categories are not mutually exclusive. Victor and Edith Turner claimed, "A tourist is half a pilgrim, if a pilgrim is half a tourist" (1978, 20). And Davidson and Gitilitz argue that while secular pilgrimage and tourism appear similar, "the visitor knows when the experience passes from the realm of tourism to that of pilgrimage" (2002, 582). Even as opportunities to visit Cuba increased under the Obama administration, tourism was not an acceptable and licensable travel category. Yet tourism has many commonalities with pilgrimage and represents a more complex form of travel than its common usage implies.

The term "purposeful travel" is broadly used by the OFAC for licensable travel categories. Tourism, however, is not purposeless and should not be discounted. Valene Smith clarifies, "A tourist is a temporarily leisured person who voluntarily visits a place away from home for the purpose of experiencing a change" (1989, 1). Tourism depends on a combination of leisure time, discretionary income, and positive local sanctions or social norms. The factor that arguably does not apply to US musicians is defining their trips as leisure time; they visited Cuba to perform. Yet this too is problematic because their concerts and festival performances were only one part of their travels to Cuba. Florida Senator Marco Rubio denounced the Obama administration's people-to-people exchanges in a floor speech on December 15, 2011, because he considered them to be a form of tourism:

> When I look at this stuff, you know what I want to say? Come on, man. This is about promoting democracy and freedom in Cuba? This is not about promoting democracy and freedom in Cuba. This is nothing more than tourism. This is tourism for Americans that at best are curious about Cuba and at worst sympathize with the Cuban regime.... This is an embarrassment. These people are getting licenses to conduct this outrageous tourism, which quite frankly borders on indoctrination of Americans by Castro government officials.[34]

One of Senator Rubio's primary criticisms of licensed trips was that they had done nothing to support their eventual goal, which the Obama administration stated was "a Cuba that respects the basic rights of all its citizens."[35]

Furthering the goal of a Cuba with more political freedoms, the administration stated, could be encouraged through purposeful travel intended to "increase people-to-people contact; support civil society in Cuba; enhance the free flow of information to, from, and among the Cuban people; and help promote their independence from Cuban authorities."[36] People-to-people trips try to avoid being characterized as tourism by following full itineraries of educational and cultural activities for travelers in order to keep them from spending time on a beach. But tourism and purposeful travel are not mutually exclusive, and tying Cuba policy to an ill-defined idea of tourism makes the policy pointless. Educational and cultural tourism is still tourism and it is certainly purposeful.

Most categories of purposeful travel contain elements of tourism. While I had a clear purpose of studying music and conducting research while in Cuba, I still felt like a tourist much of the time. I visited tourist attractions like museums, went on tours, and carried a camera. On the street, there were few if any discernible differences between Havana's many tourists and me. Critics of eased travel restrictions frown upon these touristic behaviors because they are enjoyable leisure activities that do not reflect the hardships facing many of the Cuban people. Beyond that, Rubio criticized travel to Cuba as providing much-needed currency to the Castro government, which is then used to oppress Cuban citizens and jail dissidents.[37] Rubio's fear was that US citizens travelling to Cuba would stay at state-owned beach resorts and spend money in support of a dictatorial government without ever seeing how the majority of Cubans live. Despite its critics in the United States, however, tourism transformed much of Cuban society with both positive and negative repercussions.

IMPRESSIONS AND IMPACT

Tourists from Canada and Europe have impacted the Cuban economy since the early 1990s, but the prominent presence of US citizens occurred much more recently. The musical interactions that began taking place in 2009 were made possible and justified by the Obama administration in the context of reaching out to the Cuban people. US politicians critical of expanded travel to Cuba, however, have questioned whether these trips have value or any social or political significance. President Obama himself addressed this topic when asked about the Juanes Peace Without Borders performance shortly before it was scheduled to take place: "My understanding is that he's a terrific musician. He puts on a very good concert. I certainly don't think it hurts US-Cuban relations, these kinds of cultural exchanges. I wouldn't overstate the degree that it helps."[38] In terms of immediate impacts, Obama was correct; no single concert will unilaterally bring about democratic reforms to Cuba, free dissidents, or reset a half-century of antagonistic international relations. The direct impact of these musical interactions is far more personal: by affecting an individual within the context of a larger social network, singular impressions and feelings emanate outward. Instead of transforming the governance of either country, the greatest long-term potential for these exchanges may be in impacting ordinary citizens' opinions about US-Cuban relations. As personal experiences transform one's feelings about the topic, they create a context for future relevant actions. Furthermore, the participants themselves perceive the impact and importance of these exchanges in their interactions with fellow musicians.

Beyond a shared desire to return to the country, all the US musicians who visited Cuba that I spoke with had some common impressions and experiences. One was the bewilderment of performing in events where details ranging from when it would start to what would be played and who would be on stage were negotiable. Will Magid took in stride delays during the jazz festival like the late start and power outage. He also learned that a trip to perform in Cuba requires extra time, something that he will take into consideration when he returns. He reflected, "In some ways, five days in Cuba is only like two days in the United States in terms of the amount you can get done. Things are canceled, the power is going out, and the sense of time is a little different."[39] Norah Long described similar experiences at Cubadisco:

> For the concert, the size of the hall, and the importance of the event, I expected one of those tight senses of organization: one of those "stay in your dressing room, we'll call you down ten minutes prior to when you go on, we don't want people hanging out in the wings" mentalities. But for this concert they wanted us all down in the wings before the concert even started, and I sat having to whisper or not talk for probably a full hour before I performed with everyone sort of wandering and looking on stage from the side, dancing along to some of the music, and chatting with other musicians. So that was a very interesting dynamic to watch. Just the flexibility, the go with the flow, if it happens it happens vibe that was present throughout the trip.[40]

The musicians from the Minnesota Orchestra were surprised by the easy backstage access enjoyed by the public, which violist Sam Bergman described as slightly unsettling when they first arrived. They were accustomed to well-guarded halls where they did not need to worry about who potentially had access to their expensive instruments if they were left alone. By the end of the week, however, they enjoyed the fact that Cuban music students could jump on stage to ask questions during intermission and that their Cuban friends could walk backstage to offer congratulations after the performance. A Minnesota Public Radio journalist captured an example of the musical opportunities created by this access following the orchestra's second performance. While the crew members were loading up instruments and equipment, a young Cuban musician approached a vibraphone at the edge of the stage and began to play it.[41] His brief solo allowed him to be more than just a passive observer in the musical exchange. Unlike the vast majority of classical music events in the United States of America, which are purely presentational, the concerts in Cuba provided participatory space and interaction.[42]

The quality of musicianship and dedication to music from performers and Cuban society at large awed many of the visitors. The other most commonly shared reaction between US visitors was how welcome and safe they felt, which reflected my own experiences. Everyone made some sort of a connection with Cuban citizens that made their experiences more meaningful and valuable. Those who stayed at *casas particulares* often reported developing a bond with the owner by sharing stories and music. Many had musical experiences with new acquaintances outside of their scheduled festival performances such as going to a dance club or participating in brief, informal music lessons and jam sessions. People also felt comfortable walking around the city alone and in small groups. While *jineteros* would often be annoying and could make some walks unpleasant, no one reported feeling threatened at any time.

In describing their positive experiences, travelers increase the likelihood of future exchanges. After Lisa Hittle returned from traveling with her Friends University students, another college jazz band director who wanted to make a similar trip contacted her. Hittle has since actively shared her knowledge and experiences to help educators all over the country take their students to Cuba.[43] In doing so, Hittle herself became a bridge and hub in her own expanding social network. Musical interaction encourages further musical interaction. Classical Movements, which has led the way as an organization in facilitating trips to Cuba, began receiving more inquiries about taking performing arts groups to the island than they could accept.

The company provides assistance even to groups they cannot take on as clients; they make introductions, put people in touch with their Cuban contacts, and suggest other travel providers who can organize a tour and performances.[44]

These musical exchanges have other social impacts as well. They benefit Cuban musicians and have been successful in their stated goal of reaching out to the Cuban people. Beyond the direct influx of hard currency into the Cuban economy that compensates *casa particular* owners, taxi drivers, and musicians playing for tips, there have been other material benefits. The Friends University jazz band and the Minnesota Orchestra donated musical supplies to the conservatory, which is not unusual for visiting groups from the United States. These donations greatly assist students who have trouble getting reeds, strings, and other musical resources in Cuba. Beyond material goods, Nachito Herrera argued that these exchanges are mutually advantageous for both US and Cuban musicians because it reinforces the important musical connections, similarities, and influences in Cuban and North American genres. An important contribution that these exchanges have, he explains, is that they "keep enriching the acknowledgment of both of our countries' musical styles."[45]

These exchanges also have a musical impact by increasing the musical repertoire available to performers. When arranging a tour of Cuba, Classical Movements helps their clients select repertoire and find pieces that can be performed with Cuban musicians. Sometimes this only requires acting as an intermediary that can help groups on both sides of the Straits of Florida select a piece of music known to both ensembles. More often than not, however, Neeta Helms says that this involved bringing boxes of physical sheet music to Cuba by hand. Broadband internet service in Cuba is unreliable, so they could not depend on file sharing services to send digital files.[46] Direct mail between the United States and Cuba resumed in 2016, but Classical Movements does not use it for shipping music because it is slow, expensive, and unpredictable. Still the end result of this process puts new music in the hands of Cuban performing groups, for which they are grateful. Classical Movements also commissions new works that are used in musical exchanges through their Eric Daniel Helms New Music Program; the company commissioned Tania León's *Rimas Tropicales* for the San Francisco Girls Chorus when the ensemble traveled to Cuba. The piece, which is a setting of three poems by Cuban-born writer Carlos Pintado, was premiered at the 2011 Chorus America Conference in San Francisco and then performed by the choir in Cuba a month later.[47]

The most profound story I heard about how these exchanges positively impact Cuban artists came from Norah Long. While she was in Havana for Cubadisco, she spent some time with the recording engineer for Nachito's album during the extended downtimes and breaks in the recording process. She was surprised by how straightforward he was in talking about politics and openly stating that his country needs changes in its government. He said that a malaise in Cuba prevents anyone from doing anything about it, and he pointed to the lack of incentives for anyone to try and achieve anything in his country. In response she asked what motivates all the talented musicians she had met on the island, and he told her: "Things like this. This interaction right here, and getting feedback from other people who are good at what they do, telling me I'm doing a good job. That inspires me. That motivates me to do my job as well as I can."[48]

CONCLUSION

In 2012 Nachito Herrera received an American Heritage Award from the American Immigration Council, one of three musicians to receive the prize that year. The award is given to individual immigrants for their outstanding accomplishments and positive contributions to the United States. The last Latinx musician to receive the honor was Carlos Santana. While the award was for Herrera's contributions as a musician and educator in the United States, perhaps his greatest impact has been in creating and facilitating connections that extend beyond the United States to Cuba. Classical Movements has been similarly honored. In 2014 Americans for the Arts named the company one of the ten best businesses partnering with the arts sector in the United States. Although their exchanges take performers to countries all over the world, they became a leader in facilitating musical exchanges with Cuba after 2010. Most US musicians who performed in Cuba during the Obama years depended on knowledgeable and connected individuals and organizations to make the exchanges possible. Both Herrera and Classical Movements were active in fostering these exchanges and using their connections to enable them, which strengthened their own networks.

New connections and positive experiences result in future musical interactions and other types of engagement. This has been true each time travel restrictions have been eased, allowing connections to be made. The 1977 jazz cruise gave the members of Irakere their first interaction with US jazz musicians and led to performances at festivals in the United States and elsewhere.

The jazz cruise also led to the 1979 Havana Jam festival. More recently Los Van Van was inspired to return to Miami after hearing Juanes perform in Havana. Likewise, many of the musicians who visited Cuba for the Havana Jazz Festival in 2012 or Cubadisco in 2013 and 2015 went on to advise friends and colleagues about how to visit Cuba. These connections were made at a rapid pace, and musicians have been quick to take advantage of an opportunity to perform in Cuba because of their desire to visit the island.

Musicians and other travelers have many reasons for visiting Cuba; most want to see Havana's major sites including museums, historical landmarks, and beaches on their first trip to the country. Their travel may be purposeful, but it also includes elements of tourism, which is why these trips are criticized by anti-Castro hardliners in the United States. When Cuban American politicians use examples of Americans enjoying themselves on these trips or going to events organized by the Cuban government as justifications to curtail travel, they demonstrate a partial, simplistic, and paternalistic understanding of cultural exchanges and their participants. US-to-Cuba travelers are not mindless vessels on the receiving end of Castro government propaganda. People want to visit Cuba simply because they are curious to learn more about the country and its people. Most US visitors are aware of the pervasive propaganda in Cuba and know to view it with a critical eye.

As evidence that people-to-people travel is merely tourism, Senator Rubio cited dancing as a form of entertainment and evidence that such tours were not working toward their goal of connecting with the Cuban people. Musical activity like dancing, however, can provide some of the most intense connections between people of different backgrounds. Thomas Turino has described the profound potential of musical activity while relating it to Turner's concept of communitas:

> One of the main things I seek through musical performance is a particular feeling of being deeply bound to the people I am playing with. This sense is created when my partners and I feel the rhythm in precisely the same way, are totally in sync, and can fashion the sounds we are making so that they interlock seamlessly together. The musical sound provides direct, immediate, and constant feedback on how we are doing; when a performance is good, I get a deep sense of oneness with the people I am playing with. I think that what happens during a good performance is that the multiple differences among us are forgotten and we are fully focused on an activity that emphasizes our sameness—of time sense, of musical sensibility, of common goals—as

well as our direct interaction. Within the bounded and concentrated frame of musical performance that sameness is all that matters, and for those moments when the performance is focused and in sync, that deep identification is felt as total. (Turino 2008, 18)

I experienced those feelings during FolkCuba when I sat in a room with three other students and an instructor repeating the same *batá* rhythms for hours on end until we were all able to make transitions from one rhythm to the next together, using only our instruments to communicate the changes. Melissa Deal described similar experiences of playing chamber music with Cuban students. They could not speak the same language very well, but they all played the same music and were able to connect through performance.

These exchanges benefit Cuban musicians and other individuals simply by creating connections and providing people with shared experiences. Life on an island country with limited opportunities to travel abroad creates an intense desire for connections with the outside, as Tania León previously described. When US musicians visit Cuba, they create connections that extend beyond Cuba's shores. Music creates more transnational connections, and it expands personal networks and strengthens ties within those networks. Exchanges with Cuba are not particularly profitable for companies like Classical Movements, and bringing choirs from Cuba to tour the United States actually lost them money. Yet they continue to pursue these initiatives because they believe in the positive impact that music can have. As Neeta Helms, the company's founder and president, told me, "We're always looking for the next project that will change the world just a little bit for the better."[49]

6

2016 AND THE SOUNDS OF NORMALIZATION

On August 14, 2015, the US Army Brass Quintet, along with alto saxophone and snare drum players from the US Army Band ("Pershing's Own"), performed "La Bayamesa" in Havana. Following remarks by Secretary of State John Kerry, the brass quintet played the US national anthem as the flag of the United States of America was raised. The ceremony marked the opening of the US Embassy in Havana, and Arturo O'Farrill, who had been a regular guest performer at the US Interests Section in recent years, was in attendance. The day's events included a reading by poet Richard Blanco, who was the poet for President Obama's 2013 Presidential inauguration. Blanco was the first openly gay, Latino, or immigrant person to be selected as an inaugural poet. When Blanco's mother was pregnant with him, she and his father left Cuba for Spain, where he was born; the family then immigrated to the United States in 1968. The US State Department asked Blanco, as a Cuban American, to write a poem for the opening of the embassy. Before reading his poem, "Matters of the Sea" or "Cosas del Mar," he announced that it was "for the people of both our countries who believed that not even the sea can keep us from one another." With diplomatic relations between the United States and Cuba restored, musicians and other travelers began crossing the sea separating the two nations with greater frequency than before.

In December 2015 President Obama released a statement to mark one year since announcing the major Cuba policy changes. The statement read in part:

> Today, the Stars and Stripes again fly over our Embassy in Havana. Today, more Americans are visiting Cuba and engaging the Cuban people than at any time in the last fifty years. We continue to have differences with the Cuban government, but we raise those issues

directly, and we will always stand for human rights and the universal values that we support around the globe. Change does not happen overnight, and normalization will be a long journey. The last twelve months, however, are a reminder of the progress we can make when we set the course toward a better future. Over the next year, we will continue on this path, empowering Cubans and Americans to lead the way.[1]

In January and March 2016, the administration amended the Cuban Assets Control Regulations with the goal of further engaging and empowering the Cuban people by facilitating and simplifying travel to Cuba by persons subject to US jurisdiction. The new regulations were aimed at a variety of transaction types and different categories of travel, which included easing travel for musicians wishing to perform or record in Cuba. US music aficionados wishing to see performances or accompany musicians on their trips also had greater opportunities to legally visit the island. Travel activities related to "public performances, clinics, workshops, athletic and other competitions, and exhibitions," which had previously been authorized only with a Specific License, were added as categories that qualified for a general license. Additionally, trips to Cuba to plan and organize such performances were now allowed under a general license; planning a performance in Cuba was listed as an example of an acceptable activity. The relevant section read:

> Example 2 to §515.567(a) and (b): A US concert promoter wishes to organize a musical event in Cuba that would be open to the public and feature US musical groups. The organizing of the musical event in Cuba by the US concert promoter and the participation by US musical groups in the event would qualify for the general license in paragraph (b).[2]

General licenses were also expanded to authorize transactions incident to "professional media or artistic productions of information or informational materials for exportation, importation, or transmission, including the filming or production of media programs (such as movies and television programs), the recording of music, and the creation of artworks in Cuba."[3] One of the first major products of this change was an explosive car race along the Malecón in the film *The Fate of the Furious*, the eighth installment of the big-budget *Fast and Furious* action movie franchise, which was filmed in Cuba in April 2016.[4] While filmmakers and record producers still needed to receive permission from and work with Cuban authorities to bring their projects to fruition, this change largely removed US government bureaucracy from the equation.

The 2016 policy changes also authorized people-to-people travel activities under a general license, allowing individuals to organize visits to Cuba without traveling under the auspices of a licensed organization. Travel that the US government deemed tourism was not permitted, and travelers were still required to maintain a full-time schedule of educational activities that involved interaction with the Cuban people. These changes gave individuals, families, and other groups the freedom to plan their own trips to Cuba and to set their own itineraries.[5] When musicians visited Cuba for a performance, their friends and family could now accompany them more easily under a people-to-people license. Orchestras and other performing arts ensembles could also organize people-to-people travel for their patron groups as a fundraising effort. Beyond easing restrictions on travel from the United States to Cuba, the March 2016 regulations made it legal to compensate Cuban nationals in the United States for their work or performances. The fact sheet released by the Treasury Department included a section on payment of salaries, which specifically mentions that Cuban athletes, artists, and performers "who obtain the requisite visas will be able to travel to the United States and earn salaries and stipends in excess of basic living expenses."[6] Even though the US trade embargo of Cuba remained in place, the policy changes instituted by the Obama administration opened many avenues for music-related travel and business transactions in 2016.

The year included numerous important performances and milestones in the US-Cuban relationship. Throughout the final year of the Obama presidency both official and unofficial cultural diplomacy initiatives brought performers and dignitaries from the United States to Cuba in order to celebrate the restoration of diplomatic relations. The changes that began in 2009 culminated in 2016 and resulted in celebrity musicians playing large public venues in Havana and President Obama himself visiting the island. But while performances and exchanges reflected this new political reality, the ease of travel from the United States also brought an influx of travelers and money that exacerbated some of Cuba's underlying political, economic, and technological disparities.

MAJOR LAZER, THE ROLLING STONES, AND BARACK OBAMA IN CUBA

In the span of less than three weeks, Havana experienced a large outdoor performance by US-based electronic music trio Major Lazer, a visit by President Obama, and a free concert by the Rolling Stones. On March 4, 2016, Major Lazer held a press conference in front of Havana's Anti-Imperialist Tribune, where the group's concert would take place two days later. During the media event, a BBC reporter asked DJ and producer Diplo if they felt they were part of a "Havana moment" that was happening, and if their presence in Cuba was a result of wanting to "be a part of a sort of cultural, musical, artistic moment." Diplo responded that their concert had been more than fourteen months in the making, and added, "We didn't know about Obama and the Stones coming. But we'll be sure to tell them what restaurants to eat at and stuff like that."[7] Despite Diplo's glib response, the confluence of these events in March 2016 demonstrated not only the changing political and cultural relationship between Cuba and the United States but also how Havana's connections to the outside world were changing.

Major Lazer consists of Diplo and fellow producer/DJs Walshy Fire and Jillionaire, who are originally from Jamaica and Trinidad, respectively. The musicians, who combine influences from Caribbean music with hip-hop and electronic dance music, have played throughout the Caribbean but this was their first opportunity to perform in Cuba. The documentary film *Give Me Future* records the group's visit to Cuba and captures the enthusiasm among Cuban youth for their performance. The concert was spearheaded by Fabien Pisani, the son of Cuban nueva trova singer Pablo Milanes. Pisani left Havana for New York City in 1991. In 2012 he began working with a diverse board of US and Cuban advisors to start the Musicabana Foundation with the mission "to promote Cuba as a premier destination for the discovery of new sonic horizons and a vital center of the music world."[8] Pisani was the key actor in the network that made the March 2016 performance possible, as he bridged Major Lazer's network with the institutions in Cuba that signed off on the event. Pisani first contacted the Cuban minister of culture in July 2014 to propose the concert and start the planning process.[9]

In the months preceding the concert, Diplo was concerned that because Major Lazer was an unknown quantity in Cuba, their concert may have poor turnout or the audience would be unprepared for their music. Pisani insisted he could take care of that with $1,500 and digital copies of every Major Lazer song and music video. With these basic resources and his connections in

Cuba, Pisani ensured that Major Lazer's music was distributed to young Cubans in Havana and beyond through access to a legally dubious file-sharing network that Cubans use to access international media known as the *paquete semanal* (weekly packet). This network, which emerged in Havana in 2008 and has expanded over time, is not an online digital network but a social network where individuals use portable hard drives and flash drives to copy and share data. Because access to the internet in Cuba is slow and censored by the government, this distribution network has become a primary method for Cubans to access digital music, television shows, movies, smartphone apps, and games from around the world. While the *paquete* is technically not legal, it is widely tolerated by authorities, so consumers do not have to hide possession of this media (Pertierra 2018, 14). Perhaps because of the Cuban government's willingness to turn a blind eye to this network, twenty-seven-year-old Dany Cabrera Garcia was willing to be featured producing and distributing the *paquete semanal* in the film *Give Me Future*, which documents how he included files of Major Lazer's music and concert fliers. In the film, Garcia describes using the strong internet connections at some hotels to download files, and says he has other content sources too but does not name them to protect their identities. After filling a portable terabyte hard drive with that week's data, Garcia passes it on to an associate. This person then takes it to another location where the contents are copied onto other computers and hard drives; people then use the loaded devices to distribute copies of the *paquete* to users in different neighborhoods and housing complexes for a minor fee. As an articulator in the social network surrounding this performance, Pisani not only managed Major Lazer's relationship to formal institutions like the Cuban Ministry of Culture but he also facilitated access to the informal network that could raise Major Lazer's profile through inclusion in the *paquete semanal*.

Pisani's efforts were successful. During a meet and greet with members of Cuba's electronic music community, Diplo asked the young people present if they knew Major Lazer's music and nearly all hands went up. Attendance at the free concert the next day far exceeded expectations; an estimated 450,000 people showed up. In addition to Major Lazer, the event featured performances by Cuban rumba musician Osain del Monte and electronic musician Iliam Suárez.[10] The street along the Malecón facing the US embassy and the Anti-Imperialist Tribune contained a crowd so large that it made the performers and the authorities nervous. The musicians invited Yotuel, the lead performer of the Cuban rap group Orishas, to join them on stage, but the Cuban authorities prohibited it for fear of what he might say in front of such a large crowd.[11] The concert went on without any major disruptions or controversies and was deemed a major success by those involved.

Just two weeks later on March 20, Barack Obama arrived in Cuba along with First Lady Michelle Obama and their two daughters, Malia and Sasha. It marked the first time that Air Force One landed on the island, bringing a sitting US president to the nation for the first time since 1928. The international news media provided exhaustive coverage of the Obamas' activities in Havana, which began with a rainy tour of Old Havana on the day of their arrival. The tour included a stop at the Havana Cathedral for a meeting with the archbishop of Havana, Cardinal Jaime Lucas Ortega y Alamino, who helped the United States and Cuba to negotiate the agreement that restored relations. The president's visit was in many ways a standard state visit, but the Obama administration emphasized their efforts to engage directly with the Cuban people.[12] The president's itinerary for Monday included a meeting with President Castro and a joint press conference, as well as a meeting with business leaders and a state dinner. Then on Tuesday, Obama met with members of Cuban civil society, including dissidents, gave a speech to the Cuban people at the Gran Teatro de la Habana, and attended a baseball game.[13] Music and cultural engagement were not a focus of Obama's visit, but the significance of shared US-Cuban cultural heritage came up many times. In his speech at the Gran Teatro de la Habana, where Calvin Coolidge spoke about Cuba's sovereignty eighty-eight years earlier, Obama extolled these connections: "So even as our governments became adversaries, our people continued to share these common passions, particularly as so many Cubans came to America. In Miami or Havana, you can find places to dance the cha cha cha or the salsa, and eat *ropa vieja*. People in both of our countries have sung along with Celia Cruz or Gloria Estefan, and now listen to reggaeton or Pitbull."[14] The US president also made reference to upcoming performances during his press conference with Raúl Castro when he stated, "Even as Cubans prepare for the arrival of the Rolling Stones, we're moving ahead with more events and exchanges that bring Cubans and Americans together as well."[15]

President Obama's visit, however, caused some problems for musical events and exchanges that had already been scheduled. Classical Movements sent eleven groups to Cuba in 2016, and they had organized a series of performances for the St. Olaf College jazz ensemble in Havana from March 20 to 25. Their schedule was set months before the Obama administration announced their intentions to visit the island. When the news came out, numerous travelers had their hotel reservations canceled to accommodate the increased need for security and the influx of reporters arriving in Cuba's capital to cover the presidential visit. Fortunately for the St. Olaf musicians, the years that the staff at Classical Movements had spent cultivating relationships in Cuba paid off and the performances were able to continue largely uninterrupted. In fact, the Cubans turned to Classical Movements for some musical needs when preparing for Obama's visit. The staff at Classical Movements found music for "The Star-Spangled Banner" and sent it to a Cuban choir; they also sent a conductor to train the choir on pronunciation.[16] The choir then sang the US national anthem at the exhibition baseball game between the Tampa Bay Rays and the Cuban National Team that Presidents Obama and Castro attended.

President Obama was greeted by large supportive crowds throughout his trip to Cuba, which received extensive media coverage that was mostly favorable. Back in the United States, Cuban-born pop star Camila Cabello showed her support for the president's visit on Twitter. In a reply to President Obama's tweet that he just touched down in Cuba, she simply announced to her followers "THIS. IS. AWESOME" and followed it up by stating, "i'm going to miss @BarackObama as @POTUS so much."[17] Emilio Estefan was less supportive but not outright hostile to the event. South Florida's premiere Spanish-language newspaper, *El Nuevo Herald*, asked Estefan and other Cuban and Cuban American entertainers for their opinions on the President's visit.[18] Estefan declared that while Obama's visit could bring some hope to the Cuban people, it did not signify that the Castro dictatorship is over. "We all know there is no freedom in our country," he said, adding that he would not criticize anyone who visited Cuba. Although the Estefans had visited the US naval base at Guantanamo Bay in Cuba in the 1990s, he declared that neither he nor his wife Gloria intend to return until the Cuban people have complete freedom.[19] Paquito D'Rivera was more critical. He argued that the Cuban situation could not be solved by this president or by "cultural exchanges, tourism, and partying," and added that Obama's efforts at US-Cuban rapprochement was already a failure. More than two hundred protesters in Miami's Little Havana also showed their opposition to the president's visit on the day he arrived in Cuba.[20] A poll of Miami-Dade's Cuban population showed that 48 percent opposed the president's visit while 44 percent supported it. The same poll, however, showed that Miami-Dade voters as a whole were in favor of the president's visit by a margin of 63 to 30 percent with 7 percent undecided.[21]

When the US president left Cuba on March 22, the Havana authorities had little time to change focus and prepare for the free Rolling Stones concert on March 25. As an English band, the Rolling Stones were not subject to the embargo and could have previously tried to visit and perform in Cuba, but because the band depends on back-up musicians, managers, and support staff from the United States it would have been much more difficult for them to organize a Cuban performance. One of those members included bassist Darryl Jones, who was born in Chicago in 1961. Jones had toured with Miles Davis in the 1980s and in 1994 replaced longtime Rolling Stones member Bill Wyman on bass. Jones performs and records with various other groups, but touring with the Rolling Stones is his primary job.[22] One of Jones's other bands is the musical collective Dead Daisies, which includes a rotating lineup of rock musicians, many of whom are associated with 1970s and 1980s hard rock. Jones joined the Dead Daisies in February 2015 for a concert in Cuba along with fellow Rolling Stones musician Bernard Fowler, a New York-born percussionist and vocalist; other musicians included band members from Guns N' Roses, Ozzy Osbourne, Whitesnake, and Mötley Crüe.[23] Jones's experiences in Cuba encouraged Mick Jagger to visit the island in October 2015, and the Rolling Stones management team started investigating the possibilities of a Havana concert as part of the band's 2016 Latin America tour.[24]

The Rolling Stones tour included performances in Chile, Argentina, Uruguay, Brazil, Peru, and Mexico and concluded with their first concert in Cuba. The free concert, which was held outdoors at the Ciudad Deportiva de la Habana sports complex, was originally scheduled for March 20, 2016. When the White House announced that President Obama would be arriving in Cuba on that date, the Cuban government asked the Rolling Stones to push their concert back five days.[25] The band opened their concert with an animated video of a world map; it zoomed in on Cuba before a match appeared to light the map on fire. The video then showed street signs of different cities, representing the Rolling Stones getting closer to Havana, until they eventually arrived and the musicians stepped on stage. The band opened with "Jumping Jack Flash" and played a concert featuring many of their greatest hits, as these were the songs that the Cuban audience would most likely recognize. After a performance of "Brown Sugar," the Stones left the stage before returning for a planned encore in which they performed "You Can't Always Get What You Want" with singers from Coro Entrevoces under the direction of Digna Guerra, who had been involved in numerous US-Cuban cultural exchanges in the preceding years.[26] The band concluded their concert with "(I Can't Get No) Satisfaction."

The documentary films ¡Olé, Olé, Olé! A Trip across Latin America and Havana Moon, both directed by Paul Dugdale, captured the event. While the former film addresses the planning process, logistical challenges related to

Cuba, and the reception of the Rolling Stones in different Latin American countries during their tour, the latter is a straightforward concert film. Like other contemporary music documentaries about Cuba, the music is intercut with clips focusing on classic cars, dilapidated buildings, and children playing soccer in the street. *Havana Moon* opened with these scenes as Keith Richards and Mick Jagger narrated. Jagger talks about Cuba's "weird romantic aura" as the country that stood up to the United States and the continuing attraction of figures like Fidel Castro and Che Guevara. Keith Richards states: "Obama mentioned us in his speech. So that was quite amazing. He was the opening act, I guess," before declaring, "It's about bloody time we got to Havana."[27] In *Give Me Future*, the Major Lazer documentary, Diplo has his own thoughts about the Rolling Stones playing in Cuba for the first time. He argues: "You're English. Your ass could've come here any time in the last fifty years. So why do you come now after Major Lazer? You could've already been doing it. But you're scared. Now what?"[28] The production of these documentaries allowed the musicians' management to recoup profits that could not be gained directly from a free concert in Cuba. The documentaries also fed an ongoing interest in Cuba. Although it was easier to visit the island in 2016 than it had been in decades, the perception of the country as being closed off continued. These films allowed both fans of the performers and individuals with a general interest in Cuba to get a glimpse of the island.

The Rolling Stones and Major Lazer documentaries show significant differences between the concerts, and also demonstrate a changing Havana. *Give Me Future* showed the small Major Lazer team working with Cubans to construct the concert stage and struggling to find a good mixing board and amplification equipment on the island. They were able to get everything ready for the concert, but they depended on assistance from willing and knowledgeable Cubans every step of the way. The Rolling Stones concert, on the other hand, was a huge operation. The band's entire stage was shipped to the island and required hundreds of individuals to transport it and set it up. Neither the Rolling Stones nor the Cuban government put forth the funds for such a massive undertaking, and the concert was made possible by the donations from the charity Fundashon Bon Intenshon, which is operated by Curaçao lawyer Gregory Elias. His foundation has organized and supported many other music festivals and concerts but never in Cuba. Elias argues that he had no ulterior political or economic motives for paying for the concert other than being a fan of the Rolling Stones and wanting to do something nice for the Cuban people.[29] The March 2016 concerts and the Obama visit demonstrated and perpetuated a growing international spotlight on Cuba.

This "Havana moment" could largely be attributed to the changing US-Cuban relationship, which not only encouraged US citizens to visit the island but also motivated travelers from Europe and elsewhere in the Caribbean. Technological, economic, and policy changes on the island further drove this moment. The Cuban people were finding ways to access more media and information from outside the island, and Cuban artists had been traveling abroad more frequently in the years since Raúl Castro came to power. After the success of these events, organizations like Fabien Pisani's Musicabana used images and video to encourage other musicians to visit Cuba, organize additional festivals, and make the Havana moment a lasting one.[30]

THE CULTURAL DELEGATION TO CUBA

One month after President Obama visited Cuba, the President's Committee on the Arts and Humanities (PCAH) led a delegation to Havana with representatives from the National Endowment for the Arts, the National Endowment for the Humanities, and the Smithsonian Institution. The official delegation for the United States Cultural Mission to Cuba included artists, dancers, musicians, and actors. This delegation's mission was to exercise cultural diplomacy in its most traditional sense and to lay the groundwork for future exchanges in collaboration with Cuban officials. According to the Center for Democracy in the Americas, cultural exchanges have made up nearly half of all US-Cuba exchanges, but this was the first direct government-to-government cultural mission.[31]

Ronald Reagan established the President's Committee on the Arts and the Humanities in 1982. President Reagan initially created a task force in May 1981 to investigate the possibility of restructuring both the National Endowment for the Arts and the National Endowment for the Humanities to cut public funding and increase private-sector support for programs supported by these agencies. The task force's report recommended continued public support for arts and humanities as well as the formation of the PCAH (Wu 2002, 50). Executive Order 12367 established the committee, and instructed that it be composed of the heads of numerous federal agencies including the National Endowment for the Arts, the National Endowment for the Humanities, the Institute of Museum Services, the Department of Education, the Smithsonian Institution, the National Gallery of Art, and the John F. Kennedy Center for the Performing Arts, along with citizens appointed by the president.[32] The PCAH has commissioned a number of reports on the arts since 1982, but their most public activity has been the annual presentation of the National Medals of the Arts and Humanities (Goler 2004, 111). Other recent PCAH initiatives include the National Arts and Humanities Youth Program Awards and the Turnaround Arts program, which began in 2011 under the leadership of First Lady Michelle Obama to provide arts education resources and expertise to high-poverty elementary and middle schools.[33]

Planning for the 2016 Cuba trip started with coordination between the PCAH and federal partners, and the committee enlisted the Center for Democracy in the Americas as a consultant for the cultural mission.[34] In January 2016 the group initiated meetings with the Cuban ambassador to the United States, José Ramón Cabañas, and First Secretary Bernardo Toscano. Through coordination with the Cuban embassy, the agency heads finalized the mission dates and established contacts with the Cuban Ministry of Culture. Advance trips to Havana took place from February 17 to 19 and April 3 to 6. On the first trip, PCAH staff members met with representatives from the Cuban Ministry of Culture, and on the second a small advance team finalized the itinerary and met with Cuban artists to set up opportunities for US and Cuban musicians to perform together. The delegation's final report, which was prepared by the Center for Democracy in the Americas, described the importance of these advance trips:

> These face-to-face meetings facilitated our ability to plan events and resolve problems. For example, Vice Minister Rojas expressed his concern that [the Ministry of Culture] had not received a formal invitation to participate in the Smithsonian's Folklife Festival in 2017. That enabled the PCAH advance team to take immediate action by getting in touch with the Smithsonian Institution to ensure that the Vice Minister received a formal letter the next day.[35]

The Cuban Ministry of Culture and the PCAH officially announced the mission to the public on April 14.

The PCAH invited various US musicians to participate, including violinist Joshua Bell, Motown recording star Smokey Robinson, pop and R&B singer Usher, DJ IZ, Puerto Rican soprano Larisa Martínez, musical theater performer John Lloyd Young, and singer-guitarist Dave Matthews. These musicians joined twenty-six other members of the delegation with an additional eighteen guests and ten members of the media.[36] The delegation received a briefing in Miami on April 17 before flying to Havana the following day. The first day in Cuba included lunch with the leaders of various Cuban cultural institutions and a visit to the Instituto Superior de Artes to meet with Cuban art and music students. They toured the grounds and art studios and were treated to performances by student dancers and a string quartet. Following the school visit, the delegation broke up into smaller groups, one of which took a ferry across the bay to visit the *municipio* (borough) of Regla and participate in a block party hosted by the Cuban hip-hop duo Obsesión.[37] In a series of tweets that he posted after returning from Cuba, Usher documented this trip to what he called "the Regla hood."[38] The delegation convened again for dinner at the upscale private restaurant El Cocinero on the edge of the Vedado neighborhood, where Joshua Bell, Dave Matthews, and Carlos Varela performed.

The second day included bilateral meetings between the leaders of the US and Cuban cultural agencies while members of the delegation visited either a community art project or the Institute of Cuban Art and Cinematography to learn about the film industry on the island. Travelers with the cultural mission were also able to visit another school, witness a Santería ceremony, participate in panel discussions, and see Ernest Hemingway's home. Some of the delegation members visited the EGREM recording studios, where they heard from Buena Vista Social Club guitarist Eliades Ochoa. This studio visit provided time for US and Cuban musicians to jam together and improvise. The third day also included more panel discussions and meetings, a tour of the Cuban Fine Arts Museum, and visits with the Liszt Alfonso Dance Company academy and artist studios. The day ended with dinner and a concert at La Fábrica de Arte Cubano (F.A.C.).[39]

The evening's formal concert, organized by Fábrica de Arte founder X (Equis) Alfonso, featured a children's choir and the Chamber Orchestra of Havana. The Chamber Orchestra played movements from Vivaldi's *The Four Seasons* with Joshua Bell. Bell and Larisa Martínez also performed an arrangement from Ernesto Lecuona's zarzuela "Maria La O," and Cuban pianist Harold López-Nussa accompanied delegation singer John Lloyd Young in an arrangement of Smokey Robinson's "Ooh Baby Baby." The delegation members and guests then moved into a larger hall with an atmosphere more similar to a rock concert, where Cuban musicians played music into the early hours of the next morning. The Cuban performers included X Alfonso, Síntesis (led by X Alfonso's father, Carlos Alfonso), Omara Portuondo, Harold López-Nussa, Yasek Manzano, Zule Guerra, Aldo Lopez-Gavilan, and Carlos Varela.[40] Delegation members Dave Matthews, Smokey Robinson, and Usher joined them on stage.

Varela was the Cuban musician involved most prominently in the US delegation's visit to Havana. He performed with Dave Matthews on the roof of El Cocinero during the first night of the cultural mission, and his duet with Matthews at the F.A.C. was notable for its lyrical content and the repeat performances it generated in the United States. Varela gained popularity in Cuba in the 1980s as part of the second generation of nueva trova singers. While sometimes critical of Cuban policies, trova music reflected the egalitarian ideals of socialism; *trovadores* Pablo Milanés and Silvio Rodríguez became major stars with significant television and radio exposure in Cuba (Moore 2006, 135–46). Carlos Varela grew up listening to these nueva trova singers but was also influenced by rock and roll, and as a songwriter his lyrics have been critical of the Cuban government without being overtly subversive. As the Cuban state began accepting rock performers as musical professionals around 1986, Varela was able to build an audience as a musician with a backing band and a sound reminiscent of the pop and rock styles found in the United States and Europe (Moore 2006, 162).

Varela and Matthews performed the song "Muros y Puertas" ("Walls and Doors") from Carlos Varela's fifth album *Nubes* (*Clouds*), released in 2000. *Nubes* is the artist's only solo acoustic album; Varela recorded it in Havana shortly after a tour of Spain where all his band chose to stay, which shaped the lyrics of the songs and their arrangements. The album laments the losses caused by emigration, and the lyrics to "Muros y Puertas" are also relevant to the US-Cuban relationship (Cumaná 2014, 75–76). As their performance at the F.A.C. began, Varela sang the opening lines, "Desde que existe el mundo / Hay una cosa cierta / unos hacen los muros / y otros hacen las puertas" (Since the world began / There is only one thing certain / some make walls / and others make doors). He accompanied himself on guitar while Matthews stood over Varela's right shoulder listening, and in the second verse Varela motioned for him to start playing. Matthews strummed along while reading the chords and lyrics from a piece of paper near his feet. After singing the chorus, Varela had the audience repeat the lines and then stepped back while the band vamped. Dave Matthews entered on the third verse, singing it in English. His voice was timid at first but grew louder in the fourth verse, and when he reached the chorus the audience cheered. Matthews sang it in English this time: "This is the way it's always been / And you know you know it / There can be freedom only / When nobody owns it."[41] Varela then returned to repeat the chorus in Spanish. The two musicians shook hands, and Varela kissed Matthews's hand and cheek before closing the song, which ends with the lines from the opening that translate as "Some make walls and others make doors."⁴² In 2015 Varela recorded an interview with US National Public Radio; when asked if he had a song about how people in Cuba were feeling at that time, he played "Muros y Puertas."⁴³ Varela and Matthews went on to perform this duet again in the United States in the months that followed; it became more relevant as political commentary when understood as a response to then US presidential candidate Donald Trump's call to build a border wall to prevent immigration into the United States.

By the time the US and Cuban musicians had finished performing together, it was the morning of April 21, the final day of the cultural mission. That day the Cuban Ministry of Culture hosted a closing press conference at the Gran Teatro, where President Obama had given his speech to the Cuban people almost exactly one month earlier. The purpose of the bilateral press conference was for the leaders of the participating institutions to announce new programs and initiatives to fund and support further artistic engagement between the two countries. Jane Chu, the chairman for the National Endowment for the Arts, commented on the context and meaning of the delegation's time in Havana:

> Over the past few decades, our two countries have both shared a common connection—a love of the arts—through music, art, dance, and theater. Even when we lived in isolation from each other, our appreciation for your cultural heritage has always been present. So experiencing Cuba these past few days has felt like rediscovering a long-time friend. As we've become reacquainted, we have all been captivated by Cuba's energy and spirit. We have met your artists, visited your schools, and toured your museums. Immersing ourselves in your culture has truly enriched us all.⁴⁴

She then announced that the NEA would commit $100,000 to supporting US-Cuban cultural exchanges through two existing programs: USArtists International and Southern Exposure: Performing Arts of Latin America. USArtists International provides grants to US artists in music, dance, and theater to perform in international festivals, and the 2016–17 grant cycle was the first time that artists could apply for US government funds to support performances at a Cuban festival. Southern Exposure: Performing Arts of Latin America gives grant money to US presenting organizations to book dance, music, and theater performers from Latin America, and with Chu's announcement Cuban artists would be eligible for the first time. This money would not be a onetime expenditure but represented the beginning of a long-term investment. Chu closed with the declaration, "By sharing our art forms with each other, person to person and community to community, we are creating new paths for understanding, appreciation, and fraternity."[45]

The PCAH also announced that Cuba would be recognized with the National Arts and Humanities Youth Program's 2016 International Spotlight honor and the intent to make Cuba the site for the first international Turnaround Arts school.[46] Other initiatives included a partnership with the University of Miami's Frost School of Music to offer four full-tuition scholarships to Cuban students seeking master's degrees in music, film screenings with the Sundance Institute, funds to support art conservation in Cuba from the National Endowment for the Humanities, and Cuba's participation in the Smithsonian Folklife Festival. In the final assessment of the delegation's visit to Cuba, the Center for Democracy in the Americas declared it "a very successful step in the process of building a trusting, respectful bilateral relationship that honors the accomplishments of the arts and artists in Cuba and the United States."[47] The Center for Democracy in the Americas also stated that they intended to assist the federal agencies that participated in the cultural mission to move forward with their initiatives, which would involve ongoing negotiations with the Cuban bureaucracy and navigating the various interests in Washington, D.C., including lobbyists and politicians opposed to rapprochement between the United States and Cuba. The PCAH delegation and mission to Cuba was the first formal cultural and musical diplomacy initiative toward Cuba enacted by US government agencies in the Obama years, but it took place after seven years of performances by self-declared musical diplomats who sought to create the same paths for understanding that NEA Chairman Chu described in her remarks. While 2016 witnessed the beginning of US government-funded cultural exchanges and musical diplomacy initiatives, it also saw the continuation of the unofficial efforts that started with Obama's inauguration and were further galvanized by the president's visit to the island and the restoration of diplomatic relations.

MUSICIANS ACROSS THE STRAITS AND THE FÁBRICA DE ARTE CUBANO

In June 2016 I joined the delegation for an informal musical diplomacy initiative to Havana called Musicians Across the Straits. The effort brought five musicians from St. Augustine, Florida, to perform at the Fábrica de Arte Cubano for a three-night residency. The Friendship Association, a 501(c)(3) not-for-profit organization in St. Augustine, planned the musical diplomacy effort. The organization was originally incorporated as the St. Augustine-Baracoa Friendship Association in 2000 and sought to establish a formal sister city relationship between St. Augustine and Baracoa, Cuba.[48] The Friendship Association obtained an OFAC license to engage in people-to-people exchanges, and they brought groups to Cuba annually until the Bush administration stopped issuing and renewing people-to-people licenses in 2004. The organization was unable to take the general public on trips to Cuba until policies changed under the Obama administration, but in the intervening years a license from the US Department of Commerce allowed them to deliver material aid to Baracoa such as medicine, dental equipment, mattresses, clothing, and educational materials. The Friendship Association previously worked with visual artists by bringing photographers to Cuba and exhibiting painters from Baracoa in the United States, but the 2016 effort was their first time working with musicians.[49]

Jo "Yosi" McIntyre, the Friendship Association Treasurer, proposed Across the Straits in 2015 as a campaign to celebrate the normalization of diplomatic relations between the United States and Cuba; Musicians Across the Straits was the first of multiple campaign initiatives. McIntyre and his wife, Soledad Pagliuca, were founding members of the Friendship Association and have been the driving force behind the group's numerous projects. They organized a fundraiser on September 27, 2015, that included a concert in downtown St. Augustine featuring some of the musicians who would be traveling to Cuba and a silent auction of Cuban art and other items. The event was unable to raise enough money to pay for all the musicians who wished to be involved. The reduced funding and delays in finalizing the dates for the trip meant that some musicians who are usually accompanied by full bands went to Havana as solo performers, and the original idea of programming all old Florida music was reworked.[50] The performers who traveled to Havana in June 2016 included jazz and pop vocalist Danielle Eva, classical guitarist and folk singer Sam Pacetti, old-time string musicians Elisabeth Williamson and Jim Quine, and experimental blues guitarist Michael Jordan. They were joined by Soledad, Yosi, and myself along with a delegation made up of friends of the musicians and Friendship Association members who helped fund the travel costs for the performers.

We flew from Miami to Havana on June 23, 2016. When comparing it to my trip to Cuba for the Havana Jazz Plaza Festival over three years earlier, I immediately noticed a different demographic composition of travelers on the flight and in the Havana airport. The plane was full, and there were native

English speakers all around me ranging in age from high school students to retirees. Yosi had instructed everyone with Musicians Across the Straits to say the trip was a people-to-people exchange when asked the purpose of our trip at the passport check. Security moved so quickly that they did not even ask most of us why we were there. While waiting for our baggage to come out, Yosi had no qualms about handing out flyers advertising the "Músicos Cruzando Los Estrechos" ("Musicians Across the Straits") performances and encouraging other US travelers to attend the concerts later that night. Upon exiting the airport that afternoon, we all immediately boarded a bus to the Fábrica de Arte Cubano so the musicians could do a sound check.

The F.A.C. is an old peanut oil factory that has been converted into a combination concert venue, art gallery, artist studio, and bar; it is now one of the hottest nightspots in Havana. Popularly known as La Fábrica, the space was opened to the public in February 2014 and has been the site of numerous US-Cuban exchanges. In addition to the performances by Dave Matthews and others during the PCAH cultural mission, the F.A.C. also hosted Michelle Obama in March 2016 for a public forum with Cuban students as part of the First Lady's Let Girls Learn initiative.[51] The F.A.C. has become a venue for the Havana Jazz Plaza Festival and, as a central hub of Havana nightlife, attracts international musicians who want to visit or perform there while in the city. Cuban rock and hip-hop musician X Alfonso oversaw the conversion of the former factory in the Vedado district into a venue designed to exhibit music, visual art, film, fashion, cuisine, and theatre under one roof. The concept of transforming a shuttered factory into a performance space has been popular in cities around the world for decades but was new in Cuba. As such, the F.A.C. represented a changing Havana as the government experimented with relaxing a tightly controlled economy. The space is considered a "community project" that combines elements of state-run and private business, but its runaway success has prompted some criticism on the island for being operated too much like a capitalist enterprise.[52]

The art on display also pushes political boundaries; the F.A.C. was designed to be a place where artists could present new Cuban art while raising questions about life on the island that may be uncomfortable. Herman Portocarero, the former ambassador for the European Union in Havana, described the art at the F.A.C. in his book *Havana Without Makeup*:

> The art on display is cutting edge, with strong doses of irony and tongue-in-cheek social criticism, sometimes of downright provocation, but with content mostly thoughtful and playful at the same time.

In a way, the constant testing of the flexible boundaries for artistic freedom has made for mature expression of subtle opinions, because the artists on display here don't want to deny their cubanía, or to be quoted abroad as being overtly subversive. (2017, 142)

Some of the art on display in June 2016 included a series of historic photographs of mid-twentieth-century Cuba amidst the early years of the revolution in which the Coca-Cola logo or products could be found somewhere in each photo. There was also a stationary bicycle painted white that appeared to be melting into the floor with scenes from the streets and alleys of Havana projected onto a small screen in front of it, simulating a surreal bike ride through the city.

The hours of the F.A.C. are Thursday through Sunday nights from 8:00 p.m. to 3:00 a.m., so it was nearly empty when we arrived in the afternoon for the sound check. Other than those of us who arrived on the bus from the airport, the only others we saw were the sound engineer and three staff members cutting limes to fill large tubs in preparation for mojitos and other drinks to be served that night. Upon entering the large concrete building, attendees are greeted by a bar and a narrow wooden set of stairs to visit the exhibits on the second and third floors. Across from the bar is a narrow concrete passage that leads into Sala Santiago Feliú, a low-ceilinged concrete box of a performance space with a stage at one end that hosted the St. Augustine musicians. Santiago Feliú, for whom the space was named, was a Cuban singer-songwriter and a prominent member of the nueva trova movement; Feliú died unexpectedly in February 2014 just before the F.A.C. was scheduled to open. The small space proved ideal for acoustic musicians. The second and third floors above the entrance included the primary visual arts exhibits. Further into the building one could find another bar in a wide, dark room that was used for film screenings, live theatre, and dance performances. The larger performance space where the PCAH delegation members jammed two months earlier was located even deeper in the F.A.C., through a narrow passage that opens into another section of the complex. The halls connecting each of these areas display everything from photographs and paintings to dresses and architectural designs. In many ways, navigating the F.A.C. for the first time felt like being in a maze, where the faintest intriguing musical sounds could prompt someone to explore the concrete halls until they found the music's source.

During the performances on Thursday, Friday, and Sunday nights, the US musicians attracted a diverse crowd that filled the small space. In addition to being an attractive and intimate music venue, the Sala Santiago Feliú was popular because it maintained a relatively cool temperature all night long, and one could usually sit down on folding wooden stools scattered throughout the room. While the listeners in the room likely did not come to the F.A.C. for the purpose of hearing the musicians from St. Augustine, they were made aware of who they were and where they were from by posters in the area and information on video screens at the entrance that promoted the Cruzando los Estrechos initiative. Each musician played an approximately half-hour set as people flowed in and out of the room. Some would only listen for a couple of minutes while others sat for an entire set or more. Certain performers attracted larger crowds. When Danielle Eva sang her rendition of "Wayfaring Stranger," which she has described as southern gospel meets powwow, her powerful vocals and body percussion brought many curious individuals into the room. Likewise, the Cuban audience seemed to particularly enjoy Elisabeth Williamson because one does not often hear the banjo in Havana; Williamson's dexterity on her instruments demonstrated that an older woman with gray hair can be every bit as captivating on stage as younger performers. The breakout performer from Musicians Across the Straits, however, was Michael Jordan. The guitarist created distinctive sounds with his instrument that attracted listeners who just wanted to find out what they were hearing. For many of his songs, he played his guitar flat on his lap, which allowed him not only to play the strings but also to drum on the wooden body of the instrument. Jordan built up rhythmic grooves over an extended period that would climax with crowd-pleasing, high-energy guitar solos. After his sets, young Cuban audience members wanted to ask Jordan about his guitar and posed for photos with him; his popularity was apparent enough that the performance order was changed to make him the closing act on the final night.

These musicians were not well known outside of North Florida and Musicians Across the Straits was not a government-organized cultural diplomacy effort, but many aspects were in line with the earliest models of musical diplomacy that were established during Franklin Roosevelt's administration. Non-celebrity musicians have long been the preferred cultural diplomats, and the musicians played a variety of genres with much of it falling under the umbrella of Americana. Although the idea was to showcase a variety of traditions and performance styles from the musicians' home community, they were surprised to find themselves playing not only for Cubans but also for visitors from the United States who were at the F.A.C. each night. Chartered buses dropped off groups of people who were traveling with tour companies for a night at La Fábrica as part of their people-to-people itinerary. I met several students from the United States who were part of study-abroad programs for whom the F.A.C. was one of their primary late-night hangouts. There were also US visitors who had arranged their own travel to Cuba and found themselves at the venue following the recommendations of newly made Cuban friends or as a result of the Musicians Across the Straits flyer. Some of these travelers from the United States were uninterested in the group of US musicians taking up a stage for an entire night, but others were excited by it and stayed for multiple sets.

In addition to the performances at the F.A.C., the Friendship Association took seriously its role as a people-to-people travel provider and ensured that there was a full itinerary for the travelers. We went on a guided walking tour of Habana Vieja's plazas and visited Finca Vigia, Ernest Hemingway's house. The group went to the Hotel Nacional for cocktails before going to the Fábrica one night, and we also visited the fine art museum and the old Bacardi building. On the afternoon of Saturday, June 25, during some unscheduled free time, a group of us walked to the Basílica Menor de San Francisco de Asís. The colonial-era church, which now serves as a concert hall, was the host for the fourth annual Encuentro de Jóvenes Pianistas (Meeting of Young Pianists) festival. This monthlong event featured recitals Thursday through Sunday nights from June 2 to June 26. Cuban-born pianist Solomon Mikowsky, who now teaches at the Manhattan School of Music, served as the festival's artistic director; the festival highlighted pianists from all over the world including a number of Mikowsky's current and former students. The June 25 recital featured US pianist Simone Dinnerstein performing Bach's Brandenburg Concerto No. 5 accompanied by Cuban musicians on flute and violin, a Mozart piano sonata, and a Mozart piano concerto. Other than the members of our group, the audience in the hall was primarily Cuban, including a woman of African descent who was wearing a bandana of the US flag. At the conclusion of the performance, she leapt into the aisle waving a second US flag while yelling for an encore from Dinnerstein long after the rest of the audience had ended their applause. The performance and the reaction to it were additional examples of how the changing US-Cuban relationship was reflected in Havana and how one could not help but notice the presence of US visitors and performers in Cuba's capital in 2016. My observations during the Musicians Across the Straits trip also underscored how the growing number of international visitors to Cuba was intensifying economic and technological divides in Cuban society.

TOURISTS, CITIZENS, AND TWO CUBAS

In 2016 the Cuban Ministry of Tourism reported four million foreign visitors, representing a 13 percent increase from 2015. More than six hundred thousand of those visitors were from the United States, an increase of 34 percent over the previous year.[53] The Cuban economy's dependence on tourism began after the collapse of the Soviet Union and continued through the Obama years. The balance between trying to sustain a socialist state and appealing to such a large influx of visitors from a globalized, post-Cold War world has presented challenges and contradictions. A society that claimed to be egalitarian was in reality one with clear stratifications involving multiple currencies, amenities available only to visitors, and policies that exposed underlying racial divides. In "The Janus-Faced Character of Tourism in Cuba," Sanchez and Adams argue that while tourism bolsters the Cuban economy, its negative elements may also undermine belief in and support for the island's socialist system (2010, 420). The Cuban government was skeptical and reluctant to encourage tourism during the Soviet era, likely for this reason; history has shown that governments most in need of tourism for economic reasons are often politically subverted by it. Despite the challenges tourism presents, the Cuban economy will continue to depend on international travelers for the foreseeable future. Marinas and golf courses, which were famously mocked by Fidel Castro in the early years of the revolution, are under construction along with resorts and other tourism sites. While many of these actions seem to contradict the socialist ideals espoused by the Cuban government, officials have also hoped to inspire external political sympathies through tourism, but any results have been minimal.

The Cuban government tried to curtail the threats tourism posed by limiting contact between tourists and locals, but that only created a different set of problems. For most of the 1990s and 2000s, Cubans were not legally allowed to stay in tourist hotels even if they could afford it. Under President Raúl Castro, however, policies that tried to maintain strict separation between foreigners and visitors were repealed, and those divisions have started to erode. During the Musicians Across the Straits trip, the Friendship Association hired a bus driver from Baracoa with whom they had worked many times before. He was originally scheduled to stay with another Cuban family in Havana, but a room in the hotel opened up when some delegation members decided to room together. After negotiations with the hotel staff and confirmation that the room was already paid for, the driver was able to stay in the hotel for the duration of the trip. I saw multiple new luxury hotels under construction in Havana in 2016. In the areas of Habana Vieja and Centro, new, upscale hotel buildings stand in sharp contrast with the surrounding neighborhoods of dilapidated buildings and struggling Cuban families. While it may now be legal for them to stay in these new buildings, it would be impossible for any but the richest Cubans to afford it.

Although the Cuban government announced that it would return to a single currency, the continuing use of different moneys for Cuban citizens and foreign visitors underlies and emphasizes other social and economic disparities on the island. The Fábrica de Arte Cubano only accepted the convertible peso (or CUC) used by tourists, and the cover charge of two CUCs is prohibitive for most Cubans. Once inside, drinks are also expensive. Instead of paying bartenders in cash, visitors to the F.A.C. are given a drink card when they pay their cover charge to enter the building. Bartenders stamp the card and upon exiting the building, patrons pay the amount stamped on their card. The charge for a lost card is thirty CUC (equivalent to US$30), just below the median monthly income on the island.[54] These disparities can also be found in the transportation sector. Cuba's fixed-route taxis are state-owned cars from the 1950s that drive on certain streets from one end of the city and back again. After flagging down a taxi, the passenger gets in and shares the old car's bench seat with other riders, letting the driver know when they want to get out. These taxis primarily serve Cuban citizens and often cost only twenty Cuban pesos per ride (less than one dollar). Until recently these taxis were not allowed to pick up foreigners, who were expected to take convertible-peso taxis. Since foreigners are still discouraged from using them, it remains a confusing system for outsiders to navigate. Many of my experiences with the fixed-route taxis involved riding around Havana during my first trip in 2011 with a Cuban friend named Leo, who instructed me not to talk in the cab. He later explained that my Spanish would give me away as a foreigner and they might charge me more. I saw Leo again in December 2012. He had saved enough money to lease a car that he was licensed to operate as a taxi driver for tourists and could regularly be found stationed outside hotels in Vedado.

As a black Cuban, Leo's ability to enter the tourist industry was more difficult than that of his white Cuban counterparts. Racism has a long history in Cuba that can be traced to the slave trade. Rhetoric and ideals about racial harmony have been a part of the espoused Cuban identity since the abolition of slavery and the fight for independence from Spain, but Cuban leaders put little effort into making that rhetoric a reality. The revolution gained much of its support from Afro-Cubans who were discouraged from organizing and collective action by Batista and previous leaders (Clealand 2017, 55–70). Although Fidel Castro declared that all Cubans were equal and ended legal discrimination, racism has continued into the present. Racial preference in tourism-related hiring continues to prohibit many dark-skinned Cubans from taking visible and prestigious positions in the hotel industry. Foreign journalists and scholars have pointed out how tourism is exacerbating racial and ethnic divisions in the country (Sanchez and Adams 2010, 425–26). Attention to this matter has prompted more people to acknowledge racism and has helped improve the status of black Cubans; however, the problem remains.

Another issue that has coincided with the rise of tourism is the increasing number of *jineteras* and the sex trade on the island. The Cuban state argued that prostitution was common before the revolution as a result of US capitalism and hegemony, and they claimed that the equality of socialism would eradicate sex work. The economic crisis of the 1990s and influx of tourism led to the revitalization of the sex trade, however. A common joke among Cubans is that sex is the one thing the government is not able to ration. As a male foreigner traveling alone, I found that offers were hard to avoid. The government has actively tried to curb this practice, as Sanchez and Adams explain: "The continuing existence of commoditized sexual services in socialist Cuba is an embarrassment for the government and militates against the solidifying socialist ideology and attaining national goals" (2010, 428). Yet for many of the men and women involved, the sex trade is seen as one of their few opportunities to obtain hard currency, make extra money, and get ahead in general. Both international tourists and Cuban participants are often seeking more than a quick encounter. As anthropologist Florence E. Babb describes it, foreigners may seek exotic and intimate relationships with locals, and "the Cubans involved in these entanglements are also motivated by yearnings to be swept away by romance to new places and new lives" (2010, 99).

International travelers have come to increasingly expect internet access in their hotels, and the Cuban government has started to allow higher-speed connections and wi-fi without blocking common news and social media sites in hotels. At the same time, Cubans are still generally unable to access the internet in their homes, and regular internet access is costly and censored. This is why Cubans must rely on other sources like the *paquete* to find videos, music, and software that would otherwise be streamed or downloaded. Cuban citizens with access to tourist hotels have become acutely aware of this disconnect, and demand for better internet access has increased. In summer

2015 the Cuban government launched the first paid public Wi-Fi hotspots, and by the end of 2016 there were hundreds of these hotspots and cybercafés across the island, with costs dropping from 2 to 1.50 CUC per hour.[55] These public hotspots were easy to identify because they became gathering areas for large groups of people using their smartphones or tablets to download content, browse websites, or video chat with family overseas. When walking past these cybercafés in summer 2016, young men approached me with pockets full of internet access cards for sale at prices below the official government rates. Optimism was high following the restoration of US-Cuban diplomatic relations that access to these popular gathering spots would rapidly increase. The US government eased restrictions on telecom companies, and Google expressed interest in establishing a presence on the island. But changes were slow and Cubans have still had to depend on the expensive public access points. In late 2016 the Cuban government launched a pilot program to allow home internet access, but it was limited to certain neighborhoods and remained cost-prohibitive for most potential users. Freedom House, an independent nongovernmental organization that acts as a watchdog in the areas of democracy and human rights, continues to classify the internet in Cuba as "not free" despite the modest reforms the Cuban government has introduced.[56]

The influx of travelers also fueled the number of private businesses on the island, transforming Havana's urban geography. Privately owned restaurants or *paladares*, numbered in the hundreds by 2016. On an afternoon with the St. Augustine musicians, we visited La Lamparilla, a new paladar that had been generating buzz about its food and cocktails. The paladar was decorated in bright colors and had large sliding doors facing the street that were kept open. A Coca-Cola chalkboard on the wall read in English, "We don't have wifi. Talk to each other. Pretend it's 1995." Current hit songs by US pop stars played through speakers; before we left, the waitresses of La Lamparilla insisted on performing a choreographed dance to a Bruno Mars song for our group. In addition to eliciting laughter and applause, this display caught the attention of passing tourists who decided to get a table themselves. Music can play an important role in attracting pedestrians on walking tours of Havana; many paladares depend on music because their storefronts often blend in with neighboring homes and they do not have large signs or advertisements for potential customers to see. Yet the impact of these private restaurants on life in Havana became impossible for locals to avoid. In order to meet the demands of increased tourism, paladar owners would send buyers to Havana's food markets each day to purchase the best meat and produce needed for their menus. In turn, food prices rose, and certain staples including tomatoes and onions became too expensive for much of the Cuban population. When the government made efforts to cap prices, the state-run vendors were largely unable to stock fresh produce, as it was redirected to co-ops or the black market where it could fetch higher prices.[57] In October 2016 the government temporarily suspended issuing licenses for any new paladares in an attempt to address these issues and to exercise additional control over the existing businesses.[58]

Between high-profile visits and the increased number of foreign travelers overall, 2016 demonstrated that the impacts of tourism on the Cuban population have been uneven and disruptive. International visitors created spaces for new businesses and opportunities, but those spaces were not available to most Cubans. The spaces that cater to tourists also have their own musical footprint, which reflects the increasingly noticeable stratifications in Cuban society. Businesses play international popular music to make travelers feel welcome, while charging prices that are well beyond the means of a Cuban citizen trying to survive on a state salary. The majority of music venues and clubs that feature international performers charge cover prices that keep many Cubans out. The Fábrica de Arte Cubano, for example, celebrates international popular music and culture but is priced beyond what many Cubans can spend. The disparities and differences related to the growth of tourism can be interpreted as another example of the friction from heterogeneous and unequal encounters that can anticipate and accompany new arrangements of culture and power (Tsing 2005, 5). Political changes in the United States at the end of 2016, however, added additional obstacles to an already complex situation and continue to block a clear resolution to these issues from emerging any time soon.

CONCLUSION

On November 1, 2016, Joshua Bell performed at Lincoln Center in a concert titled "Seasons of Cuba." He was joined by fellow PCAH delegation members Dave Matthews and Larisa Martínez as well as Cuban musicians Carlos Varela, Aldo López-Gavilan, and the Chamber Orchestra of Havana under the direction of Daiana García. The concert was a celebration of the renewed diplomatic relations between Cuba and the United States and of the cultural mission that took place in April. It featured many of the same pieces that the musicians played together in Havana at the F.A.C. performance. PBS television recorded the performances for broadcast and included interviews with the performers about their experiences and the musical connections between the two countries. Less than two weeks later, Carlos Varela and Dave Matthews shared the stage again, this time in a ballroom at the Hamilton Hotel in Washington, D.C., for the tenth anniversary of the Center for Democracy in the Americas. This time, when they performed "Muros y Puertas," the lyrics about building walls and opening doors were more sentimental than before. On November 8, Republican Donald Trump was elected as the next president of the United States. The Center for Democracy in the Americas and other groups that advocated for increased engagement with Cuba were now facing an uphill battle in fighting for continued cooperation between Cuba and the United States.

When asked in 2015 about President Obama's policies of engaging Cuba and reestablishing diplomatic relations, Trump said, "I think it's fine, but we should have made a better deal."[59] In September 2016, Trump changed his position. The candidate traveled to Miami and announced in front of supporters, including many Cuban Americans, that he intended to reverse the Obama administration's policies toward Cuba. The announcement received praise from anti-Castro hardliners in South Florida but was light on details. The Obama administration had negotiated agreements with the Cuban government on numerous topics beyond travel and reopening embassies. Following Trump's election, the candidate's vague statements did not address how individual issues would be addressed by his administration. Some were optimistic that as a businessman with interests in hotels and the travel industry, Trump would not damage the business opportunities that had emerged in Cuba for US companies. Others were more fearful.

The death of Fidel Castro on November 25, 2016, raised additional questions about the future of US-Cuban relations. Fidel Castro was ninety years old and his health had been declining for years. Although his brother had been president of Cuba since 2008, Fidel's presence continued to loom over the country and US-Cuban politics. Following his death, the Cuban military paraded his ashes across Cuba from Havana to Santiago on a four-day tour. The path retraced in reverse the route the revolutionary leader had taken in 1959, and crowds of Cubans lined up to see the former Cuban leader's remains as they passed.[60] Meanwhile, in Miami the exile community celebrated on Calle Ocho on November 30. Salsa music was played over amplifiers and a saxophonist played renditions of both "The Star-Spangled Banner" and "La Bayamesa." During the celebration, speakers rallied the crowd with descriptions of Castro's atrocities and indictments of the Obama administration's rapprochement with Cuba to which some members of the crowd shouted, "Viva Trump."[61]

Policies changed slowly for six years under Barack Obama and Raúl Castro, but the announcement of renewed diplomatic relations in late 2014 shocked the populations of both countries. By 2016 the significance of the policy changes could be seen and heard on the island. More US citizens and musicians were visiting Cuba, and the Cuban government was struggling to adapt to increased tourism and a changing economy. As 2016 drew to a close, however, it was unclear if the new administration would permit the full impact of the Obama-era policy changes to be realized. Ben Rhodes, who helped negotiate for renewed diplomatic relations, published a story on the social media platform Medium on December 17, 2016, arguing for the importance of building on the Obama administration's successes and not moving backwards. Rhodes wrote:

> We've increased engagement between our peoples. If Americans want to go to Cuba, their government shouldn't tell them not to, so we removed absurd restrictions on the ability of Americans to visit Cuba, and travel increased by 75 percent from 2014 to 2015; more than 500,000 Americans visited Cuba last year—including more than 300,000 Cuban Americans; ten US airlines now provide service between US and Cuban cities; and three American cruise lines have reached agreements to go as well. This travel brings revenue to ordinary Cubans; it reconciles families who've been divided; and it allows for Cubans to get access to different ideas and points of view beyond their borders.[62]

Musicians also feared that their ability to collaborate with their counterparts across the Straits of Florida would come to a close. In December 2016 Arturo O'Farrill returned to Cuba for the Havana Jazz Plaza Festival along with his family, and he once again visited the US ambassador. O'Farrill used the opportunity to return his father's ashes to Cuba. Chico O'Farrill had expressed a desire to return to the island late in life but never had the opportunity. With the future of US-Cuban relations and his ability to perform in future festivals uncertain, Arturo O'Farrill laid his father to rest at the Colon Cemetery in Havana.[63]

2016 was a turbulent year for both the United States of America and Cuba, but it also included previously unforeseen levels of US-Cuban political, cultural, and musical engagement. The US Department of Treasury relaxed travel restrictions to a point that had not been seen since the Carter administration. Individuals living in the United States could easily visit the country if they desired, and interest reached an all-time high after the reestablishment of diplomatic relations. This increased attention brought major performers including Major Lazer and the Rolling Stones to the island for notable concerts, and it also encouraged non-celebrity musicians like the group from St. Augustine to make the trip. The PCAH delegation to Cuba, which took place shortly after President Obama's own visit to the island, was the most traditional cultural diplomacy initiative between the United States and Cuba; a group of musicians, artists, and government officials traveled as official representatives of the US government to engage both the Cuban people and Cuban government institutions. This formal, official cultural diplomacy took place after years of unofficial cultural diplomacy efforts that were sanctioned by the Obama administration through OFAC licenses. The minor but significant interactions between US and Cuban musicians from 2009 through 2015 that escalated to high-profile performances in 2016 reflected the administration's approach to Cuba policy overall. The initial changes were small, but the incremental policy updates indicated a commitment to renewing US-Cuban relations that came to fruition at the end of 2014. The formal reestablishment of relations happened throughout 2015, and by 2016 the impact of normalization could be seen and heard on the streets of Havana. But before complete normalization was achieved and the US-Cuban musical relationship was restored, the Obama years came to a close.

EPILOGUE

DISSONANCE AND DIPLOMACY UNDER DONALD TRUMP

The Philadelphia Boys Choir and Chorale was scheduled to perform in Cuba in August 2016. After diplomatic relations between the United States and Cuba were reestablished, the organization's leaders and board members decided to return for the first time since 2003. The outbreak of the Zika virus that summer, however, prompted concerns from parents. The performance was delayed until January 2017, and the Philadelphia Boys Choir was one of the last groups to undertake a cultural exchange while Obama was still in office. When they were there, the choir visited and sang at the home of the US ambassador, performed with members of the Coro Nacional, and sang a new arrangement of Gershwin's *Cuban Overture*. Jeff Smith, the choir's artistic director and conductor, had long wanted to adapt the *Cuban Overture* for choir, but he was not a lyricist. The executive director suggested reaching out to poet Richard Blanco for help on the lyrics; Smith contacted Blanco, and Blanco agreed.[1]

Blanco claims to have no musical ability, and prior to Smith's reaching out, he was unfamiliar with the *Cuban Overture*. Smith sent Blanco a recording of the piece along with a paper by musicologist Andrew Lamb about Gershwin's trip to Cuba, and the two became a songwriting team that collaborated over Skype on the piece. They decided to use Gershwin's experiences as the subject matter for the lyrics, which Blanco described as a persona poem. The poet said that he tried to imagine himself as Gershwin discovering Cuba and "finding himself in a musical wonderland."[2] Blanco's text begins, "Hear the bongos and trumpets down the street. Hear the guiro, maracas, clave beat." The lyrics contain references to singing and dancing as well as imagery of the sea and tropical moonlight. Blanco said that he wanted the text to reflect a time from before Castro and Batista so that he would not have to think politically during the writing process.

While Blanco consciously depoliticized the lyrics he created for the *Cuban Overture*, he is a passionate advocate for creating connections between the United States and Cuba. The poet is a member of the advisory board for the CubaOne Foundation, which arranges trips to Cuba for young Cuban Americans. Blanco told me that millennials who are the children and grandchildren of exiles are "the inheritors of this mess." He believes in CubaOne's mission because it is important for young people to contextualize Cuba in order to find solutions and common ground for a divided population. "The people who caused the problem can't solve it," he said.[3] Since reading his poem at the opening of the US embassy in 2015, Blanco has returned to Cuba. He led CubaOne trips where the group learned about Cuban literature and visited the homes of Cuban writers and literary landmarks. He originally intended to travel with the Philadelphia Boys Choir before their exchange was rescheduled. He argues that initiatives involving music, literature, and other arts are important because the arts are the strongest bridge we have to connect disparate communities. "Arts let us connect to our shared humanity," Blanco explained. "Artists are emotional historians who can tap into something universal."[4]

Musicians I interviewed felt the same way when asked about the role music can play in international relations. Many of them even treated it as a ridiculous question—to them, the answer was obvious. Minnesota violinist Melissa Deal told me: "Even without being able to speak the common language, it was so helpful to have a common interest in music. It gave us something to talk about because musical words are similar. When you get down to it, no matter what your politics are and no matter what your living situation is, everyone plays music the same way and everyone loves music."[5] While musicians participating in musical exchanges have stressed that their performances were not political, they also believed that their performances and interactions helped make the relationship between the United States and Cuba more positive. Lisa Hittle concurred with that assessment, describing how music connected Cuba and its northern neighbor for decades, making it an ideal medium to encourage a robust international relationship in the present.[6]

The musical exchanges and cultural diplomacy initiatives that took place during the Obama administration were a contemporary manifestation of a once thriving musical discourse; they demonstrated the transnational aspirations to see that dialogue resume in full. When US policy toward Cuba changed to allow a limited amount of travel and engagement, musicians were often some of the first people to test new policies and create new transnational connections. The reforms under US President Barack Obama represent the most recent easing of restrictions toward Cuba. Presidents Carter and Clinton both increased travel between the two countries, helping facilitate musical exchanges. Like the Obama-era exchanges, concerts and tours in the late 1970s, late 1990s, and early 2000s created wide-reaching transnational networks. Following the election of Donald Trump, many feared that the Obama-era policies would represent just another temporary reprieve in the history of US-Cuban relations and that musical networks connecting the countries would once again be severed.

US-CUBAN RELATIONS IN THE TRUMP ERA

On January 12, 2017, Barack Obama's administration announced the end of the "wet foot, dry foot" policy that allowed Cubans to become legal residents of the United States if they reached land. As a result, Cuban immigrants would be treated like those from any other country.[7] It marked Obama's last policy move related to Cuba. Eight days later, on January 20, Barack Obama left office and Donald Trump was inaugurated as president of the United States. The new administration first addressed Cuba policy on June 16, 2017, when President Trump traveled to Miami with Republican politicians from Florida to once again speak in front of a group of supporters. He declared that, like he had promised, he would be "a voice for the freedom of the Cuban people." Trump railed against the reestablishment of diplomatic relations that occurred during the Obama administration, calling it a "terrible and misguided deal." He continued:

> The previous administration's easing of restrictions on travel and trade does not help the Cuban people, they only enrich the Cuban regime. The profits from investment and tourism flow directly to the military. The regime takes the money and owns the industry. The outcome of the last administration's executive action has been only more repression and a move to crush the peaceful, democratic movement. Therefore, effective immediately, I am canceling the last administration's completely one-sided deal with Cuba.[8]

The audience responded with applause and chants of, "Trump! Trump! Trump!" President Trump continued by telling a story of violinist Luis Haza, whose father was chief of police in Santiago when Castro took power. According to the story, after the Castro regime executed Haza's father, government officials demanded that the young violinist play for the regime, and he responded by playing "The Star-Spangled Banner." Luis Haza, who went on to have a successful performing and conducting career in the United States, was in attendance at the Trump rally. After President Trump told the story, he invited Haza on stage, who once again performed the US national anthem.[9] President Trump signed an order at that rally directing the Treasury and Commerce Departments to begin the process of issuing new regulations on Cuba.

Two months later, all seventeen members of the President's Committee on the Arts and Humanities resigned in protest after President Trump defended and refused to condemn the organizers of a white supremacist rally in Charlottesville, Virginia. Their resignation letter included a reference to the PCAH's work in Cuba:

> We know the importance of open and free dialogue through our work in the cultural diplomacy realm, most recently with the first-ever US Government arts and culture delegation to Cuba, a country without the same First Amendment protections we enjoy here. Your words and actions push us all further away from the freedoms we are guaranteed.[10]

Their letter included an acrostic, created by the first letter of each paragraph, that spelled the word RESIST. Cuba policy returned to the news on August 10, 2017, when the Associated Press reported that in late 2016, US diplomats in Cuba had reported hearing strange sounds that coincided with a variety of physical symptoms including severe hearing loss. The episode was initially attributed to an attack with a "covert sonic device."[11] The Cuban government denied any knowledge or involvement and argued that the health issues were an excuse for the Trump administration to damage US-Cuban relations. Experts who studied the individuals affected and their symptoms had various hypotheses, including a virus or mass hysteria, but most were skeptical that a sonic weapon was the cause.[12] The US State Department under Secretary of State Rex Tillerson responded by expelling two Cuban diplomats; after the news became public, Tillerson withdrew a majority of the diplomats from the US embassy in Havana. The State Department also issued a safety warning to US citizens advising them not to visit Cuba. The warning was downgraded in January 2018 urging people to "reconsider" travel. Although the State Department made a point not to directly accuse the Cuban government of being behind an attack, Trump himself blamed Cuba. He told reporters, "I do believe Cuba's responsible. I do believe that, and it's a very unusual attack, as you know. But I do believe Cuba is responsible."[13]

On November 8, 2017, the US Department of the Treasury Office of Foreign Assets Control released their updated guidance and regulations related to Cuba sanctions. In order to prevent economic activity from benefiting the Cuban military, the regulations stated that persons subject to US jurisdiction were prohibited from engaging in transactions with any organizations on the State Department's List of Restricted Entities and Subentities Associated with Cuba, which was released the same day. This list included eighty-four hotels along with marinas, stores, tour agencies, and other government entities that are operated by or act on the behalf of the Cuban military, intelligence, or security services. The new regulations rolled back the policy on people-to-people travel instituted in 2016 that allowed individuals to plan their own educational exchanges. The OFAC's updated guidance also added additional provisions to the Educational Travel and Support for the Cuban People categories. Educational travelers were now required to visit Cuba under the auspices of an authorized organization; if going alone, an individual must carry a certification letter stating that they are acting as the representative of the organization. Support for the Cuban People travel now required travelers to have a full-time schedule of activities that involves "meaningful interaction" with Cuban individuals; they define meaningful interaction as activities that must "enhance contact with the Cuban people, support civil society in Cuba, or promote the Cuban people's independence from Cuban authorities."[14] Despite the new regulations, any previously organized travel or business arrangements were permitted to continue even if they would not be permitted going forward.

In November 2018, Trump's National Security Advisor John Bolton, who previously worked for the George W. Bush administration and named Cuba as a threat in his 2002 "Beyond the Axis of Evil" speech, returned to the theme for a speech at Miami Dade College. Bolton declared that the Trump administration would sanction and end diplomatic relations with Cuba, Venezuela, and Nicaragua, which he called the "Troika of Tyranny."[15] Five months later on the 58th anniversary of the Bay of Pigs invasion, Bolton announced additional regulatory changes to limit travel to Cuba.[16] The US Department of the Treasury published and enacted the changes in June 2019 and effectively ended some of the largest categories of group travel. OFAC ended all general license authorizations for people-to-people travel and prohibited cruise ships that dock in the United States from visiting Cuba.

Cruises had become the most popular mode of transportation to the island for US individuals traveling for a purpose other than visiting family.[17] A number of general license categories still exist, but the Trump administration was successful in its goal of curbing US-to-Cuba travel.

Those in favor of increased US-Cuban interaction feared a complete reversal of the changes instituted by Obama, but as of summer 2019, the OFAC's policies have not gone that far. The Trump administration has been successful in reducing the number of US travelers going to the island. The Cuban government's tourism statistics showed that 95,520 US visitors traveled to the island during the first three months of 2018, a 40 percent drop from the same period in 2017.[18] Confusion over Trump's policies resulted in many people deciding not to pursue a trip to Cuba that they otherwise would have been interested in. Many people have told me that they thought that going to Cuba was illegal again. Despite their stated intent, the policies are counterproductive; by deterring individual travel and pushing people to join large group trips with licensed organizations, it hurts the casa particular owners who serve individuals and families but cannot accommodate busloads of people. These groups turn to large hotels where they can get a discount on a block of rooms, at the expense of the small business owners at the heart of Cuba's burgeoning private sector. Owners of paladares also noticed the reduced income from US visitors, but the Cuban government has increased efforts to attract Canadian, European, and Chinese travelers to make up for the reduction in visitors from the United States.[19]

The Trump White House leaned heavily on anti-Castro rhetoric when rolling out its new policies, but in April 2018 Raúl Castro stepped down as president of Cuba. It marked the first time since the Batista era that a non-Castro oversaw the country. The new president, Miguel Díaz-Canel, had served as Raúl Castro's vice president since 2013 and had been primed to take over the presidency for five years.[20] Castro will continue to exert influence in the country with a prominent position in the Communist party, but whether Díaz-Canel will try to adopt a different approach to human rights, the Cuban economy, and US-Cuban relations remains to be seen.

PLAY ON: MUSICAL DIPLOMACY CONTINUES

The situation seems dire: the new leaders of the United States and Cuba are not talking to each other, and formal diplomatic ties between the two countries have been slashed from where they were at the end of 2016 to being nearly nonexistent. Musicians, however, continue doing what they can to travel across the Straits of Florida. Performers are working to establish and maintain transnational networks while tackling the challenges of the new status quo. The resulting performances draw attention to the inconsistencies in US policies toward Cuba, making people aware that there are still legal opportunities to visit the island. Current exchanges have grown from musical interactions that took place during the Obama era, and the musicians show no sign of retreat in the face of Trump.

Rena Kraut played clarinet with the Minnesota Orchestra in Havana in 2015. When Trump announced his intention to reverse Obama's outreach to Cuba, Kraut responded with an op-ed in the *New York Times*. She referred to the Minnesota Orchestra's trip as a testament to arts diplomacy and echoed many of the points made by those in other industries about why rolling back policies that engaged Cuba were a bad idea. She continued: "We in the arts and education world would like to add our small but insistent voice. If the United States wishes to keep influence on the island—and it does—then the path forward must be to continue the dialogue started in 2014. Silencing American arts institutions hamstrings our country's most powerful method of soft diplomacy."[21]

Kraut and others who were inspired by the 2015 exchange put her words into action by forming the Cuban American Youth Orchestra (CAYO) to provide student musicians opportunities to participate in intercultural dialogue on an ongoing basis. The 501(c)(3) nonprofit organization has a large and diverse advisory board, including Minnesota Orchestra music director Osmo Vänskä, Neeta Helms from Classical Movements, and a range of business leaders, travel operators, former politicians, and communications professionals. CAYO's first academy took place in fall 2017. It brought the four founding members of the Crisantemi Quartet, who were all between the ages of nineteen and twenty-two, from Havana to Minnesota. Three of those performers played with the Minnesota Orchestra in 2015; in 2017 they joined four musicians from the University of Minnesota for a week of performances, broadcasts, workshops in music business and arts administration, and visits to Minnesota elementary schools. Together these eight musicians have agreed to advise and mentor future CAYO members.[22] In February 2018 CAYO traveled to Havana's inaugural La Ruta de Mozart festival with a string quartet from the Cleveland Institute of Music and a group of patrons and supporters. The second academy was held in April 2018, bringing a group of wind players from Cuba to Minnesota.[23] In May 2019 CAYO brought twenty-five US students to Cuba, where they joined forty-five Cuban students for the "Juntos en Armonía" ("Together in Harmony") tour. This event marked the first time that the full youth orchestra performed together, and they performed works by Dvořák, Copland, López-Gavilán, and a student composer who played violin in the group.[24]

The National Symphony Orchestra of Cuba returned to the United States for another tour in spring 2018. They returned to many of the same venues they had played in 2012, this time joined by South Korean pianist Yekwon Sunwoo, a rising classical music star and winner of the 2017 Van Cliburn International Piano Competition. Their 2018 US tour remained under the direction of Enrique Pérez Mesa; their repertoire included pieces by Cuban composer Amadeo Roldán, Spanish composer Manuel de Falla, and works by Tchaikovsky, Beethoven, Mozart, and Grieg.[25] The orchestra planned to return in February 2019. Venues had already started selling tickets for a concert featuring the National Symphony Orchestra of Cuba with jazz bassist and singer Esperanza Spalding when in April 2018 it was announced that the next tour was being canceled. The political changes and reduced US diplomatic presence in Cuba created too much difficulty obtaining visas for the performers, and organizers decided they could not plan such a high-profile tour.[26]

Visa issues also threatened to hamper a May 2018 festival at the Kennedy Center in Washington, D.C., titled "Artes de Cuba: From the Island to the World." The Kennedy Center scheduled over 400 Cuban and Cuban American artists to participate in the two-week event, and 242 of them were coming from the island. Without diplomatic staff to process visas in Havana, all the artists had to fly to Mexico City to visit the US embassy there and present their paperwork. Alicia Adams, the Kennedy Center's vice president of international programming, described the visa process as a logistical nightmare but something that was too important to give up.[27] The festival and visa process raised questions from South Florida members of Congress. Mario Díaz-Balart and Ileana Ros-Lehtinen both signed letters to the Kennedy Center accusing the organizers of featuring "pro-regime artists and propagandists" and demanded to know how artists were selected.[28] They also wrote to Secretary of State Mike Pompeo expressing concern about these artists being granted US entry when consular services in Havana are unavailable to pro-democracy and human rights activists. Rick Scott, who was Florida's governor and a Republican Senate candidate at the time, also wrote to Pompeo, urging the Secretary of State not to grant any visas to artists that he deemed "agents of the dictatorship."[29]

Despite the intertwined logistical challenges and political controversy, the festival went on and included all the artists and performers who were scheduled to appear. On May 8, 2018, for the opening night of the festival, Cuba's ambassador to the United States addressed the audience, which included various diplomats and multiple senators and representatives. Also in attendance were the former US ambassador to Cuba under Barack Obama, Jeffry DeLaurentis, and Obama's former Deputy National Security Advisor Ben Rhodes. The performers who participated in the two-week festival included Omara Portuondo, the Havana Lyceum Orchestra, Aldo López-Gavilán, Los Van Van, the Malpaso Dance Company, Yissy García, Pablo Milanes, and many others. In addition to music and dance, the festival's fifty events included theater, art exhibitions, a fashion show, a film festival, and Cuban cuisine. The festival concluded on May 20 with a performance by Arturo O'Farrill and the Afro Latin Jazz Orchestra. In a discussion with National Public Radio about his performance, O'Farrill said: "It's huge for the Kennedy Center to have this kind of festival with this kind of investment. This kind of level of involvement in artistry is unheard of. And it sends a message to the current administration and to the public that Cuba and the United States are madly in love, there was a very unpleasant divorce, but there's still a lot of love there."[30]

As the United States' National Cultural Center and a unique public-private partnership, the Kennedy Center's hosting of the Artes de Cuba festival represented a significant cultural diplomacy effort. Festival curator Alicia Adams acknowledged it as such, telling the *Miami Herald*: "Part of this is about cultural diplomacy. We're part of soft power. Arts are the best tool we have to bring people together."[31] Since first opening in 1971, the Kennedy Center has presented more than twenty festivals representing countries and regions from Europe, Africa, Australia, Asia, and Central and South America. The Cuba festival took over two years of active planning and featured many artists who had previously participated in US-Cuban musical exchanges. Following their return to Cuba, some of the participating artists met with Cuban President Díaz-Canel. In looking forward, the Cuban president told the musicians, "I don't believe that the current position will be eternal, and things like what you have accomplished in Washington can open the way."[32] While musicians work to continue cross-cultural engagement and musical diplomacy, the future depends largely on voters in the United States and the actions of leaders in both countries.

CONCLUSION

Throughout the United States there is an interest and curiosity among the public that drives a desire to hear Cuban performers and illustrates the aspiration for further US-Cuban engagement and musical interaction. Curiosity is one of many reasons people from the United States have for visiting Cuba. For some, a trip to Cuba is akin to a pilgrimage, while for others it is for leisure and entertainment. Following the late 2014 announcement that the United States and Cuba were reestablishing diplomatic relations, a spirit of celebration brought even more travelers to the island country. Most musicians still depend on well-connected and knowledgeable individuals in their personal networks to facilitate their international performances. Individuals including Nachito Herrera and Arturo O'Farrill and organizations like the Cuban American Youth Orchestra and Classical Movements have functioned as bridges between networks in Cuba and the United States; by fostering musical exchanges, these individuals are creating new connections and networks that enable further interaction. These exchanges benefit the musicians from both countries in various ways, and the social networks they create increase the likelihood of larger sociopolitical change. In her op-ed criticizing Trump's actions on Cuba, Rena Kraut wrote, "Artists have the ability to move the conversation to places corporations and politicians cannot or will not go, and to smooth the way for political change years before the document signings and handshakes."[33] Her statement echoed something Carlos Varela said at the beginning of the Obama years, when in 2009, playing for legislators in Washington, he declared: "Music is not going to move governments, but it might move people. And people can move governments."[34]

Yet the future of US-Cuban musical exchanges is uncertain in the age of Trump. A number of politicians still want to roll back all of the Obama-era travel reforms for personal and political reasons, and Cuba policy is a very low priority for most other policy makers. US policy toward Cuba primarily has been shaped by electoral considerations related to Florida and the clout of the Miami exile community, but recent movement for sustaining increased commerce and travel has come from elsewhere in the country. Politicians from Midwestern states including Minnesota have taken trips to Cuba to encourage agricultural trade and even introduced legislation to end the embargo and travel ban, but such legislative action has failed to gain traction. Musicians try to avoid politics when participating in musical exchanges, but they depend on politicians who will promote policies that allow travel to continue.

Musical interaction continues to create ties between the United States and Cuba even as diplomatic and economic normalization appears to have stalled. Thus, this story is still incomplete. Whether or not the changes that have been described in this book truly represent the "new beginning" with Cuba that President Obama called for in 2009 remains to be seen. Musical exchanges have exposed both the possibilities and limitations of current regulations, and interest in traveling between the United States and Cuba remains strong despite confusion about how the Trump administration is restricting travel. As the future of these policies continues to be debated, musicians show no signs of stopping their performances and exchanges. Through musical collaboration, performers negotiate differences and find commonalities while creating connections between individuals on both sides of the Straits of Florida. The resulting networks can be understood as a reflection of US and Cuban aspirations for positive diplomatic and transnational ties and our common desire for a more harmonious future.

NOTES

INTRODUCTION

1. At the time, I would require what the Department of the Treasury's Office of Foreign Assets Control (OFAC) called a Specific License for academic activities permitting me to spend money incident to "noncommercial academic research in Cuba specifically related to Cuba for the purpose of obtaining a graduate degree." OFAC (Office of Foreign Assets Control), US Department of the Treasury, *Comprehensive Guidelines for License Applications to Engage in Travel-Related Transactions Involving Cuba*, September 30, 2004, http://www.treasury.gov/resource-center/sanctions/Programs/Documents/cuba_tr_app.pdf.

2. "Havana Jazz Festival 2012," Cuba Tours and Travel, http://www.cubatoursandtravel.com/havana-jazz-festival-2012.

3. Adolfo Nodal, email message to author, October 12, 2012.

4. The Institute for Cultural Diplomacy uses Dr. Emil Constantinescu's definition, which states: "Cultural Diplomacy may best be described as a course of actions, which are based on and utilize the exchange of ideas, values, traditions and other aspects of culture or identity, whether to strengthen relationships, enhance sociocultural cooperation or promote national interests; Cultural diplomacy can be practiced by either the public sector, private sector or civil society." This definition is at http://www.culturaldiplomacy.org/index.php?en_culturaldiplomacy.

5. The US government's involvement is typically that of a funder and grantmaker; the New England Foundation for the Arts, Arts Midwest, and the Mid Atlantic Arts Foundation all operate international arts engagement programs that operate using federal grants, private contributions, and resources provided by partner organizations. Some of these programs send artists and musicians abroad while others bring international performers to visit a range of US communities. The decisions as to who can participate and what countries are involved are not made by government officials but by panels made up of volunteers.

6. The Music Committee ended up using their budget to support three tours of Central and South America in 1941 by the Yale Glee Club, the League of Composers Wind Quintet, and the American Ballet Caravan. The specific details of these tours and their outcomes are

thoroughly covered in Jennifer Campbell's 2010 dissertation, "Shaping Solidarity: Music, Diplomacy, and Inter-American Relations, 1936–1946."

7. Psyops (psychological operations) are military efforts to influence emotions, motives, and behaviors of individuals (and ultimately organizations and governments) to encourage behavior favorable to US objectives. They differ from musical diplomacy because of their military associations and by being more results-driven and having more specific goals than building relationships and encouraging goodwill.

8. For a list of the many well-known jazz musicians to participate in these state-sponsored tours, see Von Eschen 2004 and Monson 2007.

9. Throughout the text, italics are used for isolated Spanish words and phrases, but musical genres are not italicized. Similarly, proper nouns and titles of events and pieces of music are not italicized.

CHAPTER 1

1. See Sublette 2004 for a discussion of Cuban music with a transnational focus. The development of Cuban music, as Sublette explains, was highly dependent not only upon interactions between African and Spanish traditions but also the musical practices, cultural movements, and political upheavals in places like Haiti, Mexico, and Paris. Connections between the United States and Cuba receive special attention because their musical and political connections had been particularly important to the development of music in both countries.

2. Jazz's initial Cuban influences came through New Orleans and the Spanish influences that remained there even after Spain's control of the city had ended. Jelly Roll Morton referred to this influence that was present in his music as the "Spanish tinge" (Garrett 2008, 52). Travel also played a role in developing the connections between jazz and Cuban music. In 1900, W. C. Handy visited Cuba, where he reported seeing multiple dance bands performing, and he would later add Latin sections to some of his jazz arrangements like "St. Louis Blues."

3. Fidel Castro, "Castro Speaks to the Citizens of Santiago," January 3, 1959, Castro Speech Database, http://lanic.utexas.edu/project/castro/db/1959/19590103.html.

4. Fidel Castro, "The Havana Declaration," September 2, 1960, Castro Speech Database, http://lanic.utexas.edu/project/castro/db/1960/19600902-2.html.

5. Mark P. Sullivan, "Cuba: US Restrictions on Travel and Remittances," April 16, 2010, Congressional Research Service, http://www.fas.org/sgp/crs/row/RL31139.pdf.

6. Robert Kennedy, "Memorandum for Honorable Dean Rusk Secretary of State—Re: Travel to Cuba," National Security Archive, George Washington University, https://nsarchive2.gwu.edu/NSAEBB/NSAEBB158/19631212.pdf.

7. Gerald R. Ford Library, "Foreign Relations," President Ford '76 Factbook, http://www.ford.utexas.edu/library/document/factbook/foreign.htm.

8. For a full discussion of this issue and the complicated transnational history of "Guantanamera," see Manuel 2006, "The Saga of a Song: Authorship and Ownership in the Case of 'Guantanamera.'"

9. Bill Meredith, "Arturo Sandoval: From Cuba with Love," *Jazz Times*, October 2007, http://jazztimes.com/articles/19107-arturo-sandoval-from-cuba-with-love.

10. Arnold Jay Smith, "Voyage of the Jammed," *Down Beat* 44, no. 14 (August 1977): 46.

11. "Desde hoy, encuentro musical con artistas cubanos y norteamericanos en el Carlos Marx," *Granma*, March 3, 1979, 2; Jaime Sarusky, "Sobre el encuentro de musicos cubanos y norteamericanos," *Granma*, March 13, 1979, 4.

12. Pedraza Ginori, "Más Sobre Havana Jam 79 / Noche A Noche," *El Blog de Pedraza Ginori*, January 2, 2016, http://elblogdepedrazaginori.blogspot.com/2016/01/mas-sobre-havana-jam-79-noche-noche.html.

13. The term "ping-pong diplomacy" is a reference to the practice of table tennis players traveling between the US and the People's Republic of China in the early 1970s, which paved the way for Nixon's visit to Beijing in 1972; Jim Jerome, "Billy Joel Rocks Cuba," *People*, March 19, 1979, 34.

14. Pedraza Ginori, "¿Existió Realmente Havana Jam 79? / Havana Jam 79 Festival Really Have Existed? [*sic*]," El Blog de Pedraza Ginori, January 2, 2016, http://elblogdepedrazaginori.blogspot.com/2016/01/existio-realmente-havana-jam-79-havana.html#more.

15. Frank Meyer, liner notes to *Havana Jam*, Sony Records CD reissue, 1997.

16. Paquito D'Rivera, "Letter from Paquito D'Rivera to Kris Kristofferson and Stephen Stills," *Latin American Studies*, May 31, 2005, http://www.latinamericanstudies.org/music/paquito-carta.htm.

17. *A Night in Havana: Dizzy Gillespie in Cuba*, directed by John Holland (Docurama, 1989), DVD.

18. Mary Vorobil, "Cuban Troupe Granted Visas for Shows in US," *Miami Herald*, April 30, 1988.

19. The term "Special Period" was used by the Cuban government to refer to possible economic changes and sacrifices that would be required for the Cuban system to survive. It was originally used to describe a hypothetical "Special Period in Times of War" and how Cuba's economy would react to a US invasion. They also described a potential "Special Period in Times of Peace," which is how the government would handle extreme scarcity on the island. When the Soviet Union stopped supplying aid to Cuba, there was a period of questioning about whether or not the nation was in a special period. Then, in late 1990 the Communist newspaper *Granma* announced, "Cuba has entered the Special Period" (Hernandez-Reguant 2009, 4).

20. Manuel 2006 looks at the transnational history of the Cuban song "Guantanamera" and provides another example of the socialist state changing its stance on copyright in search of profit.

21. Larry Blumenfeld, "Rumba, Interrupted: The Bush Administration Breaks Up the Long-Running Dance between American and Cuban Musicians," *Village Voice*, January 18, 2005, http://www.villagevoice.com/2005-01-18/music/rumba-interrupted/.

22. Peter Watrous, "A Song Sails Forth from Cuba," *New York Times*, August 21, 1997.

23. Alisa Valdes-Rodriguez, "Music Builds a Bridge to Cuba," *Los Angeles Times*, March 23, 1999, https://www.latimes.com/archives/la-xpm-1999-mar-23-ca-20039-story.html; Alisa Valdes-Rodriguez, "US, Cuban Musicians Jam in Havana," *Los Angeles Times*, March 29, 1999, https://www.latimes.com/archives/la-xpm-1999-mar-29-mn-22204-story.html.

24. Ann Louise Bardach, "Kerry's Cuban Problem," *Slate*, April 26, 2004, http://www.slate.com/articles/news_and_politics/politics/2004/04/kerrys_cuban_problem.html; Isabel Vincent, "Gore punished by Cuban-Americans for Elian's return," *National Post*, November 9, 2000, http://www.cubanet.org/CNews/y00/nov00/09e2.htm.

25. The September 11 hijackers themselves were from Saudi Arabia, Egypt, Lebanon, and the United Arab Emirates, none of which were on the State Department list.

26. John R. Bolton, "Beyond the Axis of Evil: Additional Threats from Weapons of Mass Destruction," *Heritage Foundation*, May 6, 2002, http://www.heritage.org/research/lecture/beyond-the-axis-of-evil.

27. Jason Lawrence, "Cuba Travel Ban: Five Years Later," *Famuan*, March 20, 2011, http://www.thefamuanonline.com/news/cuba-travel-ban-five-years-later-1.2517442?pagereq=1#.Ukh1ymTEqFd.

28. Stephen Kinzer, "For Musicians from Abroad, Concert Schedules in Disarray," *New York Times*, April 6, 2004.

29. Jackson Browne, "Songs of Cuba, Silenced in America," *New York Times*, March 22, 2004.

30. Blumenfeld, "Rumba, Interrupted."

31. Reuters, "Audioslave Concert a First for Cuba," *New Zealand Herald*, May 6, 2005, http://www.nzherald.co.nz/lifestyle/news/article.cfm?c_id=6&objectid=10124202.

32. The performance itself can be found in the concert documentary *Audioslave: Live in Cuba*, Epic Music Video, DVD, 2005.

33. Council on Foreign Relations, "The Candidates on Cuba Policy," CFR.org, 2008, http://www.cfr.org/world/candidates-cuba-policy/p14758.

CHAPTER 2

1. Marc Frank, "Cuba allows tourism industry to hire private contractors," *Chicago Tribune*, October 9, 2013, http://www.chicagotribune.com/news/sns-rt-us-cuba-reform-20131009,0,4626537.story; Carol Pucci, "Cuba: On boulevards and back streets, its real life is revealed," *Seattle Times*, October 19, 2012, http://seattletimes.com/html/pacificnw/2019397374_pacificpcubatravel21.html.

2. "Money starts to talk," *Economist*, July 20, 2013, http://www.economist.com/news/americas/21581990-and-eventually-perhaps-one-currency-tempo-reform-accelerates-money-starts?zid=305&ah=417bd5664dc76da5d98af4f7a640fd8a; Patrick Oppman, "Cuba to do away with dual currency system," CNN, October 22, 2013, http://www.cnn.com/2013/10/22/world/americas/cuba-single-currency/.

3. Juan Tamayo, "Five years later: Cuba under Raúl: He's tinkered but it's the same old machine," *Miami Herald*, February 24, 2013, http://www.miamiherald.com/2013/02/23/3250831/cuba-under-raul-hes-tinkered.html.

4. Gay Nagle Myers, "Cuba's new visa policy greeted warmly, but warily, by industry," *Travel Weekly*, October 23, 2012, http://www.travelweekly.com/Travel-News/Tour-Operators/Cuba-new-visa-policy-greeted-warmly-but-warily-by-industry/.

5. Tamayo, "Five years later: Cuba under Raúl."

6. "Improvisación de Roberto Carcassés," YouTube video, September 15, 2013, http://www.youtube.com/watch?v=9ZT9UE5YmnI.

7. "Ministry of Culture Pardons Robertico Carcassés." OnCuba, September 18, 2013, http://www.oncubamagazine.com/culture/ministry-of-culture-pardons-robertico-carcasses/.

8. Inter-American Commission on Human Rights, "Six Reports on the Situation of Political Prisoners in Cuba." *Organization on American States*, 1979, http://www.cidh.oas.org/countryrep/Cuba79eng/intro.htm.

9. White House, "Fact Sheet: Reaching Out to the Cuban People," Office of the Press Secretary, April 13, 2009, http://www.whitehouse.gov/the_press_office/Fact-Sheet-Reaching-out-to-the-Cuban-people.

10. White House, "Remarks by the President at the Summit of the Americas Opening Ceremony," Office of the Press Secretary, April 17, 2009, http://www.whitehouse.gov/the_press_office/Remarks-by-the-President-at-the-Summit-of-the-Americas-Opening-Ceremony.

11. Bonnie Goldstein, "What Was Alan Gross Doing in Havana?" *Politics Daily*, February 11, 2010, http://www.politicsdaily.com/2010/02/11/what-was-alan-gross-doing-in-havana/.

12. Mary Murray, "Cuban Musicians Get U.S. Encore," *MSNBC*, November 3, 2009, http://worldblog.nbcnews.com/_news/2009/11/03/4376225-cuban-musicians-get-us-encore.

13. Silvio Rodríguez has been one of Cuba's most prominent singers since the late 1960s, when his folk-rock style and innovative songwriting developed a following on the island as part of the *nueva trova* movement, which combined folk music with revolutionary political content. Rodríguez and many other nueva trova musicians were influenced by the North American folk revival music of artists like Bob Dylan and Pete Seeger. For more information on Rodríguez and nueva trova, see Robin Moore, *Music and Revolution: Cultural Change in Socialist Cuba* (Berkeley: University of California Press, 2006), 145.

14. Silvio Rodríguez, "Letter written by Silvio Rodríguez to Pete Seeger," Peteseeger.net, http://peteseeger.net/wp/?p=160.

15. "Juanes," *Juanes*, http://www.juanes.net/content.bio.

16. William Booth, "Concert for Peace Draws Hundreds of Thousands in Havana," *Washington Post*, September 21, 2009, http://www.washingtonpost.com/wp-dyn/content/article/2009/09/20/AR2009092000739.html.

17. "Willy Chirino habla de Juanes," F&F Media, August 12, 2009, http://www.ffmediacorp.com/es/Prensa-2/Comunicados-de-Prensa-5/Willy-Chirino-habla-de-Juanes-12-08-09-199.

18. Jordan Levin, "Juanes: Cuba Concert Is Not About Politics." *Miami Herald*, August 25, 2009.

19. Katia Monteagudo, "Juanes Unwavering on Singing in Havana," *CubaNow*, August 24, 2009, http://www.cubanow.net/pages/loader.php?sec=4&t=2&item=7605.

20. Sara Miller Llana, "Will Massive Juanes Concert in Havana Stir Winds of Change?" *Christian Science Monitor*, September 21, 2009, http://www.csmonitor.com/World/Americas/2009/0921/p06s04-woam.html.

21. Pascal Fletcher, "Cuban exiles change tune on Havana concert—poll," *Reuters*, October 1, 2009, http://www.reuters.com/article/idUSN0126464220091001.

22. Lydia Martin and Jordan Levin, "Cubans flock to Havana plaza for Juanes concert," *Miami Herald*, September 17, 2009.

23. Representative Jim McGovern (MA), "One Million Attend 'Paz Sin Fronteras' Concert," *Congressional Record* 155:134, September 22, 2009.

24. Associated Press, "Kool and the Gang Takes the 'Celebration' to Cuba," MSNBC, December 21, 2009, http://www.msnbc.msn.com/id/34509462/ns/entertainment-music/.

25. Prensa Latina, "Cuba Grants Award to Kool & the Gang," Radio Cadena Agramonte, December 22, 2009, http://www.cadenagramonte.cubaweb.cu/english/index.php?option=com_content&view=article&id=1298&Itemid=14.

26. Frank Oteri, "What It Means to Be an American Composer," NewMusicBox, August 1, 1999, http://www.newmusicbox.org/articles/tania-leon-what-it-means-to-be-an-american-composer/.

27. Career Girls, "Composer/Conductor: 'Alma—What to Listen For,'" YouTube, January 7, 2012, http://www.youtube.com/watch?v=SyRjEoh8Nek.

28. CUNY Newswire, "Tania León Returns to Cuba for Composers Music Fest," City University of New York, September 30, 2010, http://www1.cuny.edu/mu/forum/2010/09/30/tania-leon-returns-to-cuba-for-composers-music-fest/.

29. Personal interaction with author, October 20, 2011. Tania León relayed this information in Bloomington, Indiana, during the conference "Cultural Counterpoints: Examining the Musical Interactions between the US and Latin America," held for the fiftieth anniversary of the Latin American Music Center at Indiana University. This came up in discussion after a paper I presented and a roundtable on Cuban composers in the United States that included León, Ileana Perez-Velazquez, and Orlando Jacinto García.

30. Juan O. Tamayo, "Cuban newspaper breaks ground by publishing names of exiled Cuban artists nominated for Grammys," *Miami Herald*, September 26, 2013, http://www.miamiherald.com/2013/09/26/3653015/cuban-newspaper-breaks-ground.html.

31. OFAC 2011, 20.

32. "The Berklee College of Music Awarded the CubaDisco International Prize," *Cuba Headlines*, May 15, 2011, http://www.cubaheadlines.com/2011/05/15/31309/the_berklee_college_of_music_awarded_the_cubadisco_international_prize.html.

33. For a thorough discussion on the history of the Conjunto Folklórico Nacional de Cuba, its role in the tourism industry, and ethnographic descriptions of studying with the group during the Special Period, see Hagedorn 2001.

34. "FolkCuba," *Conjunto Folklórico Nacional*, http://www.folkcuba.cult.cu/laboratory.htm.

35. OFAC (Office of Foreign Assets Control), US Department of the Treasury, *Comprehensive Guidelines for License Applications to Engage in Travel-Related Transactions Involving Cuba*, April 19, 2011, http://www.treasury.gov/resource-center/sanctions/Programs/Documents/cuba_tr_app.pdf, 20.

36. "Americans Traveling to Cuba in Record Numbers," *World Bulletin*, October 18, 2013, http://www.worldbulletin.net/?aType=haber&ArticleID=120942.

37. OFAC 2011, 30.

38. John McAuliff, "How Long Must We Wait?" *Havana Note*, June 22, 2011, http://thehavananote.com/2011/06/how_long_must_we_wait.

39. Madeline O'Connor, "Obama Bans Irish Musicians from Travelling to Cuba," *Cuba Headlines*, April 12, 2011, http://www.cubaheadlines.com/2011/04/12/30668/obama_bans_irish_musicians_from_travelling_to_cuba.html.

40. Joanne Connolly, interview by author, December 11, 2012.

41. Eizenberg previously organized exchanges between US and Cuban softball leagues and brought the Cuban dance troupe Danza Contemporanea to Boston in 2011.

42. Joanne Connolly, interview by author, December 11, 2012.

43. Without formal diplomatic relations, there is no US embassy or diplomat in Cuba. The Chief of Mission at the US Interests Section (USINT) oversees the activities of the USINT, which are similar to other embassies around the world. Numerous individuals—including scholar Henry Louis Gates, who recorded an episode about Cuba for his PBS miniseries *Black in Latin America*—attended the US Independence Day performance at the chief of mission's home.

44. Colleen Preston, "Coro de Entrevoces," *Cape Cod Online*, October 25, 2012, http://www.capecodonline.com/apps/pbcs.dll/article?AID=/20121025/ENTERTAIN/210260304.

45. Mary Beth Sheridan, "Obama loosens travel restrictions to Cuba," *Washington Post*, January 15, 2011, http://www.washingtonpost.com/wp-dyn/content/article/2011/01/14/AR2011011406748.html.

46. OFAC 2011, 22.

47. Marc Frank, "US-Cuba travel snarled by regulations, politics," *News Daily*, September 12, 2012, http://www.newsdaily.com/stories/bre88b1a9-us-cuba-usa-travel/.

48. Larry Habegger and Laurie Weed, "World watch," *Chicago Tribune*, September 2, 2012, http://articles.chicagotribune.com/2012-09-02/travel/ct-trav-0902-world-watch-20120902_1_passenger-boat-boat-captains-taxi-boats.

49. Senator Marco Rubio (FL), "Rubio Slams Abuses of Administration's People-to-People Cuba Program," Senate Floor Remarks, YouTube, December 11, 2011, http://www.youtube.com/watch?v=wmCdQAGNK-E.

50. Christine Armario, "Cuba culture trips back on as licenses are renewed," *Associated Press*, October 8, 2012, http://bigstory.ap.org/article/cuba-culture-trips-back-licenses-are-renewed; Frank 2012, "US-Cuba travel snarled by regulations, politics."

51. "Havana Jazz Festival," *Cross Cultural Journeys Foundation*, http://crossculturaljourneys.com/cuba_2013_12_18_23_jazz.pdf.

52. Ileana Ros-Lehtinen, "Ros-Lehtinen and Díaz-Balart Ask OFAC about Beyonce and Jay-Z Trip to Cuba," House.gov, April 5, 2013, http://ros-lehtinen.house.gov/press-release/ros-lehtinen-and-diaz-balart-ask-ofac-about-beyonce-and-jay-z-trip-cuba.

53. Erin McPike, "Treasury says Beyoncé and Jay-Z's trip was approved," CNN, April 9, 2013, http://politicalticker.blogs.cnn.com/2013/04/09/treasury-says-beyonce-and-jay-zs-trip-was-approved/.

54. Jay-Z, "Open Letter," Soundcloud recording, April 11, 2013, https://soundcloud.com/life-times/jay-z-open-letter-1.

55. The White House, "Remarks by The President at The White House Correspondents' Association Dinner," Office of the Press Secretary, April 27, 2013, http://www.white house.gov/the-press-office/2013/04/27/remarks-president-white-house-correspondents -association-dinner.

56. William Gibson, "Jay-Z and Beyoncé tour stokes desire to visit Cuba," *South Florida Sun-Sentinel*, June 2, 2013, http://www.sun-sentinel.com/fl-cuba-travel-congressional-push -20130602,0,7448204.story; Kia Makarechi, "Jay-Z, Beyonce's Cuba Trip Wasn't Approved by Obama," *Huffington Post*, June 19, 2013, http://www.huffingtonpost.com/2013/06/ 19/jay-z-beyonce-cuba-trip-obama_n_3467984.html; Alexa Van Sickle, "Beyonce gate: The Real Problem with Travel to Cuba," *Atlantic*, April 12, 2013, http://www.theatlantic.com/ international/archive/2013/04/beyoncegate-the-real-problem-with-travel-to-cuba/274925/.

57. News, *Tania León*, http://www.tanialeon.com/news.html.

CHAPTER 3

1. Jacira Castro, "Los Van Van," *Salsa Power*, October 10, 1999, http://www.salsapower .com/concerts/losvanvan.htm.

2. During my first trip to Havana, I met a dance instructor who used that DVD to accompany a salsa lesson and stopped to point out the protesters.

3. Timba music draws from previous Cuban dance genres like son and has a greater focus on Afro-Cuban elements like the rumba clave instead of the son clave. It sometimes uses rhythms and instruments from Santería. It also uses a drum set, which is rare in Cuban music, and draws heavily on international popular musics particularly rap, funk, soul, and rock and roll. For more information, see Perna 2005.

4. Silvana Paternostro, "Juan Formell," *BOMB* 70 (Winter 2000), http://bombsite.com/ issues/70/articles/2294.

5. Jordan Levin, "Los Van Van Leaves Politics Behind for Miami, Key West Concerts," *Miami Herald*, January 30, 2010.

6. Larry Rohter, "Miami, the Hollywood of Latin America," *New York Times*, August 18, 1996.

7. As a result of the major recording labels and studios in Miami recording music for distribution throughout Latin America, artists had to adopt the Latin Pop sound synonymous with the city. For more information on this homogenization of Spanish-language pop music, see Party 2008.

8. Jennifer LeClaire, "Latin America Makes Miami Major Entertainment Player," *Christian Science Monitor*, August 17, 1998, 3.

9. Alejandra Alvarez, "Gloria Estefan Weighs In on Juanes' Concert in Cuba," *Guanabee*, August 28, 2009, http://guanabee.com/gloria-estefan-weighs-in-on-juanes-concert-in-cuba -whi-504406026.

10. Damien Cave, "Concert Plans in Havana Start Furor in Miami," *New York Times*, September 18, 2009.

11. Pascal Fletcher, "Cuban exiles change tune on Havana concert—poll," Reuters, October 1, 2009, http://www.reuters.com/article/idUSN0126464220091001.

12. Christina Veiga, "Bell: I Didn't Cancel Concert of Musicians from Cuba," *Miami Herald*, April 12, 2011.

13. Jordan Levin, "Homestead-Miami Speedway loses court battle over cancelation of Cuban music festival," *Miami Herald*, February 14, 2013.

14. Veiga, "Bell: I Didn't Cancel Concert of Musicians from Cuba," 2011.

15. Kristina Puga, "Global Cuba Fest bridges the US and Cuba through music," NBC Latino, March 16, 2013, http://nbclatino.com/2013/03/16/video-global-cuba-fest-bridges-the-u-s-and-cuba-through-music/.

16. Neil de la Flor, "Ivette Cepeda opens Global Cuba Fest," Knight Arts, March 7, 2013, http://www.knightarts.org/community/miami/ivette-cepeda-opens-global-cuba-fest.

17. Alexandra Gratereaux, "No Protests Against Cuban Artists at Miami Global Cuba Festival," Fox News Latino, March 13, 2013, http://latino.foxnews.com/latino/entertainment/2013/03/13/no-protests-against-cuban-artists-at-miami-global-cuba-festival/.

18. Christina Puig, "Cuba Nostalgia: Festival Takes People Back to Pre-Castro Cuba," Fox News Latino, May 18, 2012.

19. The results of the 2011 FIU Cuba Poll and previous polls are available from Florida International University's Cuban Research Institute at http://cri.fiu.edu/research/cuba-poll/.

20. Oteri, "What It Means to Be an American Composer," 1999.

21. Carolina Gonzalez, "Four-month Long ¡Sí Cuba! Festival Puts on a United Front," *New York Daily News*, April 13, 2011, http://www.nydailynews.com/latino/2011/04/13/2011-04-13_cubasi14.html#ixzz1b9OsyKkA.

22. Emily Canal, "Travel restrictions might prevent some artists from attending Si Cuba festival," *Pavement Pieces*, March 20, 2011, http://pavementpieces.com/travel-restrictions-might-prevent-some-artists-from-attending-si-cuba-festival/.

23. Jon Pareles, "Mix-and-Match Ensemble Erases Borders with Enthusiasm," *New York Times*, December 2, 2012.

24. Carnegie Hall, "Chucho Valdés: Voices of Cuba," Voices from Latin America, http://www.carnegiehall.org/latinamerica/cuba/.

25. Fidel Castro, "Speech to intellectuals," Castro Speech Database, http://lanic.utexas.edu/project/castro/db/1961/19610630.html.

26. The New York Philharmonic tried to visit Cuba on two separate occasions after restrictions were eased in 2009, but plans failed because of licensing issues with the OFAC. Financial backers of the exchange were initially told that they could join the musicians in Cuba, but travel licenses could only be secured for performers. As a result, the New York Philharmonic could not secure the funding needed for the trip. Daniel J. Wakin, "New York Philharmonic Won't Go to Cuba Without Patrons," *New York Times*, October 1, 2009, http://www.nytimes.com/2009/10/02/arts/music/02orchestra.html; Daniel J. Wakin, "New York Philharmonic Cancels Cuba Trip," *New York Times*, April 5, 2011, http://artsbeat.blogs.nytimes.com/2011/04/05/new-york-philharmonic-cancels-cuba-trip/.

27. David Fleshler, "National Symphony Orchestra of Cuba to make South Florida debut in West Palm Beach," *South Florida Classical Review*, November 1, 2012, http://south-

floridaclassicalreview.com/2012/11/national-symphony-orchestra-of-cuba-to-make-south-florida-debut-in-west-palm-beach/.

28. Ruben Rosario, "Symphony tour a thrill for Cuban transplant living in White Bear Lake," *Twin Cities Pioneer Press*, September 29, 2012, https://www.twincities.com/2012/09/29/ruben-rosario-symphony-tour-a-thrill-for-cuban-transplant-living-in-white-bear-lake/.

29. Nachito Herrera, interview with author, December 8, 2013.

30. Betty Webster, "Cuban musicians get Kansas City assist after musical emergency," KCTV, October 17, 2012, http://www.kctv5.com/story/19840955/cuban-musicians-get-kansas-city-assist-after.

31. "Rep. Castor's Statement on Florida Orchestra's Trip to Cuba," US Representative Cathy Castor, press release, June 1, 2011, http://castor.house.gov/news/documentsingle.aspx?DocumentID=244025.

32. Fleshler, "National Symphony Orchestra of Cuba to make South Florida debut in West Palm Beach."

33. Rosario, "Symphony tour a thrill for Cuban transplant living in White Bear Lake."

34. Clark Morris, interview with author, October 16, 2012; Julie Schwietert Collazo, "National Symphony Orchestra of Cuba nears end of first US tour," Fox News Latino, November 12, 2012, http://latino.foxnews.com/latino/lifestyle/2012/11/10/national-symphony-orchestra-cuba-nears-end-1st-us-tour/.

35. Descriptions of performances and audience interactions are primarily based on fieldwork conducted by the author at the tour performances in Kansas City, Urbana, West Palm Beach, and at the 2012 Havana Jazz Festival. The author obtained programs for other concerts on the tour from staff at the performance venues and Arts Management Associates.

36. Benjamin Treuhaft, "About Ben," http://tunerben.com/about-ben/.

37. Diana Tsen, "HRO's Tour to Cuba," Harvard-Radcliffe Orchestra, 2011, http://www.hcs.harvard.edu/~hro/cuba.

38. Clark Morris, interview with author, October 16, 2012.

39. Jodi Duckett, "National Symphony Orchestra of Cuba makes enthusiastic debut in Allentown," *Lehigh Valley Music Blog*, October 24, 2012, http://blogs.mcall.com/lehighvalleymusic/2012/10/national-symphony-orchestra-of-cuba-makes-enthusiastic-debut-in-allentown.html.

40. Collazo, "National Symphony Orchestra of Cuba nears end of first U.S. tour."

41. Parnass, "Three Years After Arrest, American Alan Gross Still Jailed in Cuba."

42. Parnass, "Three Years After Arrest, American Alan Gross Still Jailed in Cuba."

43. Fleshler, "National Symphony Orchestra of Cuba to make South Florida debut in West Palm Beach."

44. Nachito Herrera, interview with author, December 8, 2013.

45. Yurchak explains: "This strategy functioned as a form of politics, albeit one that, paradoxically, was based on suspending the political (as defined by the state) and locating oneself in the state's zone of indistinction. We may call this the politics of indistinction to contrast it with the better-known politics of opposition and resistance. Although the relationship to power based on the politics of indistinction is not one of resistance (at least as it is usually understood, as opposition to power), it does not promote stasis either. In fact, this

relationship to state power in the late Soviet context challenged that power in unexpected ways and ultimately contributed to undermining it."

46. Manny Garcia, Jordan Levin, and Peter Whoriskey, "The Band Plays On as Protest Fails to Deter Van Van's Fans," *Miami Herald*, October 10, 1999.

CHAPTER 4

1. Anthony DePalma, "Cuban Jazz on the March, but With a Canadian Beat," *New York Times*, March 5, 1998.

2. Josef Woodard, "Chucho Valdés: Chief Messenger," *Down Beat* 80, no. 11 (November 2013): 30.

3. *Chico y Rita*, directed by Fernando Trueba, Javier Mariscal, and Tono Errando (Fernando Trueba PC, 2010), DVD.

4. Woodard, "Chucho Valdés: Chief Messenger," 30.

5. Woodard, "Chucho Valdés: Chief Messenger," 28.

6. Jordan Levin, "Bobby Carcasses opened door to jazz in Cuba," *Miami Herald*, February 24, 2010.

7. Levin, "Bobby Carcasses opened door to jazz in Cuba."

8. Although not a jazz band, Cuban dance ensembles like Juan Formell's Los Van Van perform a style that exhibits a clear jazz influence.

9. Larry Rohter, "Jazz and Politics Meet Over the Keyboard," *New York Times*, May 9, 1993.

10. Peter Watrous, "International Dissonance Aside, Harmony in Cuba," *New York Times*, December 24, 1997.

11. "Cronología," http://www.albacultural.org/cronologia.

12. Isaac Peña, interview with author, January 13, 2013.

13. Personal communication, December 21, 2012. Her sister did not share what category of purposeful travel she used.

14. Cuba Explorer Tours provides explanations for how US citizens can legally visit Cuba and resources including letter templates to use for religious, educational, and professional research licenses at http://www.legalcubatravel.com.

15. Paul Cortese, "TCU Jazz Visits Cuba," *Jazz Times*, January 24, 2011, http://jazztimes.com/articles/27077-tcu-jazz-visits-cuba.

16. Lisa Hittle, phone interview, September 27, 2013.

17. The full episode of *It's All Good with Sierra Scott* about the Friends University jazz band's trip to Cuba can be viewed at http://www.youtube.com/watch?v=0a2VZik1px8#t=538.

18. Conner Gorry, email message to author, November 29, 2013.

19. Conner Gorry, "Adventure of the Cuban Virgins: Part I," *Here is Havana*, December 29, 2012, http://hereishavana.com/2012/12/29/adventures-of-the-cuban-virgins-part-i/.

20. Will Magid, interview with author, January 10, 2013.

21. A requinto guitar is smaller than its classical counterpart and is a standard instrument in bolero ensembles.

22. "USINT Honors Jazz Luminary Arturo O'Farrill," US Interests Section Havana, December 18, 2012, http://havana.usint.gov/arturo-reception.html.

23. Ben Ratliff, "Chico O'Farrill, 79, Musician and Leader in Afro-Cuban Jazz," *New York Times*, June 29, 2001; Judy Cantor-Navas, "Chico O'Farrill to be Laid to Rest in Cuba," *Billboard*, November 11, 2016, http://www.billboard.com/articles/columns/latin/7573478/chico-ofarrill-cuba-funeral-jazz-pioneer.

24. Arturo O'Farrill itinerary; Lois Gilbert, email communication, Jazz Programmers' Mailing List, December 1, 2010; Larry Blumenfeld, "NYC Pianist Arturo O'Farrill Finds Himself in Cuba, and Brings His Father Home," *Village Voice*, February 23, 2011, http://www.villagevoice.com/music/nyc-pianist-arturo-ofarrill-finds-himself-in-cuba-and-brings-his-father-home-6430123.

25. Blumenfeld 2011.

26. "Muñequitos de Matanzas and Michel Herrera to Perform at the Chico O'Farrill School of Jazz," *Cuba Headlines*, May 14, 2011, http://www.cubaheadlines.com/2011/05/14/31292/munequitos_de_matanzas_and_michel_herrera_to_perform_at_the_chico_ofarrill_school_o.

27. Afro Latin Jazz Alliance, "The Afro Latin Jazz Alliance's Cultural Diplomacy Initiatives Unite Cuban and American Composers for GRAMMY® Award-Winner Arturo O'Farrill's New Album," press release, December 12, 2014, http://www.afrolatinjazz.org/releases.html.

28. "Statement by the President on Cuba Policy Changes," White House, December 17, 2014, https://www.whitehouse.gov/the-press-office/2014/12/17/statement-president-cuba-policy-changes.

29. Liner notes, *Cuba: The Conversation Continues*, Arturo O'Farrill and the Afro Latin Jazz Orchestra, Motéma Music, 2015; "Arturo O'Farrill & the Afro Latin Jazz Orchestra—Cuba: The Conversation Continues," YouTube, August 7, 2015, https://www.youtube.com/watch?v=1JCN7txmhCo.

30. "¿Quiénes Somos?" Abdala Studios, http://www.abdala.cu/quienessomos.aspx.

31. Upon receiving the 2016 Grammy Award for Best Instrumental Composition, O'Farrill released a statement saying, "This music is my interpretation of jazz: it's the idea Dizzy Gillespie first proposed when he said there was no difference between Latin and jazz, just a music he called universal. The suite is musically multilingual, drawing from Africa, Peru, Cuba, India, and the United States. It is montunos and ragas, tone clusters and blues. It is a nod to the past, performed now, yet firmly rooted in the future. The piece demonstrates that artistic expression that is not easily defined is the ever-changing destination of a journey without musical borders." Afro Latin Jazz Alliance, "The Afro Latin Jazz Alliance Proudly Announces Arturo O'Farrill and the Afro Latin Jazz Orchestra's 'The Afro Latin Jazz Suite' Wins the GRAMMY® Award in the 'Best Instrumental Composition, Category," press release, February 17, 2016, https://www.afrolatinjazz.org/the-afro-latin-jazz-alliance-proudly-announces-arturo-ofarrill-and-the-afro-latin-jazz-orchestras-the-afro-latin-jazz-suite-wins-the-grammy-award-i/.

32. Festejo is a celebratory Afro-Peruvian dance genre typically performed on a variety of percussion instruments and guitar.

33. Kabir Sehgal, liner notes to *Cuba: The Conversation Continues*, Motéma Music, 2015.

34. Levin, "Bobby Carcasses opened door to jazz in Cuba."

CHAPTER 5

1. Conner Gorry, email to author, November 29, 2013.

2. Ignacio "Nachito" Herrera, interview with author, December 8, 2013.

3. Heartland Concert Artists managed Nachito Herrera and all three of the singers, which is how they were connected to the Cubadisco trip.

4. Melissa Deal, interview with author, September 26, 2013.

5. Norah Long, interview with author, November 25, 2013; Of the three singers who participated in the Cubadisco trip, I was only able to arrange an interview with Long.

6. Norah Long, interview with author, November 25, 2013.

7. Melissa Deal, interview with author, September 26, 2013.

8. Norah Long, interview with author, November 25, 2013.

9. Melissa Deal, interview with author, September 26, 2013.

10. Euan Kerr, "After Thaw, Minnesota Orchestra Returns To Cuba," National Public Radio, *Weekend Edition Sunday*, May 17, 2015, http://www.npr.org/sections/deceptivecadence/2015/05/17/406993869/after-thaw-minnesota-orchestra-returns-to-cuba.

11. The Minneapolis Symphony Orchestra returned to Cuba for a second time in 1930.

12. Gordon Royce, "Jan. 15: Three-year Minnesota Orchestra deal ends 15-month lockout," *Star Tribune*, January 18, 2014, http://www.startribune.com/jan-15-minnesota-orchestra-deal-ends-15-month-lockout/240153421/.

13. "Kevin Smith appointed Minnesota Orchestra President and CEO," Minnesota Orchestra, press release, November 12, 2014, http://www.minnesotaorchestra.org/about/learn-more/press-room/1072-kevin-smith-president-and-ceo.

14. Classical Movements, "Cultural Diplomacy," http://www.classicalmovements.com/outreach.php.

15. Neeta Helms, interview with author, April 21, 2017.

16. Neeta Helms, interview with author, April 21, 2017.

17. Jenna Ross, "Marilyn Carlson Nelson named chair-elect of Minnesota Orchestra board," *Star Tribune*, September 27, 2016, http://www.startribune.com/marilyn-carlson-nelson-elected-board-chairwoman-of-minnesota-orchestra/394832811/; Euan Kerr, "'Crazy idea,' Cuban ties sped MN Orchestra's return to Havana," MPR News, May 11, 2015.

18. Neeta Helms, interview with author, April 21, 2017.

19. Neeta Helms, interview with author, April 21, 2017.

20. Because infrastructure was not in place to send the signal directly to the United States, the signal was first sent to Europe and then beamed to the United States for broadcast. This extensive effort required collaboration between engineers in Cuba, Switzerland, and the United States. "Listen to the Minnesota Orchestra perform in Cuba, May 16, 2015," Classical MPR, May 19, 2015, http://www.classicalmpr.org/story/2015/05/19/minnesota-orchestra-in-cuba-second-evening.

21. Neeta Helms, interview with author, April 21, 2017.

22. Jeff Baenen, "Trip to Cuba represents Minnesota Orchestra's revival," Associated Press, May 9, 2015.

23. Eileen Cunniffe, "Formerly Locked Out Minnesota Orchestra Musicians Invest in Management," *Nonprofit Quarterly*, December 7, 2015, https://nonprofitquarterly.org/2015/12/07/formerly-locked-out-minnesota-orchestra-musicians-invest-in-management.

24. Ross, "Marilyn Carlson Nelson named chair-elect of Minnesota Orchestra board."

25. Classical Movements, "Minnesota Orchestra Makes Historic Tour to Cuba," *Pax Musica*, 2015 Touring Year, http://www.classicalmovements.com/pax-musica-newsletter-2015.htm.

26. *Cuba Classics 2: Dancing with the Enemy*, CD, Sire, 1991.

27. OFAC 2011, 30.

28. Isaac Peña, interview with author, January 13, 2013.

29. Smith, "Voyage of the Jammed," 17.

30. Pilgrimage can also be implicit, as in the case described by Titon (1999) in which a group of singers was humbled and grateful for being invited to sing in the nation's capital, and they reciprocated by becoming tourists and paying homage to the historic sites the trip made available to them.

31. "Cuba: Music Brings Us Together," *It's All Good with Sierra Scott*, August 25, 2013, http://www.youtube.com/watch?v=oa2VZik1px8#t=538.

32. Chi Saito and Brenda K. Spevak-Saito, interview with author, October 6, 2013.

33. Pete Seeger's visit to Cuba in 1971, described in chapter 1, is an example of this type of pilgrimage.

34. Senator Marco Rubio (FL), "Rubio Slams Abuses of Administration's People-to-People Cuba Program."

35. White House, "Reaching Out to the Cuban People," Office of the Press Secretary, January 14, 2011, http://www.whitehouse.gov/the-press-office/2011/01/14/reaching-out-cuban-people.

36. White House, "Reaching Out to the Cuban People."

37. Rubio, "Rubio Slams Abuses of Administration's People-to-People Cuba Program."

38. "Obama welcomes controversial Havana concert," AFP, September 20, 2009, http://www.google.com/hostednews/afp/article/ALeqM5jjTxZZPfrNOIVuIDu99nwmCXgfCA.

39. Will Magid, interview with author, January 10, 2013.

40. Norah Long, interview with author, November 25, 2013.

41. Sam Bergman, "Cuba Diary: Leaving Havana," Minnesota Orchestra, https://www.minnesotaorchestra.org/showcase/20-cuba-diary-leaving-la-habana; Euan Kerr, "Cuba: Final thoughts," Minnesota Public Radio News, tumblr, May 22, 2015, http://mprnews.tumblr.com/post/119612203189/cuba-final-thoughts.

42. For additional information on the importance of participation in music and participational vs. presentational music making, see Turino 2010, 23–65.

43. Lisa Hittle, interview with author, September 27, 2013.

44. Neeta Helms, interview with author, April 21, 2017.

45. Ignacio "Nachito" Herrera, interview with author, December 8, 2013.

46. Neeta Helms, interview with author, April 21, 2017.

47. "Classical Movements Commissions: the Eric Daniel Helms New Music Program," Classical Movements, http://www.classicalmovements.com/commissions.htm; "RIMAS TROPICALES by Tania Leon," YouTube, September 21, 2011, https://youtu.be/NEK7O599aNo.

48. Norah Long, interview with author, November 25, 2013.

49. Neeta Helms, interview with author, April 21, 2017.

CHAPTER 6

1. White House, "Statement by the President on the Anniversary of Cuba Policy Changes," December 17, 2015, https://obamawhitehouse.archives.gov/the-press-office/2015/12/17/statement-president-anniversary-cuba-policy-changes.

2. Cuban Assets Control Regulations, 31 C.F.R. §515.567 (2016), https://www.ecfr.gov/cgi-bin/text-idx?SID=15c2cb4cf0027a0d5caa365196581b93&mc=true&node=pt31.3.515.

3. Cuban Assets Control Regulations, 31 C.F.R. §515.545 (2016), https://www.ecfr.gov/cgi-bin/text-idx?SID=15c2cb4cf0027a0d5caa365196581b93&mc=true&node=pt31.3.515.

4. *The Fate of the Furious*, directed by F. Gary Gray (Universal Pictures, 2017); Paul Heath, "'Fast 8' officially starts shooting in Cuba," *Hollywood News*, April 29, 2016, http://www.thehollywoodnews.com/2016/04/29/fast-8-officially-starts-shooting-cuba/.

5. US Treasury Department Office of Public Affairs, "March 2016 FACT SHEET: Treasury and Commerce Announce Significant Amendments to the Cuba Sanctions Regulations," US Department of the Treasury Resource Center, https://www.treasury.gov/resource-center/sanctions/Programs/Documents/cuba_fact_sheet_03152016.pdf.

6. "March 2016 FACT SHEET: Treasury and Commerce Announce Significant Amendments to the Cuba Sanctions Regulations."

7. *Give Me Future*, directed by Austin Peters (Matador Content, 2017), Apple Music.

8. The advisory board for Musicabana includes Cuban musicians Chucho Valdés and Pablo Milanés; Brazilian musician Carlinhos Brown; Spanish singer-songwriter Joaquin Sabina; US songwriter and film composer Robert Kraft; US musicologist and author Ned Sublette; and US-based event, festival, and concert producers Ashley Capps, Michael Lang, Christopher Wangro, Jill Newman, and Fabian Alsultany; "The Foundation," Musicabana, http://musicabana.com/the-foundation/.

9. Judy Cantor-Navas, "The Cuban-American Musical Detente: Inside a Native Son's 40-Year Road to Havana's Newest Festival," *Billboard*, March 1, 2016, https://www.billboard.com/articles/business/6897168/cuban-american-detente-fabien-pisana-40-year-road-musicabana-major-lazer.

10. Suárez, who is one-half of the duo I.A. Electronica, was also a founder of the ElectroBus mentioned in chapter 4.

11. *Give Me Future* (2017).

12. Ben Rhodes, Obama's Deputy National Security Advisor who was instrumental in the negotiations between the United States and Cuba, and the Obama social media team shared daily stories of the President's trip through the social media platform Medium.

They featured images by official White House photographers including many of President Obama meeting with the Cuban public.

13. "Obama's Itinerary in Cuba," *New York Times*, March 20, 2016, https://www.nytimes.com/interactive/projects/cp/international/obama-in-cuba/obamas-itinerary-in-cuba; Ben Rhodes, "Engaging the Cuban People: Here's What President Obama Will Be Doing in Cuba," Medium.com, March 17, 2016, https://medium.com/@rhodes44/engaging-the-cuban-people-here-s-what-president-obama-will-be-doing-in-cuba-3675a05cc6e4.

14. "Remarks by President Obama to the People of Cuba," White House, March 22, 2016, https://obamawhitehouse.archives.gov/the-press-office/2016/03/22/remarks-president-obama-people-cuba.

15. "Remarks by President Obama and President Raul Castro of Cuba in a Joint Press Conference," US Embassy in Cuba, March 21, 2016, https://cu.usembassy.gov/remarks-president-obama-president-raul-castro-cuba-joint-press-conference/.

16. Interview, Neeta Helms, April 21, 2017.

17. Camila Cabello, Twitter post, March 21, 2016, 1:51 AM, https://twitter.com/Camila_Cabello/status/711792265971171328; Camila Cabello, Twitter post, March 21, 2016, 1:58 AM, https://twitter.com/Camila_Cabello/status/711794089264422912.

18. Arturo Arias-Polo, "Artistas cubanos opinan sobre la visita de Obama a la isla," *El Nuevo Herald*, 19 March 2016, http://www.elnuevoherald.com/entretenimiento/gente/article66971512.html.

19. Arias-Polo, "Artistas cubanos opinan sobre la visita de Obama a la isla."

20. Monique O. Madan, "Protesters against Obama's Cuba trip take to streets in Little Havana," *Miami Herald*, March 20, 2016, http://www.miamiherald.com/news/local/community/miami-dade/little-havana/article67200622.html.

21. Bendixen and Amandi, "Channel 23 Local Issues Poll: Survey of Miami-Dade County Voters—May 2016," http://bendixenandamandi.com/wp-content/uploads/2016/05/Miami-Dade-County-Local-Issues-Poll-Part-3.pdf.

22. "Darryl Jones," Rolling Stones, http://www.rollingstones.com/artist/darryl-jones/.

23. "The Dead Daisies Head to Cuba—Rock for Peace," Dead Daisies, press release, February 9, 2015, https://thedeaddaisies.com/the-dead-daisies-head-to-cuba/; "The Dead Daisies—Revolución [Documentary Film]," YouTube, August 15, 2015, https://www.youtube.com/watch?v=FEriI95XjmI.

24. "Rolling Stones frontman Mick Jagger visits Cuba to scout out concert venues, report says," Fox News, October 6, 2015, http://www.foxnews.com/entertainment/2015/10/06/rolling-stones-frontman-mick-jagger-visits-cuba-reportedly-scouting-out-concert.html.

25. *¡Olé, Olé, Olé! A Trip Across Latin America*, directed by Paul Dugdale (Eagle Rock Entertainment, 2016).

26. Cubadebate, "Coro Entrevoces acompañará a The Rolling Stones en La Habana," *Escambray*, March 19, 2016, http://www.escambray.cu/2016/coro-entrevoces-acompanara-a-the-rolling-stones-en-la-habana/.

27. *Havana Moon*, directed by Paul Dugdale (Eagle Rock Entertainment, 2016).

28. *Give Me Future*.

29. Glenn Garvin, "Meet the lawyer who paid for the Rolling Stones concert in Havana," *Miami Herald*, March 29, 2016, http://www.miamiherald.com/news/nation-world/world/americas/cuba/article68883632.html.

30. Pisani organized the Musicabana Festival for May 2016, which promised "a once-in-a-lifetime experience with an extraordinary multi-genre bill boasting over 25 artists, bands and global DJs." Delays in approvals for participating artists and logistical challenges resulted in a much smaller festival than was initially promised, and it did not have the impact of the earlier events. After having supported the Rolling Stones concert, Curaçao lawyer Gregory Elias was approached to also fund the Musicabana Festival, which he did. Judy Cantor-Navas, "Cuban Festival Musicabana Scaled Down Significantly After Approval Delays," *Billboard*, May 4, 2016, https://www.billboard.com/articles/columns/music-festivals/7356846/cuba-musicabana-scaled-down-goverment-delays.

31. Sarah Stephens, "Final Report: President's Committee on the Arts and the Humanities (PCAH)," Center for Democracy in the Americas, May 19, 2016.

32. Executive Order 12367 of June 15, 1982, President's Committee on the Arts and the Humanities, Code of Federal Regulations, title 3 (1982): 188, https://www.archives.gov/federal-register/codification/executive-order/12367.html.

33. "What We Do," Turnaround Arts, http://turnaroundarts.kennedy-center.org/what-we-do/.

34. The Center for Democracy in the Americas is a non-partisan 501(c)3 not-for-profit organization that promotes US engagement with Cuba. The organization had previously organized delegations to Cuba for members of the US Senate and House of Representatives. According to their website, since its founding in 2006, "CDA has stood for the proposition that normalizing relations with Cuba is in the US national interest and offers the best opportunity for Cubans to write the next chapter in their own country's future. Cuba is at the center of our work because forging constructive US-Cuba relations will have a beneficial and lasting impact on both US and Cuban societies, and it sends an important signal to Latin America that the United States is ready to engage positively with the region and its people." democracyinamericas.org/about-us/.

35. Stephens, "Final Report: President's Committee on the Arts and the Humanities," 3.

36. President's Committee on the Arts and the Humanities, "United States Cultural Mission to Cuba 2016," https://www.arts.gov/sites/default/files/Delegation_Guests_Staff_Letterhead_0.pdf.

37. President's Committee on the Arts and the Humanities, "United States Cultural Mission to Cuba 2016."

38. Usher, Twitter post, April 20, 2016, 1:00 PM, https://twitter.com/Usher/status/722832348220366848.

39. Stephens, "Final Report: President's Committee on the Arts and the Humanities," 5–6.

40. George Stevens Jr., "Artists Welcome in Cuba," Huffington Post, April 27, 2016, https://www.huffingtonpost.com/george-stevens/artists-welcome-in-cuba_b_9785244.html; Stephens, "Final Report: President's Committee on the Arts and the Humanities," 6.

41. The English lyrics matched the version of the song translated by Jackson Browne for his 2014 album *Standing in the Breach*.

42. "'Muros y Puertas' Carlos Varela y Dave Matthews en la Fabrica de Arte Cubano," YouTube, April 23, 2016, https://www.youtube.com/watch?v=UiNtkCpCEnk.

43. "LISTEN: A Cuban Protest Singer On The State Of US-Cuba Relations," *All Things Considered*, National Public Radio, March 27, 2015, https://www.npr.org/templates/transcript/transcript.php?storyId=395799526.

44. National Endowment for the Arts, "Closing Ceremony Remarks from Havana, Cuba Delivered to Cuban Hosts, Members of the United States Cultural Mission to Cuba 2016, and Media," April 21, 2016, https://www.arts.gov/sites/default/files/CHU_Closing_Ceremony_Remarks.pdf.

45. National Endowment for the Arts, "Closing Ceremony Remarks"; "NEA Commits $100,000 for US/Cuban Artist Exchange Programs," National Endowment for the Arts, April 21, 2016, https://www.arts.gov/news/2016/nea-commits-100000-uscuban-artist-exchange-programs.

46. The Turnaround Arts initiative in Cuba never came to fruition. The May 2016 Final Report of the Cultural Mission stated: "the Turnaround Arts announcement was proffered as final before the Cuban government had fully agreed. Consequently, for PCAH to designate Cuba as the home of the first international Turnaround School and Cuban musician Carlos Varela as the first international Turnaround Artist, PCAH will need to engage the Cuban government in further discussions before this project is able to move forward." Stephens, "Final Report: President's Committee on the Arts and the Humanities," 8.

47. Stephens, "Final Report: President's Committee on the Arts and the Humanities," 8.

48. Baracoa is located near the eastern tip of Cuba and was the oldest Spanish settlement on the island, while St. Augustine is the oldest continuously occupied Spanish settlement in the continental United States. The organization shortened their name in 2008 to reflect a changed mandate that included Cuba more widely.

49. Jo McIntyre, personal interview, September 27, 2015.

50. Yosi and the performers originally envisioned a performance that spotlighted the music of old Florida, including songs by Florida folk musicians such as Gamble Rogers and arrangements of tunes that had been recorded by folklorists Stetson Kennedy and Zora Neale Hurston.

51. Cuban News Agency, "Michelle Obama learns about Cuban education system," Granma, March 21, 2016, http://en.granma.cu/obama-in-cuba/2016-03-21/michelle-obama-learns-about-cuban-education-system.

52. Nick Miroff and Sarah L. Voisin, "Cuba's Art Factory aims for industrial-scale hipness," *Washington Post*, December 29, 2015, https://www.washingtonpost.com/news/worldviews/wp/2015/12/29/cubas-art-factory-aims-for-industrial-scale-hipness/?noredirect=on&utm_term=.8247314cef1b.

53. "Cuba Attracts Record Visitors in 2016," *Cuba Journal*, 31 December 2016, http://cubajournal.co/cuba-attracts-record-visitors-in-2016/; Aili McConnon, "Cuba's New Luxury Hotels Look to Lure Waves of U.S. Tourists," *New York Times*, May 9, 2017, https://www

.nytimes.com/2017/05/09/realestate/commercial/cubas-new-luxury-hotels-look-to-lure-waves-of-us-tourists.html.

54. ONEI (Oficina Nacional de Estadística e Información), Cuba's national statistics and information office, calculated the average monthly income for 2016 as 740 pesos. At the rate of 24 Cuban pesos to 1 CUC, the median income can be calculated as 30.8 CUCs per month. "Salario Medio en Cifras. Cuba 2016," ONEI, Centro de Gestión de la Información Económica, Medioambiental y Social, April 2017, http://www.one.cu/publicaciones/03estadisticassociales/Salario%20Medio%20en%20Cifras%20Cuba%202016/Salario%20Medio%20en%20Cifras%20Cuba%202016.pdf.

55. "Freedom on the Net 2016: Cuba," Freedom House, May 2016, https://freedomhouse.org/report/freedom-net/2016/cuba; "Freedom on the Net 2017: Cuba," Freedom House, May 2017, https://freedomhouse.org/report/freedom-net/2016/cuba.

56. "Freedom on the Net 2017: Cuba."

57. Azam Ahmed, "Cuba's Surge in Tourism Keeps Food Off Residents' Plates," *New York Times*, December 8, 2016, https://www.nytimes.com/2016/12/08/world/americas/cuba-fidel-castro-food-tourism.html.

58. Abel Fernández, "Cuba suspends new licenses for private eateries and warns of tighter control," *Miami Herald*, October 17, 2016, http://www.miamiherald.com/news/nation-world/world/americas/cuba/article108758342.html.

59. Jeremy Diamond, "Trump shifts on Cuba, says he would reverse Obama's deal," CNN, September 16, 2016, https://www.cnn.com/2016/09/16/politics/donald-trump-cuba/index.html.

60. Ralph Ellis and Patrick Oppman, "Fidel Castro laid to rest in private funeral," CNN, December 4, 2016, https://www.cnn.com/2016/12/04/americas/fidel-castro-funeral-burial/index.html.

61. Joey Flechas, Carli Teproff, and Ariana Figueroa, "More than 1,000 in Miami rally for reform in Cuba after Fidel Castro," *Miami Herald*, November 30, 2016, http://www.miamiherald.com/news/nation-world/world/americas/fidel-castro-en/article118078168.html.

62. Ben Rhodes, "Charting a New Course with Cuba: Two Years of Progress," post on Medium.com, December 17, 2016, https://medium.com/@rhodes44/charting-a-new-course-with-cuba-two-years-of-progress-a313982284d9.

63. Judy Cantor-Navas, "Chico O'Farrill to Be Laid to Rest in Cuba," *Billboard*, November 11, 2016, https://www.billboard.com/articles/columns/latin/7573478/chico-ofarrill-cuba-funeral-jazz-pioneer.

EPILOGUE

1. Jeff Smith, phone interview, September 21, 2016.
2. Richard Blanco, phone interview, October 10, 2016.
3. Blanco, phone interview.
4. Blanco, phone interview.
5. Melissa Deal, interview with author, September 26, 2013.
6. Lisa Hittle, interview with author, September 27, 2013.

7. "Statement by the President on Cuban Immigration Policy," White House, January 12, 2017, https://obamawhitehouse.archives.gov/the-press-office/2017/01/12/statement-president-cuban-immigration-policy.

8. "Remarks by President Trump on the Policy of the United States Towards Cuba," White House, June 16, 2017, https://www.whitehouse.gov/briefings-statements/remarks-president-trump-policy-united-states-toward-cuba/.

9. "Remarks by President Trump on the Policy of the United States Towards Cuba."

10. Kal Penn, Twitter post, August 18, 2017, 10:08 AM, https://twitter.com/kalpenn/status/898547257062174724.

11. Matthew Lee and Michael Weissenstein, "Hearing loss of US diplomats in Cuba blamed on covert device," Associated Press, August 10, 2017, https://www.apnews.com/51828908c6c84d78a29e833d0aae10aa.

12. Jonah M. Kessel, Melissa Chan, and John Woo, "How an Alleged Sonic Attack Shaped U.S. Policy on Cuba," *New York Times*, Times Documentaries, https://nyti.ms/2J7HQHH.

13. "Trump says he believes Cuba responsible for attacks that hurt U.S. diplomats," Reuters, October 16, 2017, https://www.reuters.com/article/us-usa-cuba-trump/trump-says-he-believes-cuba-responsible-for-attacks-that-hurt-u-s-diplomats-idUSKBN1CL2RH.

14. "FACT SHEET: Treasury, Commerce, and State Implement Changes to the Cuba Sanctions Rules," US Department of the Treasury, November 8, 2017, https://www.treasury.gov/resource-center/sanctions/Programs/Documents/cuba_fact_sheet_11082017.pdf.

15. Alex Ward, "John Bolton just gave an 'Axis of Evil' speech about Latin America," *Vox*, November 1, 2018, https://www.vox.com/world/2018/11/1/18052338/bolton-cuba-venezuela-nicaragua-speech-troika-tyranny.

16. Niraj Chokshi and Frances Robles, "Trump Administration Announces New Restrictions on Dealing With Cuba," *New York Times*, April 17, 2019, https://www.nytimes.com/2019/04/17/world/americas/cuba-trump-travel-lawsuits.html.

17. Tariro Mzezewa, "New Rules on American Travel to Cuba Include Cruise Ban," *New York Times*, June 4, 2019, https://www.nytimes.com/2019/06/04/travel/cuba-travel-restrictions-trump.html.

18. Anthony Faiola, "In Cuba, the Great American Tourism boom goes bust," *Washington Post*, May 11, 2018, https://www.washingtonpost.com/amphtml/world/the_americas/in-cuba-the-great-american-tourism-boom-turns-to-bust/2018/05/11/53d63122-48a5-11e8-8082-105a446d19b8_story.html.

19. Oliver Bennett, "Despite Trump's efforts, Cuba continues to emerge as a prime tourist destination," *Independent*, June 20, 2018, https://www.independent.co.uk/news/long_reads/trump-cuba-us-relations-tourism-obama-miguel-diaz-canel-havana-castro-a8388021.html.

20. "Miguel Díaz-Canel: The man succeeding the Castros," BBC News, April 19, 2018, https://www.bbc.com/news/world-latin-america-43795286.

21. Rena Kraut, "Trump Is Wrong to Pull Back from Cuba," *New York Times*, June 16, 2017, https://www.nytimes.com/2017/06/16/opinion/trump-is-wrong-to-pull-back-from-cuba.html.

22. 21C Media Group, "Cuban American Youth Orchestra (CAYO)—New Cultural Exchange Program—Launches with First CAYO Fall Academy," October 16, 2017, http://21cmediagroup.com/2017/10/16/cuban-american-youth-orchestra-cayo-new-cultural-exchange-program-launches-with-first-cayo-fall-academy-oct-29-nov-5/.

23. Cuban American Youth Orchestra, "2018 Impact Report," April 2018, http://cayomusic.org/wp-content/uploads/2018/04/CAYO-Annual-Report-2018-web.pdf.

24. 21C Media Group, "Cuban American Youth Orchestra (CAYO) Made Historic Debut Last Month on 'Juntos en Armonía/Together in Harmony' Cuban Tour," press release, July 1, 2019, https://21cmediagroup.com/2019/07/01/cuban-american-youth-orchestra-cayo-made-historic-debut-last-month-on-juntos-en-armonia-together-in-harmony-cuban-tour/.

25. "Direct from Cuba! National Symphony Orchestra of Cuba @ Lehman Center," *Riverdale Press*, March 7, 2018, http://riverdalepress.com/stories/direct-from-cuba-national-symphony-orchestra-of-cuba-lehman-center,64957; "The National Symphony Orchestra of Cuba is joined by the 2017 Van Cliburn gold medal pianist for Moss Arts Center performance," *Virginia Tech News*, March 12, 2018, https://vtnews.vt.edu/articles/2018/03/mac-cubaorchestra.html.

26. Stephen Raskauskas, "Visa difficulties force Esperanza Spalding, National Symphony Orchestra of Cuba to cancel Chicago concert," WFMT, April 4, 2018, https://www.wfmt.com/2018/04/04/visa-difficulties-force-esperanza-spalding-national-symphony-orchestra-of-cuba-to-cancel-chicago-concert/.

27. Mimi Whitefield, "Politics collides with art as Kennedy Center prepares for Cuban culture festival," *Miami Herald*, May 4, 2018, http://www.miamiherald.com/news/nation-world/world/americas/cuba/article210253224.html.

28. Mario Díaz-Balart, Twitter post, April 27, 2018, 6:20 PM, https://twitter.com/MarioDB/status/989992807308890112.

29. Whitefield, "Politics collides with art as Kennedy Center prepares for Cuban culture festival."

30. Marisa Arbona-Ruiz, "'Still a Lot of Love': Arturo O'Farrill on Cuba-U.S. Artistic Relations," NPR Music, June 1, 2018, https://www.npr.org/sections/altlatino/2018/06/01/615950192/still-a-lot-of-love-arturo-o-farrill-on-cuba-u-s-artistic-relations.

31. Whitefield, "Politics collides with art as Kennedy Center prepares for Cuban culture festival."

32. "Díaz-Canel: US Hostility to Cuba Won't Be Eternal," teleSur, May 24, 2018, https://www.telesurtv.net/english/news/Diaz-Canel-US-Hostility-to-Cuba-Wont-be-Eternal-20180524-0025.html.

33. Kraut, "Trump Is Wrong to Pull Back from Cuba."

34. Ginger Thompson, "Trying to Sway America's Cuba Policy with Song," *New York Times*, December 28, 2009, http://www.nytimes.com/2009/12/29/world/americas/29cuba.html.

REFERENCES

Abreu, Christina D. 2015. *Rhythms of Race: Cuban Musicians and the Making of Latino New York City and Miami, 1940–1960*. Chapel Hill: University of North Carolina Press.

Acosta, Leonardo. 2003. *Cubano Be, Cubano Bop: One Hundred Years of Jazz in Cuba*. Translated by Daniel S. Whitesell. Washington, DC: Smithsonian Books.

Arús, María A. Cabrera. 2019. "The Material Promise of Socialist Modernity: Fashion and Domestic Space in the 1970s." In *The Revolution from Within: Cuba, 1959–1980*. Edited by Michael J. Bustamante and Jennifer L. Lambe. Durham, NC: Duke University Press, 189–217.

Askew, Kelly M. 2002. *Performing the Nation: Swahili Music and Cultural Politics in Tanzania*. Chicago: University of Chicago Press.

August, Arnold. 2013. *Cuba and Its Neighbours: Democracy in Motion*. New York: Zed Books.

Babb, Florence E. 2010. "Sex and Sentiment in Cuban Tourism." *Caribbean Studies* 38 (2): 93–115.

Baker, Geoffrey. 2011. *Buena Vista in the Club: Rap, Reggaeton, and Revolution in Havana*. Durham, NC: Duke University Press.

Ballantine, Christopher. 1984. *Music and Its Social Meanings*. New York: Gordon & Breach.

Baranovitch, Nimrod. 2003. *China's New Voices: Popular Music, Ethnicity, Gender, and Politics, 1978–1997*. Berkeley: University of California Press.

Bardach, Ann Louise. 2009. *Without Fidel: A Death Foretold in Miami, Havana, and Washington*. New York: Scribner.

Bleiker, Roland. 2005. "Of Things We Hear but Cannot See: Musical Explorations of International Politics." In *Resounding International Relations*. Edited by M. I. Franklin, 179–95. New York: Palgrave Macmillan.

Bohlman, Philip. 1993. "Musicology as a Political Act." *Journal of Musicology* 11: 411–36.

Bohlman, Philip. 1996. "Pilgrimage, Politics, and the Musical Remapping of the New Europe." *Journal of the Society for Ethnomusicology* 40 (3): 375–412.

Bosin, Joshua. "Miami's Mambo: The 'Cuba Affidavit' and Unconstitutional Cultural Censorship in an Embargo Regime." *University of Miami Inter-American Law Review* 36, no. 1 (2004): 75–113.

Brinner, Benjamin. 2009. *Playing Across a Divide: Israeli-Palestinian Musical Encounters*. New York: Oxford University Press.

Broyles, Michael. 2011. *Beethoven in America*. Bloomington: Indiana University Press.

Buch, Esteban. 2003. *Beethoven's Ninth: A Political History*. Chicago: University of Chicago Press.

Campbell, Jennifer L. 2010. "Shaping Solidarity: Music, Diplomacy, and Inter-American Relations, 1936–1946." PhD diss., University of Connecticut.

Candea, Matei. 2011. "'Our Division of the Universe': Making a Space for the Non-Political in the Anthropology of Politics." *Current Anthropology* 52: 309–34.

Carpentier, Alejo. 2001. *Music in Cuba*. Translated by Alan West-Durán. Edited by Timothy Brennan. Minneapolis: University of Minnesota Press.

Chun, Sung-Chang, and Guillermo Grenier. 2004. "Anti-Castro Political Ideology among Cuban Americans in the Miami Area: Cohort and Generational Differences." *Latino Research @ ND* 2 (1): 1–9.

Clealand, Danielle Pilar. 2017. *The Power of Race in Cuba: Racial Ideology and Black Consciousness during the Revolution*. Oxford: Oxford University Press.

Crandall, Russell. 2008. *The United States and Latin America after the Cold War*. Cambridge, MA: Cambridge University Press.

Cumaná, María Caridad. 2014. "A Singer Who Uses the Guitar as a Camera: The Cinematic Quality of Carlos Varela's Songs" in *My Havana: The Musical City of Carlos Varela*. Edited by María Caridad Cumaná, Karen Dubinsky, and Xenia Reloba de la Cruz. Toronto: University of Toronto Press, 68–78.

D'Rivera, Paquito. 2005. *My Sax Life*. Evanston, IL: Northwestern University Press.

Davidson, L., and D. Gitilitz Davidson. 2002. *Pilgrimage: From Ganges to Graceland, An Encyclopedia*. Edited by L. Davidson and D. Gitilitz Davidson. Santa Barbara, CA: ABC-CLIO.

Duany, Jorge. 1999. "Cuban Communities in the United States: Migration Waves, Settlement Patterns, and Socioeconomic Diversity." *Pouvoirs dans la Caraïbe* (Martinique) 11: 69–103.

Dunaway, David King. 2008. *How Can I Keep from Singing?: The Ballad of Pete Seeger*. 2nd ed. New York: Random House.

Edmondson, Laura. 2007. *Performance and Politics in Tanzania: The Nation on Stage*. Bloomington: Indiana University Press.

Erikson, Daniel P. 2009. *The Cuba Wars: Fidel Castro, the United States, and the Next Revolution*. 2nd ed. New York: Bloomsbury Press.

Fernandes, Sujatha. 2006. *Cuba Represent!: Cuban Arts, State Power, and the Making of New Revolutionary Cultures*. Durham, NC: Duke University Press.

Franklin, M. I. 2005. "Introductory Improvisations on a Theme: Resounding International Relations." In *Resounding International Relations*. Edited by M. I. Franklin, 1–28. New York: Palgrave Macmillan.

Garcia, David. 2006. *Arsenio Rodríguez and the Transnational Flows of Latin Popular Music*. Philadelphia: Temple University Press.

Garcia, Maria Cristina. 1996. *Havana USA: Cuban Exiles and Cuban Americans in South Florida*. Berkeley: University of California Press.

Garrett, Charles Hiroshi. 2008. *Struggling to Define a Nation: American Music and the Twentieth Century*. Berkeley: University of California Press.

Gidal, Mark. 2010. "Contemporary 'Latin American' Composers of Art Music in the United States: Cosmopolitans Navigating Multiculturalism and Universalism." *Latin American Music Review* 31 (1): 40–78.

Goehr, Lydia. 1994. "Political Music and the Politics of Music." *Journal of Aesthetics and Art Criticism* 52 (1): 99–112.

Goff, Patricia M. 2013. "Cultural Diplomacy." In *The Oxford Handbook of Modern Diplomacy*, 419–35. Edited by Andrew F. Cooper, Jorge Heine, and Ramesh Chandra Thakur. Oxford: Oxford University Press.

Goler, Robert I. 2004. "Cultural Policy and Philanthropy." In *Philanthropy in America: A Comprehensive Historical Encyclopedia*, vol. 1, 109–12. Edited by Dwight Burlingame. Santa Barbara, CA: ABC-CLIO.

Granovetter, Mark. 1973. "The Strength of Weak Ties." *American Journal of Sociology* 78: 1360–80.

Gronbeck-Tedesco, John A. 2008. "The Left in Transition: The Cuban Revolution in U.S. Third World Politics." *Journal of Latin American Studies* 40 (4): 651–73.

Hagedorn, Katherine. 2001. *Divine Utterances: The Performance of Afro-Cuban Santería*. Washington, DC: Smithsonian Institution Press.

Hernandez-Reguant, Ariana. 2004. "Copyrighting Che: Art and Authorship under Cuban Late Socialism." *Popular Culture* 16 (1): 1–29.

Hernandez-Reguant, Ariana. 2009. "Writing the Special Period: An Introduction." In *Cuba in the Special Period*, 1–18. Edited by Ariana Hernandez-Reguant. New York: Palgrave Macmillan.

Hess, Carol. 2013a. "Copland in Argentina." *Journal of the American Musicological Society* 66 (1): 191–250.

Hess, Carol. 2013b. *Representing the Good Neighbor: Music, Difference, and the Pan American Dream*. Oxford: Oxford University Press.

Iturralde, Iraida. 2007. "In Search of the Palm Tree: An Afternoon with Tania León." In *Cuba: Idea of a Nation Displaced*, 223–34. Edited by Andrea O'Reilly Herrera. Albany: State University of New York Press.

Jorgensen, Estelle R. 1990. "Music and International Relations." In *Culture and International Relations*, 62–71. Edited by Jongsuk Chay. Westport, CT: Greenwood.

Joseph, Gilbert M. 1998. "Close Encounters: Toward a New Cultural History of U.S.-Latin American Relations." In *Close Encounters of Empire: Writing the Cultural History of U.S.-Latin American Relations*, 3–46. Edited by Joseph M. Gilbert, Catherine C. LeGrand, and Ricardo D. Salvatore. Durham, NC: Duke University Press.

Kinkley, Jeffrey C. 2007. *Corruption and Realism in Late Socialist China*. Stanford, CA: Stanford University Press.

Kirshenblatt-Gimblett, Barbara. 1998. *Destination Culture: Tourism, Museums, and Heritage*. Berkeley: University of California Press.

Knoke, David, and Song Yang. 2008. *Social Network Analysis*. 2nd ed. Thousand Oaks, CA: SAGE.

Lamb, Andrew. "Gershwin's Cuban Vacation." Academia.edu. http://www.academia.edu/10986708/Gershwins_Cuban_Vacation_written_pre-2006_.

LeoGrande, William M., and Peter Kornbluh. 2014. *Back Channel to Cuba: The Hidden History of Negotiations between Washington and Havana*. Chapel Hill: University of North Carolina Press.

Leppert, Richard, and Susan McClary, eds. 1987. *Music and Society: The Politics of Composition, Performance, and Reception*. Cambridge: Cambridge University Press.

Loiacano, Catherine. 2010. "A 'community' divided: Cuban-American attempts to influence Jimmy Carter's Cuba policy, January 1977-May 1978." *American Diplomacy* (September 6).

Macleod, Donald. 2002. "Disappearing Culture? Globalisation and a Canary Island Fishing Community." *History and Anthropology* 13 (1): 53–67.

Maggin, Donald L. 2005. *Dizzy: The Life and Times of John Birks Gillespie*. New York: Harper Entertainment.

Manuel, Peter. 1987. "Marxism, Nationalism and Popular Music in Revolutionary Cuba." *Popular Music* 6 (2): 161–78.

Manuel, Peter. 1994. "Puerto Rican Music and Cultural Identity: Creative Appropriation of Cuban Sources from Danza to Salsa." *Ethnomusicology* 38 (2): 249–61.

Manuel, Peter. 2006. "The Saga of a Song: Authorship and Ownership in the Case of 'Guantanamera.'" *Latin American Music Review* 27 (2): 121–47.

Marks, Edward B. 1934. *They All Sang*. New York: Viking.

Martí, José. 1891. "Our America." In *Selected Writings*, 288–96. Edited and translated by Esther Allen. New York: Penguin.

Martí, José. 1895. "Letter to Manuel Mercado." In *Selected Writings*, 346–49. Edited and translated by Esther Allen. New York: Penguin.

Maxwell, Joseph. 2005. *Qualitative Research Design: An Interactive Approach*. 2nd ed. Thousand Oaks, CA: SAGE.

McClary, Susan. *Feminine Endings: Music, Gender, and Sexuality*. Minneapolis: University of Minnesota Press, 1991.

Monson, Ingrid. 2007. *Freedom Sounds: Civil Rights Call Out to Jazz and Africa*. Oxford: Oxford University Press.

Moore, Robin D. 1997. *Nationalizing Blackness: Afrocubanismo and Artistic Revolution in Havana, 1920-1940*. Pittsburgh, PA: University of Pittsburgh Press.

Moore, Robin D. 2006. *Music and Revolution: Cultural Change in Socialist Cuba*. Berkeley: University of California Press.

Myers, Helen. 1992. *Ethnomusicology: An Introduction*. New York: W.W. Norton.

Nielsen, Nanette. 2018. *Paul Bekker's Musical Ethics*. New York: Routledge.

Ninkovitch, Frank A. 1981. *The Diplomacy of Ideas: U.S. Foreign Policy and Cultural Relations, 1938-1950*. Cambridge: Cambridge University Press.

Ortíz, Fernando. 1974. *La Música Afrocubana*. Madrid: Ediciones Júcar.

Party, Daniel. 2008. "The Miamization of Latin-American Pop Music." In *Postnational Musical Identities*, 65–80. Edited by Ignazcio Corona and Alejandro L. Madrid. New York: Lexington Books.

Peréz, Louis A., Jr. 1999. *On Becoming Cuban: Identity, Nationality, and Culture*. Chapel Hill: University of North Carolina Press.

Peréz, Louis A., Jr. 2008. *Cuba in the American Imagination: Metaphor and the Imperial Ethos*. Chapel Hill: University of North Carolina Press.

Pérez Firmat, Gustavo. 2012. *Life on the Hyphen: The Cuban-American Way*. Revised ed. Austin: University of Texas Press.

Perna, Vincenzo. 2005. *Timba: The Sound of the Cuban Crisis*. Burlington, VT: Ashgate.

Pertierra, Anna Cristina. 2018. *Media Anthropology for the Digital Age*. Medford, MA: Polity Press.

Picard, David, and Mike Robinson. 2006. "Remaking Worlds: Festivals, Tourism and Change." In *Festivals, Tourism and Social Change: Remaking Worlds*, 1–31. Edited by David Picard and Mike Robinson. Tonawanda, NY: Cromwell Press.

Pike, Fredrick B. 1995. *FDR's Good Neighbor Policy: Sixty Years of Generally Gentle Chaos*. Austin: University of Texas Press.

Pollack, Howard. 1999. *Aaron Copland: The Life and Work of an Uncommon Man*. New York: H. Holt.

Pollack, Howard. 2006. *George Gershwin: His Life and Work*. Berkeley: University of California Press.

Portes, Alejandro, and Alex Stepick. 1993. *City on the Edge: The Transformation of Miami*. Berkeley: University of California Press.

Portes, Alejandro, and Ariel C. Armony. 2018. *The Global Edge: Miami in the Twenty-First Century*. Berkeley: University of California Press.

Portocarero, Herman. 2017. *Havana Without Makeup: Inside the Soul of the City*. Brooklyn: Turtle Point Press.

Prell, Christina. 2012. *Social Network Analysis: History, Theory, and Methodology*. Los Angeles: SAGE.

Rockefeller, Stuart Alexander. 2011. "Flow." *Current Anthropology* 52 (4): 557–78.

Rodriguez, Olavo Alén. 1998. "Cuba." In *The Garland Encyclopedia of World Music*. Vol. 2, *South America, Mexico, Central America, and the Caribbean*. Edited by Dale A. Olson and Daniel E. Sheehy, 822–39. New York: Garland.

Root, Deane L. 1972. "The Pan American Association of Composers (1928–1934)." *Anuario Interamericano de Investigacion Musical* 8: 49–70.

Sanchez, Peter M., and Kathleen M. Adams. 2009. "The Janus-Faced Character of Tourism in Cuba." In *Tourists and Tourism: A Reader*, 419–38. 2nd ed. Edited by Sharon Bohn Gmelch. Long Grove, IL: Waveland Press.

Smith, Valene. 1989. "Introduction." in *Hosts and Guests: The Anthropology of Tourism*, 1–17. 2nd ed. Edited by V. Smith. Philadelphia: University of Pennsylvania Press.

Spinazzola, James. 2011. "Tania León." In *Women of Influence in Contemporary Music: Nine American Composers*, 251–98. Edited by Michael Slayton. Lanham, MD: Scarecrow Press.

Stallings, Stephanie. 2009. "Collective Difference: The Pan-American Association of Composers and Pan-American Ideology in Music, 1925–1945." PhD diss., Florida State University.

Stoeltje, Beverly J. 1992. "Festival." In *Folklore, Cultural Performances, and Popular Entertainments*, 261–71. Edited by Richard Bauman. Oxford: Oxford University Press.

Sublette, Ned. 2004a. *Cuba and Its Music: From the First Drums to the Mambo*. Chicago: Chicago Review Press.

Sublette, Ned. 2004b. "The Missing Cuban Musicians." *Cuba Research and Analysis Group*. June 24.

Sublette, Ned. 2004c. "Rumba Diplomacy in the Age of Bushismo." *World Policy Journal* 21 (1): 75–84.

Titon, Jeff Todd. 1999. "'The Real Thing': Tourism, Authenticity, and Pilgrimage." *World of Music* 41 (3): 115–39.

Tsing, Anna. 2005. *Friction: An Ethnography of Global Connection*. Princeton, NJ: Princeton University Press.

Turino, Thomas. 2008. *Music as Social Life: The Politics of Participation*. Chicago: University of Chicago Press.

Turner, Victor. 1969. *The Ritual Process*. Chicago: Aldine.

Turner, Victor, and Edith L. B. Turner. 1978. *Image and Pilgrimage in Christian Culture*. New York: Columbia University Press.

Von Eschen, Penny M. 2004. *Satchmo Blows Up the World: Jazz Ambassadors Play the Cold War*. Cambridge, MA: Harvard University Press.

Washburne, Christopher. 2012. "Latin Jazz, Afro-Latin Jazz, Afro-Cuban Jazz, Cubop, Caribbean Jazz, Jazz Latin, or just . . . Jazz: the politics of locating an intercultural music." In *Jazz/Not Jazz: The Music and Its Boundaries*, 89–107. Edited by David Ake, Charles Garrett, and David Goldmark. Berkeley: University of California Press.

Wu, Chin-Tao. 2002. *Privatising Culture: Corporate Art Intervention Since the 1980s*. New York: Verso.

Yurchak, Alexei. 2008. "Necro-Utopia: The Politics of Indistinction and the Aesthetics of the Non-Soviet." *Current Anthropology* 49 (2): 199–224.

Zimmer, Dave. 2000. *Crosby, Stills & Nash: The Authorized Biography*. Cambridge, MA: Da Capo Press.

INDEX

academic travel to Cuba. *See* educational travel to Cuba
Acosta, Leonardo, 85
Afro-Cuban Jazz Suite, 105, 108
Afro Latin Jazz Orchestra, 104–10
Afro Latin Jazz Suite, 108–10, 187
Alcohol prohibition, 5–6, 125
allure of Cuba, 124–30
"Alma" (León), 42
American Civil Liberties Union (ACLU), 26, 55, 62
Americans for the Arts, 134
"Arenas d'un Tiempo" (Leon), 42
Arnaz, Desi, 8
Artes de Cuba festival, 172–73
Audioslave, 27–28
Authentic Cuba Tours, 96
Azpiazu, Don, 5–6

Balkan Bump. *See* Magid, Will
Ballet Nacional de Cuba, 65
Baracoa, 152
Basílica Menor de San Francisco de Asís, 156
batá, 44–45, 86, 103, 136
Batista, Fulgencio, 8
Bauzá, Mario, 7, 83
"Bayamesa, La," 48, 71, 122, 137, 162
Bay of Pigs, 10
Beethoven, Ludwig van, 74, 122
Bell, Joshua, 147–48, 161

Bell, Lynda, 61–62
Berlin, Irving, 5, 125
Bernstein, Leonard, 122
Beyoncé (Knowles-Carter), 50–51
Blanco, Richard, 137, 165–66
bolero, 100–101
Bolton, John, 25, 169
Brooklyn Academy of Music, 65–66
Brouwer, Leo, 14, 86; Leo Brouwer Festival, 41–42
Browne, Jackson, 27
Buena Vista Social Club, 23–24, 82, 103, 118, 128, 148
Bunnett, Jane, 81–83, 96, 97
Bush, George H. W., 19
Bush, George W., xi, 24–28

Cabañas, José Ramón, 147
Cabello, Camila, 143
cajon, 45
Campa, Will, 93, 99
Canadian travelers in Cuba, 81–83
Carcassés, Bobby, xi, 33, 82, 92, 108, 110
Carcassés, Roberto, 33–34, 62, 85, 87–88
Carter, Jimmy, 12–17, 41
Casa de la Cultura (Vedado), 86–87, 92–93
Casa del ALBA Cultural, 92
casa particular, xiii, 32, 45, 128, 132–33
Carter, Shawn. *See* Jay-Z (Shawn Carter)
Castro, Fidel: death of, 162–63; illness and surgery, 28, 31; meeting with Dizzy

Gillespie, 18; revolutionary movement of, 8–9; "Words to Intellectuals" speech, 67

Castro, Raúl: confirmation as president, 31; economic changes under, 31–32, 153, 158, 160–61; end of presidency in 2018, 170; political changes under, 32–33; provisional presidency, 28; relationship with US, 107

Caturla, Alejandro García, 4, 122

censorship in Cuba, 34, 42

Center for Democracy in the Americas, 146–47, 151, 162, 192

Chamber Orchestra of Havana, 148, 161

"Chan Chan," 23, 103

Chico y Rita, 83–84

China, xxii, 52, 71

Chirino, Willy, 37

Classical Movements, 115, 120–24, 132–33, 134, 136, 142–43

Clinton, Bill, 20–24, 64–65, 121

Clinton, Hillary, 37

Cold War, xvii, 20

Cole, Natalie, 3

Cole, Nat King, 3, 86

Cole Español, 3

"Comparsa, La" (Lecuona), 72

commodification of culture through festivals, 95

communitas, 126–27, 135

"Conga" (Miami Sound Machine), 59

Conjunto Folklórico Nacional, 18, 44–45, 181

Cooder, Ry, 13, 23–24

Coolidge, Calvin, 142

Copland, Aaron, xvii, 5, 172

CorHabana International Choir Festival, 47

Coro de Entrevoces, 48, 122, 123, 144

Cowell, Henry, 4

Cramer, Larry, 82

Creole Choir of Cuba, 65

Crisantemi Quartet, 171

Cruz, Celia, 15

"Cuarto de Tula," 103

Cuba Explorer Tours, 94, 186

Cuba Nostalgia Festival, 63

Cuba: The Conversation Continues, 106–10

Cubadisco, 39, 44, 116–24

CubaOne Foundation, 166

Cuban Adjustment Act, 11

Cuban Americans: desire to visit Cuba, 127, 166; political influence of, 57–67; travel restrictions on, 34–35, 40–42

Cuban American Youth Orchestra, 171

Cuban Assets Control Regulations. *See* Office of Foreign Assets Control

Cuban Five, 33–34, 107

Cuban Liberty and Solidarity Act. *See* Helms-Burton Act

Cuban Missile Crisis, 10, 76

Cuban Overture (Gershwin), 72, 165–66

Cuban Revolution, 8–10

cultural diplomacy, xiv, 121, 124, 146, 155, 176. *See also* musical diplomacy

currency in Cuba, 21, 32, 158

danzón, 73

Dead Daisies, 144

Deal, Melissa, 116, 136, 166

Delgado, Isaac, 56

Department of State: Bureau of Educational and Cultural Affairs, xviii; Division of Cultural Relations, xvi; performances in Cuba facilitated by, 36–40

Department of Treasury. *See* Office of Foreign Assets Control

Diaz, Telmary, 62, 65

Díaz-Balart, Lincoln, 25–27

Díaz-Balart, Mario, 51, 172

Díaz-Canel, Miguel, 170, 173

Dinnerstein, Simone, 156

diplomatic relations between US and Cuba, reestablishment of, 107, 120, 137–38, 152

Diplo. *See* Major Lazer

DJ IZ, 147

D'Rivera, Paquito, 13, 16, 19, 65, 85, 87, 143

economic embargo of Cuba, xxii, 9–11, 139; efforts to end, 26, 174; publications and recordings, 19

economy of Cuba, 31–32
Educational Travel Alliance, 47–48
educational travel to Cuba, 23–25, 42–46, 96–98, 169
EGREM (Empresa de Grabaciones y Ediciones Musicales), 14, 116, 117, 148
Eisenhower, Dwight, 9–10
ElectroBus, 100, 190
Eleguá, 112. *See also* orishas (in Afro-Cuban religious practices)
Elhai, Robert, 118
Ellington, Duke, xviii, 7, 97
Encuentro de Jóvenes Pianistas, 156
Escuela Nacional de Arte, 122
Estefan, Emilio and Gloria, 58–60, 143
Eva, Danielle, 152, 155

Fábrica de Arte Cubano (F.A.C.), 148, 153–56, 158
Fania All-Stars, 15
Fate of the Furious, 138
Feliú, Santiago, 154
Ferrer, Ibrahim, 27
festivals, study of, 89
Florida Orchestra, 67, 70–71
Florida Travel Act, 26
flow, xx, 53
FolkCuba, 44–45, 128, 136
Formell, Juan. *See* Van Van, Los
Four Seasons (Vivaldi), 148
Freedom Flights program, 11, 41
friction, xx, 53, 115, 123, 161
Friendship Association, 151–52
Friends University jazz ensemble, 96–98, 114, 127, 132
Fuego Cuban Music Festival, 61–62

García, Daiana, 161
Gershwin, George, 72–73, 165–66
Gillespie, Dizzy, xviii, 7, 12–14, 18–19, 84, 88
Give Me Future, 140–41, 145
Global Cuba Fest, 62–63
González, Elián, 24
Good Neighbor policy, xv–xvii, 35
Gorry, Conner, 98–99, 114

Grammy Awards, 27, 110, 187. *See also* Latin Grammys
grant programs, 150, 176
Gross, Alan, 35, 75, 107
Guaguancó (López-Gavilán), 73
"Guantanamera," 12, 23, 48, 103, 177
Guerra, Digna, 47–48, 144
Guevara, Ernesto "Che," 8

Haden, Charlie, 88
Harrison, Benjamin, xv
Harvard-Radcliffe Orchestra, 74, 121
Havana Jam, 14–16, 87, 135
Havana Jazz Plaza Festival, xi–xiii, 18–19, 44, 49; history of, 87–89; in 2012, 89–104, 112; in 2014, 107; musical genres present, 103–4; venues, 92–93, 153
Havana Moon, 144–45
Haza, Luis, 167–68
Helms, Neeta, 121, 133, 136, 171
Helms-Burton Act, 22
Henry, Bruce, 117
Herrera, Ignacio "Nachito," 68–79, 95, 112, 115–19, 133, 134
Hittle, Lisa, 96–97, 114, 132

I.A. Electrónica, 100
"(I'll See You in) Cuba" (Berlin), 5, 125
improvisation, xi, 103
Insight Cuba, 49–50, 52
Instituto Superior de Arte, 97, 148
Interactivo. *See* Carcassés, Roberto
internet access in Cuba, 159–60. See also *paquete semanal*
Irakere, 13–15, 86–87, 134

Jacox, Maurice, 117
Jagger, Mick, 144–45
Jay-Z (Shawn Carter), 50–52
jazz, 6–7; 1977 cruise to Havana, 12–14, 86, 125, 134; history in Cuba, 83–87; as pan-American music, 109. *See also* Havana Jazz Plaza Festival; Latin Jazz
Jazz at Lincoln Center Orchestra, 39, 105, 113

Jelly Roll Morton (Ferdinand Joseph LaMothe), 83
jineteros, 90, 128–29, 132
Joel, Billy, 15
John F. Kennedy Center for the Performing Arts, 172–73
Johnson, Lyndon B., 11
Jones, Darryl, 144
Jordan, Michael (guitarist), 152, 155
José Martí Anti-Imperialist Plaza, 28
Juanes (Juan Esteban Aristizábal Vásquez), 36–39, 55, 60, 113, 130, 135

Kansas City, Missouri, 70
Kennedy, John F., 10–12
Kennedy Center. *See* John F. Kennedy Center for the Performing Arts
Kerry, John, 137
Kool and the Gang, 39, 113
Kraut, Rena, 171, 174
Kristofferson, Kris, 14–15

Ladies in White, 77
Latin America, US relations with, xv
Latin Grammys, 42, 60, 110
Latin jazz, 6–7, 103–4
Lecuona, Ernesto, 72–73, 148
León, Tania, 40–42, 54, 64–65, 133, 181
Leonard, Neil, 44
Long, Norah, 117–19, 131, 134
López-Gavilán, Guido, 73, 172
López-Nussa, Harold, 148
Lucumí. *See* Santería

Machín, Antonio, 6
Machito (Francisco Raúl Gutiérrez Grillo), 7–8
Magid, Will, 98–100, 114, 131
Mahanthappa, Rudresh, 108–9
Major Lazer, 140–42, 145
mambo, 7–8, 63
"Manisero, El" (Simons), 5, 82
Manolín "El Médico de la Sansa," 56
Marks, E. B., 5–6
"Maria La O" (Lecuona), 148

Mariel boatlift, 17, 57
Martí, José, xv–xvi. *See also* José Martí Anti-Imperialist Plaza
Martínez, Larisa, 147–48, 161
Matthews, Dave, 147–50, 161–62
McCain, John, 30
Mendelssohn, Felix, 73
Miami, Florida: biculturalism in, 57–59; changing attitudes towards Cuba, 60–61, 63, 78–79, 127; concerts and festivals in, 55–56, 61–63; Latin music industry, 59–61; local government policies related to Cuba, 56, 58; protests of musicians, 37–38, 55–56, 62–63; Trump rallies in, 167; waves of immigration, 17, 57–58
Miami Sound Machine, 58–60
Mikowsky, Solomon, 156
Milanes, Pablo, xix, 14, 63, 140, 148, 173
Ministry of Culture, Cuban, xix, 9, 34, 36, 77, 121, 141, 147, 150
Minnesota, 68–69, 116–24, 171
Minnesota Orchestra, 120–24, 132, 171
Minnesota Public Radio, 122, 132, 188
Muñequitos de Matanzas, Los, 20, 27, 65
"Muros y Puertas" (Varela), 149–50, 162
Museo Nacional de la Revolución, 48, 97, 128
Musicabana Foundation, 140, 146, 190, 192
musical diplomacy, definition of, xiv
Music Bridges project, 23
Musicians Across the Straits, 151–56

Natalie Cole En Español (Cole), 3
National Arts and Humanities Youth Program, 147, 151
National Choir of Cuba, 47–48, 122
National Endowment for the Arts, 146, 150
National Endowment for the Humanities, 146, 151
National Symphony Orchestra of Cuba, 66–79, 102, 112–13, 116–19, 172
New Orleans, Louisiana, 13, 83, 110, 177
New York City, 6–8, 64–66, 110
New York Philharmonic, 184

NG La Banda, 93
Night in Havana, A, 18, 88
Nubes (Varela), 149
Nueva trova, xix, 149

Obama, Barack: 2008 campaign, 28–30; 2012 reelection, 78–79; administration of, xi, 34–36; on music, 131, 142; visit to Cuba, 142–43
Ochoa, Eliades, 148
O'Farrill, Arturo, 27, 104–10, 114, 137, 163, 173, 187
O'Farrill, Chico, 104–5, 163
Office of Foreign Assets Control: 2011 Cuba regulations, 43–49; 2016 Cuba regulations, 138–39; general license to visit Cuba, 40, 43–46, 121, 138, 169–70; initial policies under Obama, 36; specific license to visit Cuba, 46–48, 121, 176; under George W. Bush, 24–26; under Kennedy, 11; under Trump, 169–70
Office of Inter-American Affairs, xvii
¡Olé, Olé, Olé! A Trip across Latin America, 144–45
"Ooh Baby Baby" (Robinson), 148
"Open Letter" (Jay-Z), 52
Operation Mongoose, 11
Organization of American States, 34
orishas (in Afro-Cuban religious practices), 45, 48, 81, 112. *See also* Santería
Orishas (rap group), 141
Orquesta Aragón, 14–15, 122

Pacetti, Sam, 152
paladares, 32, 160–61
Pan-American Association of Composers, 4–5, 65
Pan-Americanism, xiv–xvii
paquete semanal, 141
Parker, Charlie, 105
Peace Without Borders, 36–39, 55, 60, 130
"Peanut Vendor, The." *See* "Manisero, El"
people-to-people travel, 23–24, 43, 49–52, 129–30, 139, 152, 156, 169
Perez, Manuel, 83

Pérez Mesa, Enrique, 67, 172
Philadelphia Boys Choir, 165–66
pilgrimage, 126–30, 189
Pintado, Carlos, 133
Pisani, Fabien, 140, 146, 192
Pitbull (Armando Christian Pérez), 52, 142
Platt Amendment, xvi, 4
Plaza de la Revolución, 36
political music, xxi, 75–78, 185
Pompeo, Mike, 172
Portuondo, Omara, 27, 118, 148, 173
Pozo, Chano, 7, 13, 18, 83–84
Prado, Pérez, 7
President's Committee on the Arts and Humanities, 146–51, 168
Presidential Proclamation 5377, 17–18, 20, 27, 36. *See also* Reagan, Ronald
Primitive Love (Miami Sound Machine), 59
Prokofiev, Sergei, 122
psyops, xvii, 177
purposeful travel, 129–30
Puente, Tito, 8

Quine, Jim, 152

race in Cuba, 84–85, 158–59
Reagan, Ronald, 17–19, 146
recording industry, 8, 58–60, 117
Regla, Havana, 148
Regla de Ocha. *See* Santería
Rhapsody in Blue (Gershwin), 72–73, 112
Rhodes, Benjamin, 52–53, 163, 173, 190
Richards, Keith, 145
Rimas Tropicales (León), 133
Robinson, Smokey, 147–48
Rodríguez, Arsenio, 7
Rodríguez, Silvio, xix, 14, 34, 36, 108, 148, 180
Rodríguez, Tito, 8
Roldán, Amadeu, 4, 6, 72, 172
Rolling Stones, 143–45
Romney, Mitt, 78–79
Roosevelt, Franklin D., xv–xvii
Ros-Lehtinen, Ileana, 25–27, 39, 51, 172
Rubalcaba, Gonzalo, 18, 88
Rubalcaba, Guillermo, 82

Rubio, Marco, 50–52, 129, 135
rumba, 4–7, 20, 41, 45, 73

San Francisco Girls Chorus, 133
Sandoval, Arturo, 13, 18–19, 85, 87–88
Santería, 20, 44–45, 148
Seeger, Pete, 12, 36
Septeto Nacional, 65
sex work in Cuba, 159
¡Sí Cuba! Festival, 65–66
Simons, Moisés, 5
Sintesis, 81–82, 103, 148
Smithsonian, 146–47
socialism and music, xxii
social networks, 114–16, 119–20, 123, 132–34, 141
son, 5–7, 15, 23, 63
Sonidos de las Américas, 64–65
Southern Exposure, Performing Arts of Latin America, 150
Soviet Union, xxii, 9, 12, 20, 78
Special Period, 20–22, 89, 178
St. Augustine, Florida, 151–52
"Star Spangled Banner," 71, 122, 143, 162, 168
State Department, US. *See* Department of State
State Sponsors of Terrorism, US list of, 17, 26
Stills, Steven, 14–16
St. Olaf College, 116, 142–43
Summit of the Americas, 34

Tampa, Florida, 67, 70–71, 73
Teatro Karl Marx, 15
Teatro Mella, 13, 81, 92–93, 112
Teatro Nacional, 44, 118, 122
Tillerson, Rex, 168
timba, 22, 55, 183
Tin Pan Alley, 5
tourism, Cuban: accusations of cultural exchange as tourism, 51, 129; festivals in, 95; history of, 21, 157; music in, 44; under Raúl Castro, 32, 157–61
tourist, definition of, 129
travel ban, 11–12, 17, 24, 26; efforts to lift, 42

Trio Los Vigilantes, 100–103, 114, 125
Trump, Donald: 2016 campaign, 150, 162; administration of, 167–73
Turnaround Arts, 147, 151, 193
Turner, Victor and Edith, 126

US Army Brass Quintet, 137
USArtists International, 150
US Embassy in Havana, 137, 168. *See also* US Interests Section in Havana
Usher, 147–48
US Interests Section in Havana, 12, 48, 104, 106, 137, 182
US university programs in Cuba, 45–46, 156

Valdés, Bebo, 3, 84
Valdés, Chucho, 3, 13, 27, 39, 66, 83, 85–88, 103, 114
Van Van, Los, 22, 27, 55–56, 61, 79, 135, 173
Varela, Carlos, 27, 148–50, 161–62, 174
Varèse, Edgard, 4, 72
Vedado, Havana, 44, 90–93, 148
visas for Cuban artists, 36. *See also* Presidential Proclamation 5377
Voice of America radio, xviii, 84
Voices from the Heart, 47–48, 115

weak ties, 114
West Palm Beach, Florida, 75
wet foot, dry foot policy, 22, 167
Williamson, Elisabeth, 152, 155

X Alfonso, 38, 148, 153

Yale Alumni Chorus, 121
Young, John Lloyd, 147

ABOUT THE AUTHOR

Photo credit: Mary Beth Johnson (2020)

Timothy P. Storhoff is ethnomusicologist and orchestra administrator living in Winston-Salem, North Carolina. Originally from Fargo, North Dakota, Timothy is currently the Director of Philanthropic Services for the Winston-Salem Symphony. He has worked as an arts administrator, project manager, and grantmaker for state government and non-profit cultural organizations. Timothy holds a Bachelor of Music in Bassoon Performance and a Bachelor of Arts in American Studies from the University of Iowa. He received his Master of Music and PhD in Musicology from the Florida State University.

www.ingramcontent.com/pod-product-compliance
Lightning Source LLC
Chambersburg PA
CBHW030342240426
43661CB00052B/1713